OTHER LITERATURE IN TRANSLATION
FROM CATBIRD PRESS

Toward the Radical Center: A Karel Čapek Reader,
edited by Peter Kussi, foreword by Arthur Miller

War with the Newts by Karel Čapek, trans. Ewald Osers

Three Novels by Karel Čapek, trans. M. & R. Weatherall

Tales from Two Pockets by Karel Čapek, trans. Norma Comrada

Talks with T. G. Masaryk by Karel Čapek, trans. Dora Round,
edited by Michael Henry Heim

The Four Sonyas by Vladimír Páral, trans. William Harkins

Catapult by Vladimír Páral, trans. William Harkins

What Ownership's All About by Karel Poláček,
translated by Peter Kussi

Jewish Voices, German Words: Growing Up
Jewish in Postwar Germany and Austria,
ed. Elena Lappin, trans. Krishna Winston

Joseph von Westphalen

Diplomatic Pursuits

Translated from the German by
Melanie Richter-Bernburg

CATBIRD PRESS

See page 302 for the translator's acknowledgments

CATBIRD PRESS
16 Windsor Road, North Haven, CT   06473
800-360-2391; e-mail: catbird@pipeline.com
Our books are distributed by
Independent Publishers Group

Library of Congress Cataloging-in-Publication Data
Westphalen, Joseph von, 1945-
[Im diplomatischen Dienst. English]
Diplomatic pursuits / Joseph von Westphalen ; translated from
the German by Melanie Richter-Bernburg.
— 1st English-language ed.
ISBN 0-945774-28-1 : $14.95
I. Richter-Bernburg, Melanie. II. Title.
PT2685.E825I413   1995
833'.914—dc20   94-42791 CIP

1 How attorney Harry von Duckwitz is overcome by uneasiness and has growing doubts about the meaning of his profession. About green, gray, and black telephones, what Harry thinks of his girlfriend Helen's absence, and how his clients become ever more suspect to him. In addition to some information about his origins, his carryings-on as a student, his breakfast habits, and his preferred means of locomotion.

No way! It couldn't go on this way. Harry von Duckwitz got up from his desk and walked over to the open window. He hadn't studied law for years just to sit in an office now, dictating reports that went by the name of briefs. Not at seven in the evening, in May, in this weather.

Frankfurt, mid-seventies, 1975 to be exact, but what difference does the year make compared to the weather and the season. It's the way late spring turns to early summer on a warm evening without a trace of twilight that goads your sense of longing into aimless motion and makes you feel your soul stirring once again.

Duckwitz had been working in these offices for almost a year. It was by no means hell, but it was no way to live, in the long run. Not that he had expected heaven on earth—he was past that age. He didn't expect anything at all. If he ever had. What do you expect out of life? A fairly reasonable question actually, but when you heard it, or said it out loud, it sounded obscene. You really had to have gone to the dogs not to find it presumptuous. You might be able to ask yourself such questions, but not too often. To expect fulfillment, from your job no less, was ridiculous.

And yet, he'd been lucky. A flourishing law firm in a good location on the edge of downtown Frankfurt. An old building—that was important. Nice parquet floors. Nothing against skyscrapers on a city skyline, but he didn't want to work in one. He was no insect. Here there were sensible partitioned windows that could be opened wide. The soothing roar of traffic rose reassuringly from below. At least something was going on in the streets. There were even trees outside the windows, linden trees. They were in blossom now, and their sweet country scent mingled pleasantly with the smells of the city.

The two secretaries had left at five, as usual. "Good night. See you tomorrow, Herr von Duckwitz!" Both his colleagues and the legal intern had taken their leave at six. With a sense of relief and a trace of respect and friendly commiseration, they called out: "Don't work yourself to death!"

Now the cleaning lady had also disappeared, her last act having been to check the earth in the potted palm with her knuckle: "Doesn't need water, it's still okay." Right now she was busy in the dermatologist's office one floor up. You could hear her vacuuming and shoving furniture around. Maybe she worked twelve or thirteen hours a day, too, like Duckwitz. He probably earned four or five times as much as she did. And that dermatologist up there, the quack, probably raked in ten times as much.

But the problem wasn't grotesque differences in income. In earlier years, he had taken to the streets to protest such injustices. That was once upon a time.

Duckwitz closed the window. Frankfurt was known as an ugly city, but he just couldn't see it that way. Recently some people had been calling it an honest city. If ugliness could be turned into honesty, then it had to follow that a lie is something beautiful.

He went back to his desk and concentrated on a damage claim made by a builder against an electrician, and on criminal charges brought against a lapsed alcoholic for some ludicrous break-in. He would like to have walked back and forth as he was dictating to his machine, but oddly enough, even though he was alone in the office, that still seemed too pompous. Not yet thirty, he wasn't about to begin strutting around officiously, as if he were some actor playing the part of a brooding celebrity attorney waiting for a flash of inspiration.

This, by the way, was a bigger problem than the cleaning lady's wages: his image. It wasn't an agonizing problem, but it had been on his mind. He was just the sort of successful young lawyer he and Helen had jeered at only a short time ago. Success was as low as you could go, that much had been clear. There had to be something fishy about anyone who was successful in this society.

Who knows, maybe that's why Helen had turned away from him. Maybe she didn't like living with a successful young lawyer who spent less and less time with her. Harry wasn't sure. But what should he have done? There was no alternative. He just slid into success. Other people slide into failure. You slide this way, you slide that, maybe you slip and fall. The whole thing's just one big skating party. But after all, the fault of success is easier to take than the fault of failure.

Nevertheless, Harry did everything he could to avoid creating the impression of being a successful young lawyer. He was very careful not to change: threadbare sports coats instead of suits, his rusty old car, and no new apartment. But the question was, could he hold off the inevitable that way?

He still had some time for skeptical self-examination, though he'd rather have been examined by Helen. That wouldn't be so exhausting. Anyway, you had to be careful not to look like you were part of the establishment, if you actually were. Or wasn't he?

At some point resistance becomes foolish. Why shouldn't you at least buy a better car? Are you a monster just because you take your accountant's advice and start driving a Mercedes or a Volvo? What's wrong with a new jacket, and what's really so objectionable about a new suit? What would old photo albums and old movies be without the suits? You couldn't imagine those great seedy detectives from the thirties and forties without the suits. It was undoubtedly childish to put up such resistance to suits and decent cars. And while wearing a tie is really stupid, it's also stupid to resist so hard. As if wearing one made you a jackass.

Those were the big questions. But for the time being there weren't any answers. He'd have to discuss them with Helen. It was a dirty trick for her to have taken off like that. Harry took out a sheet of paper and wrote: "Dear Helen, I need an image consultant. Good pay. Won't you take the job?"

He put the unfinished letter into the drawer where he kept his personal belongings, then took down some commentaries in order to dictate a couple of letters. One of the commentaries was called *Rules for the Allocation of Public Works Contracts*. The opening pages bore a resplendent dedication by the author: "In deep gratitude to my dear wife, especially for the many years of patience and consideration that made this 7th edition possible."

A commentary is the crowning achievement of a legal career. He would never let things go that far, Harry told himself. He wouldn't write a commentary on contracting rules or anything else, and he certainly wouldn't have the gall to dedicate such drivel to any dear woman, wife or otherwise. He put the books back on the shelf. He should specialize, then he wouldn't have to work so hard. Only first he'd have to find out which branch of civil or criminal law suited him best.

Still, something just wasn't quite right. The business about success was really a joke, and he still felt strong enough to laugh off the suspicion that he belonged to the establishment. But he'd rather have laughed about it with Helen—laughing alone could easily sound a little bitter.

The problem was that while you might be able to evade the image of the successful young lawyer, you couldn't get around the rules of the justice game. That terrific fellow who angrily kicked a car after the driver nearly ran him over would never have obtained his rights, even if he was right to do what he did. Naturally, the driver of the swanky limousine filed suit for damages right away. A dented door. Seven thousand marks worth of damage from a single kick, according to one expert's estimate. Even the judge had been amused at that: such an expensive car and such thin metal? Nevertheless, you don't kick car doors. Only if you've actually been hit can a lawyer claim it was a reflex reaction. Or better yet, that it involved a mere "excess of justifiable self- defense." When Duckwitz had the rare opportunity to throw terms like that around in court, he really enjoyed his profession. But the plaintiff had suddenly withdrawn his complaint—didn't want to give the name of the witness, that is, of the woman who had been sitting next to him in the car. Aha!

That was just it. Instead of setting up a monument to the defendant's awesome kick, instead of sentencing the driver to thirty lashes on the soles of his feet, the whole thing ended without the least sense of triumph. If his client's adversary hadn't been so pitifully afraid of the questions his wife would ask about the woman passenger, Duckwitz could have helped the car kicker get his due. But how? What judge would have been willing to find for his heroic client on the grounds that, in this case, car doors may be kicked? Yet only this way can justice take on a higher meaning!

There was simply no end to the tricks and the schem-
ing, the deliberate silences and the diversionary tactics. You
employed ruses and evasions and indulged in petty charges
of procedural error in a half-hearted search for half-truths.
No brilliance, not a hint of justice, no ideas, just this snoop-
ing and fiddling and messing and rummaging around.
Ridiculous mental gymnastics for hairsplitters. Okay, okay,
he'd known that. He'd had time to prepare himself for this
nonsense as a student, as a legal intern, even as an associate
in the firm. But it's one thing to know about the nonsense
and something else to engage in it yourself.

What he hadn't known was that the clients would be
the worst part. You couldn't drive them away, after all,
because you lived off them; but they were horrible—indignant as plaintiffs, weepy as defendants. His law firm had a
reputation for being liberal, and so most of the people who
showed up were either abused, disadvantaged, or insolvent.

This morning he'd represented a supermarket cashier
who was fired. Sure you're supposed to put everything you've
got into helping such a wretched creature. But in court it
turned out that she was slow, clumsy, regularly late for work,
and always chattering; she couldn't remember a thing, and
she couldn't add. She was simply out of place. She was one
of those women who drive you insane when you're standing
in line because she doesn't know the price of the merchan-
dise, has to ask another cashier about every stick of butter,
and nothing moves. Customers had complained. The manager's description had been absolutely credible. He'd been
fair. She'd been given proper notice. It was hard, but then
that's life. The only thing was, the very friendly store manager had not sent her notice by registered mail, and Harry
had been forced to drum it into his client's head that she
received the letter on January 2 and not punctually on
December 31. With no effort at all, Duckwitz had been able
to get a settlement of twelve thousand marks for this incom-

petent goose. Her boss, on the other hand, an Italian, was penalized because he didn't know that in this case he had to send a registered German letter mailed at a German post office. And the result of this cheap victory was that the manager had to pay Duckwitz two thousand marks in legal fees out of his own pocket. It just couldn't go on this way.

Worst of all were the divorces. Duckwitz evidently exerted some kind of mysterious attraction on the kind of man who thinks he's been cheated by his wife both sexually and financially. After umpteen years of married hell, he didn't feel like stuffing half his hard-earned income into the maw of that deceitful beast.

Duckwitz always nodded but thought to himself: if you get married, you've got it coming. In court, his adversaries, that is the women, turned out to be absolutely fabulous; his clients, on the other hand, turned into foul and nasty characters, an imposition on any sensible woman. Why wasn't it the women who came to his office? Was there some hidden contradiction between a beautiful client and a liberal law office? It was sort of romantic to be thought of as a liberal lawyer in a liberal law firm, but if the result of this dubious reputation was that he attracted only miserable wretches, then thanks but no thanks. In that case he'd rather wage non-ideological battles on behalf of beautiful women and pick the pockets of slippery characters for the rest of his life. Someone has to take up the cause of beauty, damn it!

Recently, he'd found himself confronted in court by a woman whose eyes were so green that he could have allowed the most hair-raising assertions to pass without objection. And right in front of this woman he had to paste together a legally convincing case out of the disgusting charges made by his awful client. The green eyes rested on the man with mild disdain. If she'd only take a pistol out of her purse and shoot him! thought Duckwitz. He'd offer to defend her on the spot. He moved as far away from his client as he could in order to avoid being caught in the rays of this beautiful green disdain. He tried to sneak into his remarks some secret signs of sympathy for his opponent but stopped when he noticed that, as the laws of rhetoric would have it, he was helping his client. He'd have to represent the man so miserably that she'd win on all counts. Only she wouldn't know who it was she had to thank for the victory. Duckwitz would be the loser, and women like that don't like losers. Her lawyer would have to be the one to tell her that Duckwitz let her win. Then she'd call to thank him, and Harry would say equivocally, "Don't mention it!" Naturally he'd go out to dinner with green-eyes. And pretty soon he'd be gazing at her and asking: Say, what is it about me that always makes me wind up with such atrocious clients?

It was already too late for the movies now, a quarter past nine. Green-eyes' name was Wagner. There were a lot of Wagners. Duckwitz looked in the file for her first name and address. The Wagner Case. Then he checked the phone book. There they were, right after the divorce, still peacefully united. Sybil and Hubert. Where do people actually live after a divorce? Calling Sybil Wagner now would be stepping completely out of line. It would be unseemly, and unseemly was exactly what he wanted to be.

When he got home, Harry contemplated his telephone. He hadn't gone out to dinner, not alone. No fun in that. There had to be a little conversation at dinner or you might as well wolf down something right from the refrigerator. That's what he'd just done. Somehow it was odd to think of your body as if it were a car. Simply fill up the tank and off you go. But where to?

He wouldn't call Helen. She'd have to do it, she was the one who left. And besides, there was no hurry. He wasn't even thirty yet.

Harry was proud of his old black telephone. Bakelite. You have to keep the most obtrusive kinds of progress from taking over. Keep up the battle against pointless innovation. Someone had come up with new telephones even though the old ones were still perfectly good. His receiver was as heavy as a dumbbell, and there was a cradle that still deserved the name. If you wanted to, you could drop or slam down the receiver, you didn't have to fit it into some ridiculous well. When the dial turned, it sounded like those old radio mystery stories with the detective about to come in and save the day. Harry's splendid phone had belonged to the previous tenant. There was always static on the line, and the telephone repairman had wanted to replace it. "Well, you're finally going to get a new one!" he said cheerfully, pulling out his screwdriver. "Are you crazy?" Duckwitz barked so indignantly that the man packed up his tools and left.

It was annoying that there were no old black telephones at the office, although compared to his miserable clients, that was a mere trifle. Harry didn't think even a telephone should be a matter of indifference to someone who considers himself a thinking being. An office that doesn't have black telephones carries less weight, the same way the new telephones pack less weight. If you have to spend hours on the phone at the office every day, you need one you can really get hold of, not some toy that goes sliding around every time you make a call.

When the office was furnished a year earlier, he'd had a say in things. Some crook from that monopoly Siemens had wanted to talk them into a touch telephone, said touch telephones were the latest development. The first one had been installed for the President just that year, June of seventy-four, and then they'd gone into production. "Out of the question," Duckwitz had said. He was no bookkeeper and he wouldn't punch numbers. Even where the telephone was concerned, he wanted to be free—free to dial, not to hunt and peck. Then there had been the question of color: gray, green, or an absolutely impossible orange. The man

from Siemens had recommended green, fern green. Friendly.
If not black, then gray, thought Harry. Why would you
want fern green in an office? What rubbish! An office isn't
a forest. Some factory psychologist or business school grad
had thought that one up in order to demonstrate to the
members of the board that he was indispensable. It looks
friendly, he said. The greener the workplace, the harder your
employees will work.

Needless to say, they had fern green telephones in the
office, because the only ones who were there when the
phones were delivered were the secretaries, and they had
naturally chosen green. Helen, by the way, had once interrupted Harry's hymn to the old black telephone with a nasty
comment: she just couldn't help herself, she said, it reminded her of the Gestapo and Hitler's headquarters. "You
really know how to ruin things," Harry had replied.

Harry didn't need an alarm clock. He always slept well
and woke up refreshed after just a few hours' sleep. That's
why he couldn't stand people who yawned the whole morning and complained about how hard it was to get up. He
woke up before six this particular morning, with the sun
shining into his room. A clean shirt, the same sports coat
and pants as yesterday. It was good to be a man, it made
things easier.

Harry left his apartment. His place wasn't bad, and the
stairway was even better. A beautiful, broad wooden staircase
from a time when houses weren't built by idiots. And there
was no drop into an underground parking lot by elevator. It
was a May morning. A walk along the river. A pretty good
head on his shoulders—good enough for remembering, turning off, taking things in. It could have been worse. Eyes still
good, a full head of hair, no lisp. What more could you
want?

If you ignored the nitpicking, the haggling, and the
dirty tricks you had to use to obtain your rights, or rather to

help your undeserving clients obtain their undeserved rights, then it was pleasant to be able to use your head, to make waves, to stir up sympathy, to look the judge straight in the eye and push things so far that the prosecutor's mouth began to resemble a carp's. Those were the real triumphs!

What was terrible was having to wear those gowns they call robes. Just one more reason to quit this job someday. On the other hand, it wasn't such a bad thing that the legal system made itself look ridiculous by insisting its representatives dress up as if for Carnival. Since most sentences were handed down by judges in robes, it made them seem sort of playful. It just couldn't be true that some clown in a smock could send another person to a real jail for seven long years. Somehow that just couldn't be true. Maybe that's even what made it bearable.

Lawyers don't wear robes in the States. But that doesn't help the Americans at all. They're a stupid bunch. Except for blues and jazz, they haven't produced much. A few dozen nice love songs. Not bad. And of course some movies. And then the protest songs. Really good pop songs had always been a protest against something. If it wasn't against war, then it was against the callousness of narrow-minded Americans who support their presidents' wars. Or against the naive, gum-chewing obedience of GIs who slaughter and are slaughtered in some strange corner of the world. That miserable war in Vietnam had been over for two years now, at least on paper. The Yankees had actually withdrawn in seventy-three. Napalm was already a thing of the past, Ho Chi Minh just the echo of a battle cry at a demonstration, and way in the back of your mind a few memories of horrible old news photos. What was left were some songs by Bob Dylan, Joan Baez, Janis Joplin, Jimi Hendrix, and the Doors, a few wild jabs and chords on the guitar. At first those singers had been considered incredibly rebellious, but then it turned out that the rebelliousness of the pop musicians was either an act or unintentional. Nothing but an invention of fans and euphoric journalists. There must have been something authentic about them, though, in spite of the fact that they were always high. Some of their versions of old songs were still amazingly powerful. They flung the notes at you in a way that was somehow believable, that still made you hard and soft and proud and resistant.

Harry walked along the river to the art museum and then turned back. The time had come to have a tape deck installed in his car. The time had come to take up his trumpet again. The record player needed to be repaired.

If it's true that criminal political systems breed explosive music, then it's surprising that Nazism didn't produce a popular musical protest. Why hadn't some German musician in exile come up with the idea of turning that corny song about Lilli Marleen into a raving protest, with an assassin dreaming how she'd blow up the whole pack of Nazis? "Outside the barracks / Hitler's standing by. / I'll kill him now, / And none will question why. / The light from the lamp is bright as day's— / I'll shoot him there, right in the face. / For you, Lilli Marleen." A musical vision of justifiable assassination with an accusatory trumpet paraphrase, then back to the trenches with that song on the BBC!

Why didn't anyone write music like that during the war, or maybe even afterward? The resistance in Germany, with its officers and its communists, was pretty ineffective, and "coming to terms with the past" was just a compulsory exercise for public speakers and intellectuals. Historians and psychoanalysts had plenty of explanations for Germany's past, but what was really missing were a couple of great songs that everyone liked and everyone could whistle, songs that turned back and cried out in anger against National Socialism, that smashed the past to bits with the sheer force of their rhythms.

Harry thought about his trumpet, about the jazz band they'd had at school, and how it still wasn't too late to take up the trumpet in some cause here in Frankfurt. He could probably still manage to play the "West End Blues." But the way things were now, what with the office and all—well, it just couldn't go on this way.

Near Harry's apartment there was a little bakery that opened at seven in the morning. He almost always ate breakfast there, and every morning he had the same struggle with himself about whether or not to ask the waitress: Are you busy tonight? Every morning he was in love with her. But he was old enough to know there was no point to it. That kind of love only works in the bakery's coffee shop or, on warm spring days like this one, at the little tables they put out on the sidewalk.

Carola. Of course he didn't call her Carola. He didn't call her at all. He simply raised a finger when he wanted to order something or pay his bill. He had the same thing every morning, coffee and a roll with butter. He loved Carola for that, too—for not saying "The usual?" and for not bringing him the same thing each time without saying a word. No, every morning she stood at his table and smiled as if she expected him to order something special, and each time he said: "A pot of coffee and a biscuit with butter."

Harry didn't like the expression "coffee for one." It sounded too much like a resort café. Saying "coffee for one" was almost as bad as asking someone what he expects out of life. So he just said "a pot of coffee." And he didn't like the word "roll" either, so he said "biscuit," the way they do in the south. Harry had grown up in southern Germany, near the Bavarian Alps. Beautiful. He had no quarrel with his childhood. People had said "biscuit" there and had laughed at "Prussians," who said "roll." It was good to be in Frankfurt, to be a Prussian by birth, and to call a roll a biscuit.

As far as those things were concerned, Harry was content with his life.

Carola had accepted the fact that he wanted to distinguish himself from the coffee-for-one-and-a-roll people. When she was in a good mood, she said with a touch of irony, "Here's your pot of coffee and your biscuit." She said it again today. They gave each other a conspiratorial look, and Harry asked himself if he shouldn't give it a try after all.

Harry and the baker's girl. If only he didn't have this mess of ridiculous titles. Show me your passport, she would say on the trip they'd take to Venice or Paris. "Dr. Harry Baron von Duckwitz." It was ridiculous. People used to talk about pride of rank, but that was a thing of the past. Now there were other barriers.

Kissing, stroking, screwing, even being quiet together—great. Going to the movies would be okay, too. But having a glass of beer or wine afterward would already be a problem. What do you do with all your associations? He wasn't even sure that Carola would understand what he was saying. And he could hardly imagine going with her to a museum to look at old paintings. Unless the weather was good and the museum was almost empty. Maybe she'd come along, even be interested and curious. But then he might start holding forth. Awful. He could only go to see paintings alone, or with Helen. Passing by all of modern art without a word. It was great to ignore all the rubbish and know it wasn't worth a damn, to feel this elation because you hadn't fallen for all the junk the museum directors and critics had been talked into. Then on to the Old Masters. You couldn't allow yourself to fall for everything there, either. There was a lot of cheap stuff. Just don't show any awe—point out the poorly painted figures with a chuckle, the ludicrous mythical scenes, the Christian nonsense, the diminutive saints. The Old Masters had succeeded more or less by accident at what was really important: a windowsill with a hand towel and a vase, a small dog in a corner, and mountains turning blue toward the horizon—the end of the world. The things that seemed to be the least important to them turned out to be the best, no question about it.

That was the way life with Helen had been. They were on the same wavelength, at least for a couple of years. When you were a student, you had time. You crammed once a year, really hard, and then you had a lot of time again. Helen had studied this and that, languages, theater, mostly art. They slept together, talked and screwed, ate and drank. They didn't have much money, but it was enough. They weren't happy, but they weren't unhappy either. They went to the movies, to art exhibits, and listened to records—when you were in your twenties, you thought you were too old to go to pop concerts. At that age, you can't imagine what it will be like having a job and having to earn a living. Enough money for a tank of gas always seemed to come from somewhere. What did gas cost before the '73 oil crisis? Less than 60 pfennigs a liter?

Harry drew war orphan's benefits. Both his parents were dead; he hadn't known them at all. He thought that wasn't so bad, but Helen thought otherwise: "You can't be normal under those circumstances. If you grow up without a mother, you just have to be a little cracked!"

Harry had told her about his aunts and Villa Huberta, about his childhood near the Alps and the Austrian border, about buying chocolate in Salzburg and feeling like a smuggler bringing it across the border. Later on it had been rum, 160 proof, and he'd hoped it wouldn't cause impotence the way some people said it did.

One of his aunts had given Harry an ancient motorcycle for his twenty-first birthday, in October of 1966. Harry had admired it when he was little. It had belonged to one of his aunt's favorites who didn't come back from the war.

With that motorcycle, Harry had been a king and Helen a queen. It had two huge cylinders, one on each side, and a pancake engine that made a deep rattling sound. It needed repairs constantly, and the spare parts dealer had been more important to him than the university. He'd been just as important as the demonstrations against the Yanks' war in Vietnam.

Harry spent a couple of semesters in Berlin avoiding the draft. "The army, join the army, you're in the army now"—it was enough to make you sick. "Conscientious objector," "fundamental objection to war service," this twisting of words had been out of the question for him. You shouldn't have to subject yourself to a room full of malicious people asking trick questions. On the other hand, taking care of sick people for several months of his life hadn't been much of an alternative.

It was in Berlin as well that he must have been fathered, if everything had gone according to Hoyle. It was a riddle to him how anybody could think about screwing under those circumstances. His father was a doctor at a hospital in Berlin. Harry's aunts swore to him later that his father hadn't been a Nazi. He'd been killed in one of the big bombing raids on Berlin at the beginning of February 1945. Three thousand tons of high explosives, 22,000 dead. He had evidently sired Harry shortly before that, because Harry was born in Berlin in the peaceful month of October.

In 1946, Harry's half-brother, Fritz, came into the world, a product of his mother's incredible lust for life. She died in childbirth. Fritz grew up with foster parents in the Rhineland, and Harry was sent to live with his aunts in Bavaria, where he was well taken care of. There was deep snow in winter and tall grass in the meadows in summer.

Memories of his childhood had put Carola's charms in the shade. Harry took a newspaper off a hook. May 16, 1975, the racehorse Halla had just turned 30. Incredible that a horse could be six months older than Harry himself! In 1956, Winkler had won a gold medal on Halla, in spite of the fact that he was riding with a torn stomach muscle. It had been a hot subject at the time. "The fellow's fantastic!" said Aunt Frieda, who once rode horses herself, supposedly like the devil. But that was before the war, the First World War. Aunt Ursula saw things differently. Raising her smoke-roughened voice, she said: "That idiot! That damned Stalin-grad-, hang-tough-mentality!" And then Aunt Huberta let him have it as well: "It's his own fault, the conceited ape!" Aunt Frieda fell silent, outvoted. Harry's classmates and his teacher tended to be on the side of Aunt Frieda and her declarations of respect, while Harry, who was usually on Aunt Ursula's side, enjoyed calling the noted victor a bastard and a conceited idiot. Ten-year-old Harry clearly sensed that his swearing impressed the others. He'd learned to curse from his aunts. Each and every one of them a countess or a baroness, they spoke of nothing but bastards, S.O.Bs, idiots, windbags, wimps, and losers.

At the next table, Carola was waiting on a customer who had raised his backside from the chair and was search-ing his pockets for money. Carola stood there calmly with a large wallet in her hand, looking vaguely up and down the street. Harry was thinking that you should only take up with a woman when you can be pretty sure that after your second number, when you're forced to take a little breather, you can fill up an hour or so by making fun of something together— like the stupidity of steeplechases, the cruelty to the horses, and those disgusting riding boots and spurs.

The newspaper reported that the trial of the terrorists from the Red Army Faction would begin in Stuttgart in a few days. Harry had been bitterly disappointed that he couldn't get in on the trial as a lawyer. It would have been a real pleasure to stand up to the bastards prosecuting the case. And he'd have had clients he wanted to defend! How right they were to call the people in power "pigs." They have their solitary confinement, their high-security prison tracts, but they let the old Nazis off the hook.

Duckwitz paid his bill. He was so angry he couldn't even manage a forced smile for Carola. You couldn't treat a handful of show-offs as if they had rabies (after all, they only shoot things up because they believe in a better society!) and at the same time let concentration-camp killers run around loose and leave the worst of the Nazi judges in office. Sure, sure, you can't do anything about it, and there's no point in making the case in court, however eloquently, since it would simply make the judge and the prosecutor yawn. And only the leftist journalists who didn't have the slightest idea about how justice works would include his impassioned remarks in their stories. At least Helen would have read his name in the newspaper once in a while: "RAF attorney Duckwitz succeeds in getting court to subpoena new witnesses," or "Judge So-and-So excluded for partiality at request of RAF attorney Duckwitz."

Maybe Helen would have been in court for the final arguments, rushing over from that odd town in northern England where she'd taken a university teaching job. Without so much as batting an eyelash, she'd said: "I think the separation will do us good." And she asked Harry if he realized that for a long time they had simply been coexisting.

No, he replied, he hadn't noticed. And he didn't think it was so bad just to coexist.

"Thanks," Helen had said, "but not with me." And then she was gone, unfortunately not without adding: "You live your life and I'll live mine!" What an ugly thing to say after all that time.

Harry went over to his car. It was a VW Bug, of course. Nothing new-fangled. Helen had always been wild about Bug convertibles. They'd probably have had an argument now. Why should Harry work so hard and earn so much money if he wasn't even going to buy a more comfortable car? Harry thought a convertible was too trendy, too much like everyone else. The young lawyer who comes dashing up in a convertible. No thanks. He'd lose his credibility entirely. Harry certainly didn't think he had much credibility anyway, but it was a different kind.

He would have preferred to ride his motorcycle to the office, but he would have felt ashamed. The papers were full of stories about businessmen, doctors, even lawyers riding motorcycles to work. Even portly and aging state premiers allowed themselves to be given motorcycles, mounted them, and rode around looking like the dung beetles they were. Just a few years ago it had been unusual, and you would have looked like a shabby old pensioner. But all of a sudden it was in. All kinds of people were winding up dead or half-dead, and insurance was getting more expensive all the time. Harry would wait until the fad had passed.

It was a sunny morning in spring, warm and dry—and his car wouldn't start. This was its latest trick. It was what you got if you couldn't part with your old things. If Harry had been a member of the Automobile Club, he could have called road service. But the Automobile Club was obviously a kind of mafia, and if a normal driver was already the bottom of the barrel, what did that make a club that included millions of them!

It was seven-thirty. He was to be in court for a hearing at nine. It took twenty minutes to get to the office on foot, across the river and past the town hall. The question was, how should he cross the Main? One of the car bridges, or the old "Iron Footbridge"? These were the tough decisions. Being determines consciousness, he thought, and the kind of bridge you take determines your mood. A pedestrian bridge makes you more introspective. Harry decided he had been introspective enough already and chose the loud, heavily traveled vehicular bridge. Even if Harry loathed Sunday afternoon carwashers, car waxers, and car buffs—those typically German monstrosities—he didn't mind the cars themselves or the stench they created in the morning. While they might be unhealthy, they were a sign of life and movement. The quiet corners of the old city, where cars had been outlawed, seemed dead by comparison.

Harry was in his office just before eight. The secretaries weren't in yet. Yesterday the last to go, today the first to arrive. It couldn't go on this way.

Duckwitz concentrated on the court proceedings scheduled for nine that morning. Builder v. electrician. The wiring had been done incorrectly. In all probability the company that was being sued was a small, friendly operation that didn't get bogged down in details. Duckwitz would have to pick the company's sympathetically relaxed attitude to pieces because this asshole of a builder didn't want to pay the additional costs for relocating the plugs. Why did he have to build a house anyway!

There were noises out on the stairs and at the door, jingling keys and the sound of voices in the entryway. It was the prettier of the two secretaries and the legal intern. Duckwitz could hear everything they said through his partly opened door. "It's all just a façade, all just an act," said the secretary. "Believe me, he's as cold as ice." Duckwitz envisioned some disco hotshot who'd tried to put the make on the two chicks the night before. He could hear one of them rummaging around in her purse, then it was quiet. Probably putting on lipstick. Next came the ritual of making coffee.

"And those clothes he was wearing yesterday!" said the intern. Duckwitz imagined one of those grinning young faces you see in ads for banks.

"The same shirt as the day before," the secretary said.

"Now you're exaggerating," said the intern.

"I've got eyes!"

"Does he smell?"

"That's all we'd need."

There wasn't much doubt, they were talking about him. The secretary was right about the shirt. The things they notice! She was busy settling down at her desk, while the intern, that harmless, loyal soul, went to her office. The coffee machine gurgled and steamed, and the conversation seemed to be over when the intern called out: "It did make me mad that he wasn't along the last time everyone in the office went out together."

You too, thought Duckwitz.

The secretary poured a cup of coffee, stirred it, and said: "Do you think he's asked me just once in all these months how I am?" She took a sip. "He doesn't think about anything but his career. I can't stand guys like that."

2

How Duckwitz makes known his decision to enter the diplomatic service, takes various examinations, and soon learns to appreciate the advantages of his new way of life.

Once Harry tore a fingernail he'd cut awkwardly while in too much of a hurry. Filing your nails in peace was also a thing of the past. He thought about his school days. One time a teacher asked what happened at the Congress of Vienna; another boy answered: "A bunch of diplomats sat around filing their nails, that's all." It was a nice image, and Harry remembered it. Then he recalled that just before they finished high school, a career adviser had come to talk to them. Harry told him he had no idea what subject he should study since life was pointless anyway. The adviser replied that under those circumstances, and with Harry's name, he would recommend a career as a diplomat.

All of this occurred to Harry once again. As a joke, he called the Foreign Office in Bonn and had them send him some information. He glanced through a brochure labeled *Advice to Applicants: Careers in the Senior Diplomatic Service.* Just for fun, he filled out the application.

It had been a normal, boring day, one like so many others recently. He'd spent it going through clients' files and earning money he couldn't spend. He still hadn't taken his record player to be fixed, and he still hadn't installed a tape deck in his old VW. He was still eating breakfast at the bakery, and Helen was still in northern England. Things had come to a standstill and threatened to stay that way.

A short time later he was notified that on September 12, 1976 he should appear for the written qualifying examinations in Frankfurt. Harry loved exams. They had always come easy to him. This time it was especially pleasant because he was going into the exam without any real stake in it, on a mere whim, the way you buy a lottery ticket that doesn't promise much but doesn't really cost you anything either. He didn't tell anyone at the office.

Harry learned shortly afterward that he had passed the exam. Evidently he had successfully translated both into and out of French and English the texts on butter pricing policy and the French atom bomb. And the baloney he'd written in a set essay about relations between China and the Soviet Union didn't seem to have bothered anyone. Answering the questions hadn't been easy. "Explain why the German Reich has not been eliminated as a subject of international law"— that had been okay. But then came, "Name four of the topics that were discussed at the U.N. Conference on Maritime Law" and "By what means are EC agricultural markets protected from cheap imports?" That was a pretty hairy question. But even if Duckwitz didn't have much time to spare at the office, he had always managed to read the newspaper. He read it thoroughly and had a good memory, and so he was well-informed even about things he wasn't particularly interested in. And since he also knew who Paul Klee and Karl Jaspers were, as well as the composers of *The Four Seasons* and *Così fan tutte*, he had scored more than the minimum number of required points.

Three hundred applicants had taken the written examination, he was told, and one hundred had passed. He was requested to appear at the Foreign Affairs Training and Advanced Education Center in Ippendorf, near Bonn, as soon as possible for the oral examination. The selection committee would then "be able to gain a comprehensive and differentiated impression of the personality and intellectual abilities of the applicants," after which it would recommend an elite of 30 to 40 people to "The Federal Minister of Foreign Affairs," as they loftily called their cabinet minister.

The two partners in his law firm couldn't believe it when he told them about his plans. "You're crazy!" they said. Even making allowances, the diplomatic service is the pits. What a club! A bunch of peacocks! Harry glanced over at the secretary who had carped behind his back about his lack of collegial feeling. Even she seemed to regret that he was leaving.

When his colleagues realized that he was serious about it, they tried a different tack. What would the office do without Harry and his expertise? He was a pearl among lawyers, they couldn't let him throw himself before the swine at the Foreign Office!

They used Harry's own arguments against him for a while, but he didn't feel like discussing it. He didn't want to hurt them. His old aversion to notions like hard work and ambition were none of their business. All he said was: "Some people go to see a guru in India. I'd rather enter the diplomatic service."

"How about the Foreign Legion!" said one of his colleagues.

"I'd rather represent this strange country we call the Federal Republic of Germany than keep on representing smart alecks in court," said Duckwitz. And besides, nothing had been decided yet.

The oral part of the selection process was supposed to last several days. He took the train to Bonn. During the short trip he had a chance to think about this odd flirtation with a diplomatic career. After all, he was about to make an important change in his life. Were his aunts behind it? Did he have to prove something to them in the absence of a father? The psychoanalytical approach was actually Helen's specialty. Was it his poor but feudal childhood that was coming through here? Did the image of the slightly decadent diplomat seem more in keeping with a Baron von Duckwitz than did that of a lousy lawyer? It was hard to believe his upbringing could have left behind any trace of attitudes like this, but it didn't make much difference anyway. If there's one thing that makes you drowsy, it's a train ride, and Harry soon dozed off.

As the taxi left the capital proper and approached the Foreign Affairs Training and Advanced Education Center in Ippendorf, Harry began to feel a little giddy. You can escape from people you don't like, but you're at the mercy of architecture. Not only was the center's location oppressively peripheral, but the angular cement building with its terrible mixture of styles from the fifties and sixties aroused the most unpleasant associations. Such sprawling, secretive structures, thought Harry, should be reserved for fanatical Jesuits or pink-cheeked college boys from Connecticut, for high-ranking NATO officers or the lean, mean products of transcendental schools of management. The landscaping of the rather barren park areas around the center was hopeless, and the outer walls of the building had dark patchy marks left behind by the rain. The only thing missing was graffiti proclaiming in red that you were now leaving the Western Sector.

In his welcoming remarks, the director of the center gushed about the recently completed building. For years, the diplomatic elite had been receiving its training in run-down barracks, he said, but that was a thing of the past. In addition, the members of the intermediate levels of the diplomatic service were now also being trained in this bulding, "that is, those young men, pardon me, men and women, who come to us directly from high school and who are later part of the everyday life of our embassies abroad and our headquarters here at home." It's time to overcome prejudices and barriers, he added.

Duckwitz found the selection process quite enlightening. He came to understand completely what he had only suspected on first sight of the towering cement block of the center. His suspicions had been confirmed by the insipid neckties and somewhat acidic joviality of the past five days: any trace of what is generally understood as diplomacy was timidly avoided here. Aristocratic bearing, cigarette cases, flirting with the few women applicants like a character in a Lubitsch film, or an extra champagne piccolo at their shared lunch were totally out of place. What they were looking for was a self-assured but modest manner, unobtrusive clothing, and a dutiful head full of knowledge about national and international law, history, politics, and economics. What they wanted were the go-getters and the salesmen types being sought by every personnel manager of every large company: healthy and energetic, though perhaps not as tough as the ones for Esso and Hoechst. They rather tactlessly made no secret of the fact that top people were, unfortunately, rare here because they had already been wooed away by industry and the major banks. It made all the applicants feel about two inches tall and absolutely second-rate. The unemployed teachers of English, French, and History who had chosen a diplomatic career because of the unforeseen surplus of teachers in the country squirmed uncomfortably in their seats.

Duckwitz also had his problems. With his aristocratic title and his law degree, he was an exact fit for the stereotype of the diplomat the Foreign Office was trying to shake off. But he was able to argue credibly in a number of conversations that he thought of the Foreign Office as a "mere service agency." "Oh, not just that," the director of the center interjected with a smile; it was clear to him that you weren't supposed to grasp merely cocktail glasses these days, but a little something more.

In spite of a few clever answers, Duckwitz wasn't sure where he stood. Things were starting to get interesting.

The real gems among the applicants were a farmer who showed up in blue jeans and tennis shoes, and a conscientious objector with a full beard. Since these exotic types would allow the Foreign Office to demonstrate its tolerance and openness, it was clear that they would be among the chosen.

During a panel presentation, Duckwitz was finally able to brush aside the reservations people had about him. The subject was American intervention in Vietnam, an old hat, and the discussion wasn't getting off the ground because everyone seemed to agree that intervention had been in keeping with national and international law and was morally right in any case. The discussion flagged, and the farmer, who had to play the role of moderator, broke out in a sweat. He timidly tossed out some bait, asking whether military intervention might not possibly have its disadvantages. As he asked the question, he cast an apologetic glance toward the examining committee at the back of the auditorium. No one took the bait. Then Duckwitz pulled himself together and launched into an attack on Nixon. He could see the kitchen of his old college commune, and Helen's flaming words now erupted from his mouth: "We cannot insist on a strict interpretation of the principles of international law in a case that is judged emotionally by the people. The magnitude of these emotions forces us to talk about the emotion itself and not about ivory-tower legal concepts!"

At last the discussion took a lively turn. The others attacked Duckwitz's arguments, adduced all kinds of points for consideration, added that you could not ignore the balance-of-power issue, and the conscientious objector said that he would always defend the free West, naturally without the use of force. Everyone stepped to the fore, everyone had to demonstrate his intellectual ability and vitality to the psychologist and the director of the center. Quicker than you can count to three, each one of them turned into the Foreign Minister or Chancellor of the Federal Republic. But no one came close to Duckwitz that day. In the subsequent evaluation of the presentation, the psychologist praised the courage and skill he demonstrated in taking over the leadership of the discussion at just the right moment. The director said with a threatening grin: "Let's hope that's not what you really think."

Following his excursion into the absurd world of aptitude testing, Duckwitz returned to Frankfurt. The handful of cases he had to wrap up were the last straw. As childish as the trained and untrained diplomats in Bonn had been, the prospect of winding his way through the foreign world of diplomacy was beginning to seem appealing.

•   •   •

While in training, they were called "attachés." The dashing term contrasted oddly with the plastic chairs in the classrooms where they subjected themselves to language courses and lectures on national and international law. All of the trainees had rooms of their own at the center, even the ones who were married, though they usually lived at home if their marriage was intact. When the Deputy Foreign Minister came to Ippendorf for a chat, even the farmer put on a suit.

Most of the attachés measured their daring by the length of their sideburns. Even at a time when the sideburns of some political party chairmen were thick and bushy, attachés stuck to the unwritten law that sideburns should not extend below the earlobe. How vulgar! While the free world was discussing the clitoris, the subject of discussion in Ippendorf was the tip of the earlobe. And the high point of originality was a midnight dive into a swimming pool by a formally dressed attaché at a summer party in Bad Godesberg. Harry was able to rise above that level without too much effort.

While he was in training, Duckwitz stayed in touch with Helen, who was still in northern England. There were occasional letters, postcards, and telephone calls. They saw each other once when Helen was on her way to southern France, where she had angled a lively job helping prepare for the summer festival in Avignon. Their meeting fell kind of flat. Harry had armed himself against Helen's reproaches. He was prepared for wild accusations, thinking she might ask whether he had gone absolutely mad joining this bunch of snobs. He had worked out his line of defense, and then was disappointed when her attacks failed to materialize. She thought it was a little strange, but not so bad. "So what profession is ideal?" she said before disappearing in the direction of Avignon.

Harry didn't even manage to get in his hymn to the joys of irresponsibility. Because that's what he really liked about it. Only a lunatic would have been convinced by the instructors' comments about the meaning and importance of the diplomat's job. It was absolutely clear that all their talk was just another indication of its insignificance. All the bull they gave you about the colossal responsibility of the diplomat was designed to hide how little responsibility he actually has. And that was the best part of it. As a lawyer he'd had to bear real responsibility, and it had been a bother.

Harry enjoyed the year. Of course it was ridiculous to spend twelve months as if you were at a weekend training seminar; but it was pleasant not to have to bother about anything. He finally had some time. He had his record player repaired and listened to old records. Not much new since the beginning of the seventies. None of the pop music of the last few years was worth mentioning—thirty percent of it was rehash, seventy percent was absolute hogwash. That much was clear.

From time to time he read an old novel, he enjoyed the English and French courses, and he took a little Spanish. Once in a while he got together with his brother Fritz, the poet. Although Fritz lived in Cologne, they didn't get together very often. They didn't have too much to say to one another. Harry just didn't feel like bothering with the stuff Fritz wrote.

Fritz considered Harry's decision a pretty good one. At first Harry thought his brother was making fun of him. "No, why?" asked Fritz. "Being a diplomat isn't so bad." A lot of diplomats had been poets, and poets diplomats, there had to be some kind of affinity between them. Besides, Fritz liked the word "foreign"; it had so many connotations, you could almost turn it into a poem. If you're foreign, you don't belong. The foreigner is a great symbolic figure, a less senti-mental version of the hackneyed outsider.

After making this comment, Fritz left, as usual without any warning. Harry lay on the bed in his room at the Train-ing Center in Ippendorf. All of a sudden he sensed some-thing like brotherly feeling. Maybe he needed to be just a little "foreign" in order to be comfortable? Even as a school kid, he'd liked being an External Pupil. Not belonging. The only high school near Villa Huberta was a boarding school. Two-hundred pupils locked inside, and Harry was the only one who could go home at the end of the day. He wasn't sent to bed, didn't have to put up with the shoving in the chow line, he merely disappeared into freedom.

Maybe he'd been uncomfortable as a lawyer because he couldn't step out of line. You had to stand behind your client one hundred percent. And now he was taking on a job that he could profit from but in all good conscience did not have to take seriously. Harry thrived. He could do the things expected of him with his left hand. The feeling of being above it all was priceless. True luxury isn't money but being able to indulge in your own thoughts. And there was plenty of opportunity for that here.

He sent Helen a card: "Bonn is my India. Here I have found illumination." Marx had been absolutely wrong with his diatribes against the alienating effects of labor. It was the other way around: work that doesn't alienate you turns you into an imbecile. "Just look at business executives, Helen," he wrote, "at lawyers—as dull as dumdum bullets. And what do they do? They greedily immerse themselves in their non-alienating labor."

Helen sent him a return postcard quoting a neatly impudent remark, unfortunately without giving the source: "As for me, I am broadly uneducated." Harry hung the card on the wall above his bed.

When Harry had completed his training and his first diplomatic post abroad was up for discussion, the man in the Personnel Office asked: "Do you have any preferences?"

Duckwitz shook his head. "It's all the same to me. Just far away."

"If only it were this easy all the time!" said the man from Personnel.

A week before he was supposed to leave, Duckwitz learned that he was being sent to the embassy in Yaunde, Cameroon, where he'd be responsible for Economic and Legal Affairs.

"You'll get along just fine there," someone said.

3 *How Harry von Duckwitz misbehaves at a dinner party at the embassy in Yaunde, Cameroon, and how the people he would least have expected to, take it amiss. How he refuses to light a lady's cigarette, and how he is not at all interested in spreading German culture abroad. In addition to some unexpected insights on the meaning of religion, church towers, the pyramids, and the artistic value of Sanella Margarine picture cards. Along with some information on Duckwitz's colleague Hennersdorff and the advantages of hierarchy, as well as a number of recollections of Duckwitz's former girlfriend Helen. Finally, how Duckwitz has to defend himself against the old charge of triviality.*

The embassy of the Federal Republic of Germany had availed itself of the opportunity of a visit by a German Member of Parliament to host a dinner party. The M.P. was traveling in the company of an amply endowed lady who was supposed to breathe new life into the Goethe Institutes abroad. She, in turn, was accompanied by a man described as a distinguished professor of German literature. He looked suspiciously tough and wiry. Harry von Duckwitz, Counsellor for Economic Affairs and the number three man in the embassy, was seated next to the woman from the Goethe Institute and was wondering why she'd chosen to wear a ruffled dirndl dress, fit for a princess, here in the middle of Africa. It was a dress that would have been out of place anywhere in the world, and it emphasized curves in all the wrong places. Despite this vagary of taste, she was pleasant enough to chat with, and to Duckwitz's Prussian ears the slight Viennese lilt to her speech lent their conversation the faded glamor of a bygone era.

Duckwitz had just been advising the Goethe woman against going to an African folk performance when the moment for dessert arrived. One after the other, the guests at the table crooked their necks to make room for the arms of the black waiters serving the dessert. Strawberry creme Bavarian topped with whipped cream—nothing exciting, of course, but here in far-off Cameroon like a greeting from home, one the Europeans at the table received with childlike pleasure.

After Duckwitz had taken the first bite of dessert, his usually animated face froze. The lady on his right smiled expectantly, for the witty diplomat's look suggested he was good for another bon mot as soon as he'd swallowed his first sweet spoonful. Instead, Duckwitz let the dessert flow back onto his plate as silently as lava. If he hadn't finished with a loud spitting noise, the others might never have noticed. As it was, the whole table looked up. "Damned bastards!" he said, every eye riveted on him. The two African cabinet ministers and their wives evidently thought he was going to make a speech—they placed their silverware politely on their plates, wiped their mouths with their napkins, and leaned back with an air of attentive courtesy. "Damn this shit!" said Duckwitz hotly. "I'll bet there's a package of Dr. Oetker Instant Something-or-Other behind this!" Duckwitz said that he would be the last person in the world to mourn the good old days when the foreign missions flew in Helgoland lobster and fresh strawberries for their dinner parties. But that revolting, old-fashioned posturing had been replaced by an instant- and fast-food mentality that was no less disgusting. This pudding, for instance, would be an imposition on anybody's tongue!

The four high-ranking Cameroon officials probably didn't understand a word. The last German colonials had left Cameroon in 1916, and there were only a few old men in the country who still spoke German. When they were younger, they'd served chilled drinks to the gentlemen from Biberach and Breslau, but now that their human dignity had been restored by the passing of several decades, they raved about the old days. The dark-skinned natives among the guests were young. They spoke that wonderful black French and English that sounds more authentic than the language of Paris and London. They applauded when Harry stopped speaking, a few others clapped ironically or with a sense of relief, and the embarrassing moment soon passed. "This won't happen to me again," the ambassador said with a trace of gratitude after dinner. "That depends on what you serve," said Duckwitz.

They took their coffee on the terrace. The ambassador was talking with the M.P. about the climate. Down on the coast, in Duala, he said, the heat and humidity are almost unbearable. He felt sorry for his poor colleagues at the embassy's branch office there.

Duckwitz didn't feel like talking to anyone anymore. He sat down in a corner and picked up a newspaper. The Goethe woman and the jeans-clad professor—who evidently taught literature at some incredibly progressive university— stood around looking lost. Then, with as much nerve as embarrassment, they simply sat down at Duckwitz's table. The wicker chair groaned under the Goethe woman's weight. A cigarette already dangling from her lips, she began searching through her abomination of a purse for a cigarette lighter. Duckwitz had the feeling that, once she'd lit her cigarette, she would ask him about the incident at the table. The professor took in everything with birdlike glances.

When the Goethe woman finally found her lighter and blew her first cloud of smoke into the African night sky, she actually did ask whether Duckwitz thought he'd done the right thing at the table. She may have sounded particularly irritated because Duckwitz, though he was her host, had not made the slightest move to light her cigarette. The Austrian accent that had spread such a pleasantly carefree atmosphere only a moment ago suddenly seemed pedantic. Duckwitz didn't feel like answering her questions, so he asked one of his own: "Do you know why I didn't light your cigarette?" She shot back a reply: "Probably because it makes you feel like an emancipated man!" "Not at all," said Duckwitz. "It's because you smoke Marlboros!" Anybody who would smoke an American weed sold through ads showing horse-buggers, he said, wasn't about to get a light from Harry von Duckwitz.

The Goethe woman sniffed: God knows she didn't care at all for instant foods, she said, not at all, but what Duckwitz had done was no way to show distaste. It had been absolutely revolting! He was only destroying his own credibility, and he wouldn't get anywhere with his silly aristocratic uncouthness. It was. . ., it was. . . She searched for the right word and finally found it—it was a mere petitesse. She pronounced the word as if it were a Viennese specialty. Duckwitz didn't want to argue with this old biddy from the Goethe Institute, and besides, what he'd done didn't have anything to do with the dessert. She'd never understand that. She was probably one of those upstanding old Social Democrats who suffer under the illusion that you can still achieve something with party work and adult education. You can get along with any plumber, with any laborer, better than with these narrow-minded intellectuals who live in as much fear of committing a social blunder as any other narrow-minded person.

The jeans-clad professor jumped into the conversation at this point, saying that he certainly hadn't found Duckwitz's behavior scandalous, though he had found it alarmingly frivolous. He had to ask himself whether that was the right way to demonstrate resistance to the political establishment. He said he was anything but satisfied with the way things were, but he found this form of criticism to be totally lacking in political perspective. Duckwitz was quite taken with the professor's comments—the man had, after all, judged his provocation to be a political act.

The jeans-clad professor turned to the Goethe woman, and as if what he had to say was of no concern to Duckwitz—who wouldn't understand it anyway—he lectured: "Throwing up is, of course, an old metaphor for rejection, but this was completely out of place." The professor evidently considered Duckwitz a character in a novel, to be interpreted any way he pleased! What a ridiculous jacket he had on! "Your jacket," said Harry as cuttingly as possible, "is also a metaphor, even more so than your slacks. May I inquire as to the meaning of the metaphor?" The professor refused to be ruffled. As a matter of fact, he became quite affable, telling Duckwitz that he was wearing a parachutist's jacket from California. Sky diving was a passionate hobby of his, and the best place for that was California, where he was about to take another course.

Intellectuals who play soccer are incomprehensible enough, thought Duckwitz, but a sky-diving professor of literature—that's just too much! He didn't have to sit here and let himself be censured by ignoramuses and jocks who called themselves progressive and earned enough money as academics to pay for trips to California! He didn't have to let himself be hauled over the coals by Marlboro-smoking, sky-diving optimists! He'd show them all! Well, maybe he wouldn't after all. Old-fashioned conservatives, like the ambassador and his wife, would never understand that he wasn't merely an entertaining clown. And these progressives with their expansionist desires, who think a violation of the rules is a violation of good sense, would never understand that the situation can be made bearable by just one thing: constant misbehavior and the violation of rules and manners, custom and tradition.

The Goethe woman and the jeans-clad professor finished their coffee and in muted voices began lamenting the current state of European culture. In Latin America, said the professor, writers cultivate quite a different tradition of myth. All of a sudden he sounded like a washing-machine salesman, snobbishly pointing out the unsurpassed cleansing power of the new Miele 2000. Duckwitz chimed in and asked why, if they really thought European culture had gone to the dogs, they were so busy trying to transport it to every corner of the globe.

The professor laughed out loud, rubbing his leg and turning to Duckwitz: "Pragmatism!" he exclaimed. And the Goethe woman went into a long explanation that was indeed very pragmatic. Duckwitz hated responses like that, the kind that don't tell you anything you don't know already. A response had to be witty. You could come up with sensible answers yourself—assuming you weren't a complete idiot. In any case, these two representatives of pragmatic reason were totally lacking in wit. About the only thing they did have was a feel for literary wordplay of a kind Duckwitz didn't understand, didn't even want to understand. Harry thought with horror about the incomprehensible literary productions of his rhymer of a brother.

In any case, Professor Parachute and Aunt Petitesse had no feel for Duckwitz's antics, certainly not for antics that miscarried. The business with the pudding he'd choked up might have miscarried, but these two masters of interpretation, who were getting all worked up over the lack of a literary avant-garde, didn't understand a thing about the antics of desperation. They evidently did think they understood something about innovation, which was what they were talking about now. "Contemporary literature lacks innovation," they said. Here they were, two people whose profession was the German language, and they sat there heedlessly using borrowed words like "hobby" and "innovation"! What

difference is there between them and the head of the loan
department at a bank, or engineers at Mercedes Benz, or the
data freaks at Siemens? They don't ever think things are
innovative enough, either! That's why they're constantly
coming up with new automobile designs and ever more
idiotic telephones. And that's why literature keeps getting
more idiotic. All these new books are indigestible because
not one damn soul trusts himself to use ordinary language,
because poets don't dare try to capture their observations in
downright ordinary words. And if someone uses ordinary
language, they say he lacks the power of observation! It was
in order to distinguish themselves from journalists that
writers began using artificial language in the first place, and
now they were upset because no one was interested in their
books!

   "Harry, you don't understand," his brother Fritz had
once said to him. He'd come to visit Harry and Helen when
they were students in Frankfurt, and he'd brought along a
book as a present. Harry opened to a page at random and
read out loud: "Yellow is either alive or it isn't. Don't let
yourself be tamed! Hold on! The Self will have its day! Go
down as upright as possible so that it all comes back up!"
There you have it! Harry had said to his brother. He told
Fritz he could stay only if he took the book with him when
he left the next day. Harry picked out another sentence and
read: "I've had it up to here with a sense of security!" Harry
was irritated: "What hogwash!" Not as bad as napalm
maybe, but that's about all you could say for it. Nobody
could understand a thing like that. Writers were just putting
up smokescreens, and everyone else went groping around in
them. And because no one understood a thing, everyone
thought the haze was the non plus ultra of literature! Harry
said that even as a school kid he'd known when a writer was
trying to put something over on a reader. And calling on his
mercilessly reliable memory, Harry recited with pleasurable

contempt a few lines from a poem by Hermann Hesse that he'd had to learn in school: "Strange, in the fog to wander / Life is lonely / No one knows the other / Each has himself only." That was still the basic poetic feeling, said Harry. It used to be pure kitsch. Now writers have become so refined, they simply make the kitsch a little less comprehensible. Harry said he preferred his kitsch straight.

And now here he was, years later, with two characters wanting to export innovative West German cultural kitsch to Cameroon, and he was supposed to help them do it. Duckwitz was in charge of finding additional space for the Goethe Institute in Duala. This would give the Goethe woman a suitable answer for any bureaucrat or passer-on of requests who objected that there was not yet a site for the new institute. "Herr von Duckwitz, who is in charge of Legal and Economic Affairs at the German embassy," she would say, "has indicated there is a reasonable property available for the purpose." That's what he was good for, to serve as henchman to these two smart-asses. He wouldn't lift a finger for their foolish institute! German culture, innovative or not, should stay where it is. You have to fight this missionary zeal, otherwise you're liable to find yourself arranging dramatic readings for has-been German actors in the middle of Africa. Europeans have peddled their intolerable Christianity long enough! What's left of the Third World should at least be spared their latest line of cultural products.

Duckwitz was going to let the professor and the Goethe woman think he would do everything he could for them. No point in explaining there's no point, he thought. There was even less point in telling them that he objected to their plan on what could be called ideological grounds. And that wasn't quite it either. He objected because the two of them got on his nerves. If the woman sitting there had been pretty and if the man had possessed a sense of irony, that is, if they had been people Duckwitz could get on with, the export of West German culture would probably have seemed quite bearable.

Harry longed again for Helen's company. She was in far-off Germany doing God knows what. He'd always liked listening to her criticisms. She wouldn't have criticized his pudding number, but he'd have had to watch out if he'd later claimed it had been the "antics of desperation." Helen would have had a thing or two to say about the "antics of desperation"!

Helen might have been able to make it clear to these two incomprehensible champions of literature that the actual spitting out of pudding might be more meaningful and artful today than the devoted repetition of inane art-world banter. In the meantime, though, the Goethe woman and the professor had almost passionately agreed that the hundredth birthday of some Dadaist or Surrealist, in any case some terribly avant-garde figure, should be celebrated next year or the year after that in Goethe Institutes all over the world.

The others had gone inside, but the doors remained open. How reasonable the babble of human voices sounded when you could only understand a snatch of conversation here and there. As if all was right with the world! Unfortunately, the sky was overcast. When he was little, Harry believed that in Africa the sky was always clear. It was easier to get lost in your thoughts if you could look up at the stars. Or bats. Watching bats at twilight wasn't bad either. Actually, there should be bats here in Africa, too. He'd asked a zoologist about it recently. It turned out that you just couldn't see them in Cameroon because nightfall comes so quickly near the equator.

It had grown cool. Harry turned up his collar and pulled his jacket around himself more tightly. It was pleasant not to feel any responsibility for anything. Like guests he should have been looking after but wasn't. For even more regrettable than the lack of stars and bats was the fact that among the more than thirty guests at this dinner there wasn't a single woman he was attracted to. Sitting alone out on the terrace would be much more pleasurable if there was a chance that some woman with whom he'd exchanged a long look at the table would unexpectedly appear on the terrace, as if by chance, and exclaim: Oh, there you are! What are you doing out here? And he would reply: You may not believe it, madam, but I'm just in the process of summing up my theory of art.

Where art was concerned, Duckwitz had limited but, to his way of thinking, incisive knowledge. He felt that he could, in good conscience, talk about art. He told everyone who would lend an ear that in contrast to natural phenomena or new technologies, art is best judged by non-specialists, since distance leads to insight. That's the advantage of a work of art as compared with a technical invention: the opinion of the layman is more valuable than that of the specialist. As an indefatigable reader of newspapers, Duckwitz was fairly well informed about what was going on in the art world and thus had enough information to deliver his witty tirades against the absurdity of modern art. When his remarks drew the applause of culturally conservative lovers of good old art, though, Duckwitz would suddenly turn and attack their "eternal values."

From his trips with Helen, Harry knew a lot about the architectural styles of the past. He'd never been able to spend more than one minute in a Gothic cathedral without feeling sick to his stomach. For him, this had become a universally valid argument against Gothic art: it's revolting and inhumane, he liked to say; its sole aim is to turn men into worms and snails. In Harry's opinion, Baroque palaces weren't any more humane. As a student, he had naturally called their dimensions "fascist."

Then, on one of the art history expeditions he'd taken

with Helen in the late sixties and early seventies, he'd
noticed that there were churches that either didn't let in
enough light or were so high you couldn't decipher the
paintings on the ceiling with even the best of eyes. In short,
the history of art was just one long history of nonsense, and
Helen was studying a nonsensical subject. By comparison,
Harry would say, his law studies made pretty good sense,
though artistic nonsense did have its advantages. After all,
what would Cologne and Strasbourg be without their somber
cathedrals, what would Munich be without its Frauenkirche,
Würzburg without its palace? And even the most miserable
provincial holes they passed through would lack something
without their church towers. You had to hand it to the
church: hypocritical as it was thoroughly corrupt, at least it
had brought forth church towers.

In Harry's opinion, the only thing worse than Christianity was Islam, because it was so terribly vital. The good
things about Christianity were its mendacity, its complete
state of decay, its insufferable Catholic popes and the jokes
they call cardinals, and the fact that it had become completely watered down. Christianity was nothing more than a
morbid, inconsequential relic. In any case, Harry didn't know
anyone who would lay claim to being a practicing Christian.
In fact, these days the very idea of a "practicing Christian"
was enough to make you laugh yourself silly! But those
damned Muslims weren't even hypocritical! They confessed
to their religion with almost canine devotion, turning in all
seriousness toward Mecca, falling punctually to their knees,
and behaving like cockroaches in heat. It wasn't funny but
awful to see them worship a monster called Allah who'd
been invented by some uppity prophet. Freedom of worship
was one of the weaknesses of the democratic constitution,
though it was clear that you couldn't deal with religions by
prohibiting them. That only made them more intractable.
Once religion had caught on, it was as hard to get rid of as

nuclear waste. It took forever for the radiation to die down. Only after Christianity had been around for 1200 years did it reach its aggressive phase, with the Inquisition, and only after 1700 years and the Enlightenment did it begin to lose its punch. Islam was a good 500 years younger. If there was some kind of half-life for monotheistic religions, then you had to figure it would take another 200 years, 1700 plus 500, for Islam to lose its virulence, for Muslims to turn into normal human beings you could joke with about God and the world.

But even if Islam did turn men into insects, what would Middle Eastern cities be without the minarets and the bleating of the muezzins—pre-recorded or live from fanatic throats? Harry would be the first to stand up for the preservation of mosques and minarets, because they were part and parcel of the nonsense. Nonsense provided a backdrop. Without the backdrop, life would be even more disagreeable.

Cameroon wasn't as permeated by Islam as some other countries in black Africa. If you could believe the statistics, there were nearly twice as many Christians as Muslims in Cameroon. When the ambassador deigned to show his German guests around the capital, he made sure to point out the new church. It was the latest atrocious monument to missionary zeal, and it was considered to be one of the proudest, most modern sights of Yaunde.

•   •   •

Like any other bureaucracy that seeks to exact respect from those who serve it, the German Foreign Office told its diplomats only at the last minute which of the foreign missions would be home to them for the next three years. Diplomats complained about the chicanery, but without any real indignation. They were like well-behaved children who, in their supreme impotence, accept with no more than a giggle the ridiculous dictates of their parents. Duckwitz had also accepted the practice with a shrug of his shoulders. It was no way to treat people, of course, but it did spare him a decision. As for the others, only a few of them protested, because the moment of surprise brought a bit of color to the drabness of a diplomat's everyday life.

Duckwitz had had just enough time to buy himself a couple of books about Cameroon. He found it reassuring that nearly half the population had refused to be fast-talked into adopting a foreign religion and still clung to their old animism. In fact, he was beginning to think it was a piece of luck that he'd been sent to Cameroon. Though the political situation was pretty catastrophic and the president was, of course, a power-hungry autocrat, though the regime had the gutless opposition under control and organized the usual electoral fraud, in comparison with other countries in Africa there was less mindless pomp, less coercion, less swindling, and less bloodletting. Power didn't run quite as wildly amok as it did in the neighboring Central African Republic, there were no religious wars as in Sudan, and there was no mass butchering of political opponents as there had been in Uganda. There had been rumors of a bloodbath recently in the northern part of Cameroon, possibly a few hundred dead, but that was nothing compared with the thousands slaughtered in Rwanda and Burundi. Uganda, Rwanda, Burundi—what idyllic-sounding names, and how hellish the reality behind them! Cameroon had even been favored by nature, with no disastrous droughts or famines like those in Chad and Ethiopia. Military leaders didn't crave power the same way they did in Nigeria, and there was no civil war that left behind a sea of dead as had the attempted secession of Biafra. Corruption was grotesque in Cameroon, but it wasn't boundless.

"The situation is stable," the ambassador had always

written reassuringly at the end of his regular reports to the Foreign Office in Bonn. And one way or the other he was even right with his naive assessment. But since Duckwitz had come to the embassy as the number three man and counsellor for economic affairs, and since he had begun supplying the ambassador's information, a few critical remarks had found their way into the reports. "The situation is comparatively stable" was the new conclusion to the ambassador's comments—that was better, that was good. "Comparatively" was more cautious and more diplomatic, and above all it was more accurate.

"How do you know all this?" the ambassador had asked recently when Duckwitz handed him his assessment of the country's economic situation. The figures and economic forecasts were ones you could find in Germany in any reputable paperback on the Third World in any good bookshop in any university town. Duckwitz phoned an official from Cameroon's Economics Ministry who'd been taken out of the loop, checked the numbers, and brought them up to date. You should always rely on people who've been cut off or removed from office, on the frustrated and the powerless. They're the ones who know best. And because they're embittered, they're happy to supply you with information.

"You have to know the right people," Duckwitz told the ambassador with as straight a face as he could muster. The ambassador was delighted: Duckwitz was an excellent man; the embassy really needed people like that; Duckwitz was well informed. The ambassador's wife, on the other hand, thought Duckwitz was a commie. The ambassador dreaded commies, but better a commie than that number two man in the embassy. He was responsible for cultural affairs and relations with the press, but all he was interested in was his collection of African sculpture. Besides, his name was Mayer. What an impossibly common name for someone in the senior diplomatic service!

Cameroon, Duckwitz found, was rather like a snug little nest—it felt downright homey at times. Maybe it was because even the incredible pace of modernization couldn't keep him from recognizing the Africa he remembered from the Sanella Margarine picture cards he'd collected in the early fifties, nearly a quarter of a century ago. The happiest moments in the life of the 6- to 8-year-old Harry von Duckwitz had been the afternoons when he'd begged his aunts to let him go to the Edeka Market to buy margarine, and he'd come back with the newest cards: zebras and gnus at the watering hole, ritual dances, at home with the black king Mua Mingo. And of course there was an excursion to see Dr. Albert Schweitzer, the oganga of Lambaréné. There was even an airplane that took the child-hero on a margarine journey to Africa, flying him over the darkly enticing wilderness of the continent. Twin-engined and good-natured as a bumblebee. Then there were the cityscapes of Addis Ababa and Capetown: the dignity of blacks and whites sauntering along dusty streets past block-long American cars. It had been a happy afternoon when he got a new picture, and a great day when he could paste all one hundred of them in his album!

The anonymous painter of the pictures on Sanella Margarine cards must have been a great artist, one who recognized the inner nature of Africa. He was a thousand times greater than his contemporary, that renowned bungler Raoul Dufy. Dufy's paintings of Paris looked like album covers and didn't have a thing to do with the real France. Or might it be that the Sanella pictures had made such an impression on him as a kid that he couldn't see Africa any other way now?

Quite apart from the Sanella pictures though, there were, strangely enough, parts of Cameroon that reminded Duckwitz of certain landscapes at home. There was one place in the foothills of Mount Cameroon that looked like a stretch along the Rhine near Coblenz as seen from the train by a certain light. And on the outskirts of Yaunde there was a place where you could almost think you were in Stuttgart.

Of course, no one else saw the similarities. Helen was the only person he could have confided in about such things. For some reason there was never anything like that in the personals: "Seek wife for exchange of ideas about similarities." It certainly didn't speak highly of prospective marriage partners to neglect that as a requirement; after—and in addition to—the screwing, it was the best part. Duckwitz, as an avid newspaper reader, had naturally taken note of the personals, the one true mirror of middle-class yearning. In any case, Harry thought that an exchange of observations about similarities was among the most pleasant of human pastimes, that it was a sign of love and understanding to be able to put your heads together and try to figure out who this or that person looked like.

•   •   •

Duckwitz rose from his wicker chair. Enough. Enough musing, enough ruminating. His brother was a rhymer and he was a ruminator. They came from the land of rhymers and ruminators.

Duckwitz's colleague Hennersdorff, who was talking to the M.P. and a black cabinet official in another corner of the room, looked like the mailman who had once—seven, eight, no, it was ten years ago—delivered the mail to Helen's commune in Frankfurt. They didn't receive any letters, but they did get the *Peking Observer* on thin foreign paper. Even the most rabid Marxists among them didn't read it.

A person's observations about similarities were more valuable when he could exchange them with someone. They were insignificant, yet like little discoveries. They helped you

get on, they made life richer. It was such a relief when you
finally remembered who the military attaché, that dud,
actually looked like. Of course! That actor with the bristly
crewcut, the one who was in so many French films in the
sixties, maybe even in the fifties. The one you still saw as a
character actor and whose name you could never remember.
His exact double was standing right there, wearing that
absolutely ludicrous uniform. Totally out of place. He should
be swept out with a broom. His only redeeming virtue was
that he recalled to mind that strangely familiar actor. But
there was no Helen to help savor the recollection.

Good old Hennersdorff, a reincarnation of their former
mailman—Duckwitz could have hugged him. Hennersdorff
hadn't attended a university. He'd applied to the diplomatic
service straight out of high school. Since he didn't have a
degree, he wasn't a member of the "senior civil service," as
Duckwitz was, but only a member of the "higher civil
service"—which sounds good if you don't know anything
about it, but actually translates into less influence and, above
all, a smaller salary. It was said that people in the senior
civil service looked down on those in the higher civil service.
Sometimes that was true, sometimes not. During Duckwitz's
training for the senior civil service, the attachés had formed
a more or less separate group. The way the instructors told
them not to look down on the members of the "higher," the
"intermediate," and particularly the "inferior civil service" had
been a model of condescension. But everyday diplomacy
evened out a lot of things and didn't leave much room for
pretension. The few really intelligent people, no matter what
path of diplomatic service they had chosen, quickly realized
that they were all just small fry. This created a bond.

Still, all the talk about the condescending behavior of
senior diplomats was so embarrassing to Duckwitz that he
was as friendly as could be toward everyone in the lower
ranks. It was his way of making recompense for privileges he

felt he hadn't earned. It had been a privilege, for instance, to grow up an orphan without an exacting, neurotic father and a mother eaten up with anxiety. It had been pleasant to grow up in an ingratiating landscape, in an old house with the wonderful name Villa Huberta, under the lax supervision of his smoking, drinking, card-playing, frivolously cursing aunts. It had been a privilege to be able to finance his university education with a combination of orphan's allowance and war-orphan's benefits and not to have to be a burden on anyone—least of all himself. He was a burden only to that monstrosity, the state, and you don't have to feel grateful to the state. It had been a privilege to have time to think about himself and to realize that everyday events are just so much hocus-pocus.

With all his privileges, he had yearned, as a student, to help those less well favored by fate, which is presumably why he went into law. It was also the reason why he was drawn to Helen and to the other flaming leftists she lived with in Frankfurt. For years, he had warmed himself at their fires. Later, as a lawyer, he would help those deprived of their rights. As a student, there wasn't too much you could do. One thing had been to distribute leaflets outside a factory at five in the morning. Duckwitz did it once. Never again. He'd believed he had to undergo such an initiation rite in order to justify himself as Helen's boyfriend and as a long-term guest at the commune. But outside the factory he'd felt unreal, as if he were a figure in one of those stirring socialist woodcuts from the 1920s or a drawing by Käthe Kollwitz. Harry von Kollwitz, the red baron, in the act of distributing leaflets! No, that didn't help. It wasn't even funny. He found it patronizing to inform workers about their supposedly miserable situation. His instincts told him to never, ever do it again.

It was only years later, as a lawyer, that he realized how perverse the whole thing was. He was in the process of successfully defending the rights of a worker against an employer who was exploiting him. Harry realized how passionately he had gone into the case and how, in the course of the proceedings, it became ever more obvious that the worker was a lazy bum and that the employer had been fair and a gentleman, but would come out on the short end of the stick following Harry's fiery summation.

This was one area where he and Helen were less in agreement than they were on the similarities between bus passengers and certain actors, actresses, and politicians. They'd argued into the seventies about the best way to improve conditions. Harry had reproached Helen for her interest in art history and French cathedrals, for babbling instead of doing. Helen countered by telling him that after a short burst of revolutionary thinking, he'd reverted to the bourgeois cynicism he'd grown up with.

In addition to this intellectual disagreement, an unusual feeling of sexual dissatisfaction suddenly crept into their relationship. For years, semester after semester, they'd screwed whenever they felt like it. All of a sudden, Helen was saying she felt Harry's advances were bothersome. The catastrophe was that she called them "advances." What had come naturally before was now an advance and seemed a little sleazy. She nagged him about his obvious hunger for sex and told him he joked so much it killed her desire. If he gave her a pat when she wore her tight blue jeans or her daring leather pants, she punished him the next day by wearing a baggy, asexual dress that made her look like a member of the Salvation Army or a guru groupie. And then, because he naturally didn't pat her in that outfit, she reproached him for being obsessed with externals. No, she told him, he wasn't one of those men who had only his own pleasure in mind, one two and off he went. That was all she needed! But the way he stroked her lately was so mechanical.

Harry said that her reproaches were enough to make a

normal man impotent but that he was, thank God, sufficiently robust to withstand them. He should have taken up with another woman right away, proven to himself and to Helen that it wasn't his fault but hers, for reading too many feminist books. He told her he could hardly bear anymore even to hear the words "emancipation," "woman," "women's literature," "women's pub," or "women's solidarity."

"That's just typical!" Helen shouted at him. "You're getting more and more reactionary!" This drove them apart.

• • •

When he was a lawyer, there was no hierarchy. There were colleagues and companions, adversaries, clients, and judges, but there was no hierarchy—no superiors, no subordinates. The secretaries at the office did not aspire to become lawyers. Now that he was a civil servant, there were rungs on a ladder and seniority and people of higher rank and different career tracks and different levels. Here there was hierarchy, and here you could finally show how little you thought of it. Hierarchy had always been the enemy because it ran counter to antiauthoritarian ideas of equality and justice. From within the hierarchy, he now realized that the constant complaints about it had been all wrong. Hierarchy was the enemy, but it was an abstract and necessary enemy. It provided useful rules of order you could constantly ignore. Since everyone within the hierarchy hated it, you could make yourself popular by violating its unwritten laws as often and as blatantly as you liked. Hierarchy produced brownnoses and conformists, but no one liked a brownnose or conformist. Duckwitz enjoyed being able to approach his boss as an equal. After all, that's what distinguished a civil servant from a stag: he didn't drive you out of his territory, he accepted you immediately as an equal—which was easy, since he never

forgot that he was the boss and that you were no threat.
Because you didn't cringe like a dog, he didn't treat you like
one. Those were the secret rules of the game. They worked
only as long as there were enough of those other characters
who went bowing and scraping down the hall, entering the
offices of their superiors with backs bent in deference.

At official functions, the ambassador was stingy with
the whisky. As if he had to pay for it himself. German beer,
German wine, but not even a run-of-the-mill scotch.
Duckwitz got himself two ice cubes from the refrigerator in
the small kitchen next to the reception room and went to
the broom closet, where he'd hidden a bottle of scotch
behind a bucket. Content, he returned to the others holding
a full glass. Hennersdorff's wife was droning on to Austria's
honorary consul about the virtues of Vienna's Lipizzaner
horses. The woman was an absolute phenomenon. In spite
of her good figure, she possessed not one shred of eroticism.
It was somehow reassuring, thought Duckwitz, that a
superior pair of legs just wasn't enough. Hennersdorff was
still talking to the M.P. and the black cabinet minister and
was looking a little pained. He worked harder than
Duckwitz and earned less money. At first, Duckwitz had
tried to make up for the injustice by being particularly kind
to Hennersdorff—as part of his own boycott of hierarchy.
The only thing that had curbed his efforts was his concern
that such kindness might seem exaggerated. But now such
artificial considerations had evaporated, and Hennersdorff
and Duckwitz were linked by a somewhat distant but sincere
friendship.

As if he realized that Duckwitz had been watching
him, Hennersdorff returned the look with a clear sign of
helplessness as the M.P. went on talking. He made as if to
quack by holding two fingers up to his mouth, which meant
that he had to interpret for the other two but would join
Duckwitz as soon as possible.

Duckwitz thought Hennersdorff should actually be called "von" Hennersdorff. His name cried out for that mark of aristocracy, more in any case than did the name Duckwitz. Duckwitz was an absolutely unaristocratic name, and the "von" in front of it just sounded ludicrous; it went perfectly with Hennersdorff. He'd said that to Hennersdorff at a party soon after arriving in Yaunde; Hennersdorff's wife, with her good figure and her complete lack of eroticism, hadn't known quite how to react.

Hennersdorff was loyal. When you weren't loyal yourself, this gave you something to lean on. When Duckwitz called the ambassador a jackass and his wife a water buffalo, Hennersdorff wasn't the kind who would smile at him roguishly. In order to settle the business of the "senior" and the "higher" civil service from the beginning, Duckwitz had tried to dismiss the distinction with a touch of irony. I think the word "high" sounds much more distinguished than "senior," he'd said. The next day, Hennersdorff had put his calling card on Duckwitz's desk along with a note: "From this moment on, I shall be 'von' Hennersdorff, Member of the Exalted Foreign Service." Since then, Duckwitz had taken Hennersdorff to heart. He would like to have been on familiar terms with him, but for some reason this affront to the prevailing conventions of the foreign service would have seemed like pandering.

In Duckwitz's opinion, Hennersdorff's marriage was an unhappy one: you can't be anything but unhappy if you're married to a woman like that. She didn't talk, she bellowed and shouted, usually about her three children and the breeding of horses. Once Duckwitz screwed up his courage and asked Hennersdorff why his wife talked so loudly. Hennersdorff hadn't even noticed. For a long time she'd lived with her mother, who was hard of hearing, and she probably got used to it, Hennersdorff said. Sometimes Duckwitz the bachelor spent the evening with the Hennersdorffs. He'd have enjoyed it much more if it hadn't been for this awful woman, whose first name was Rose and whom Duckwitz privately called Rugosa Rose, because she jutted up so straight.

Hennersdorff left the M.P. standing with the black government minister. For lack of an interpreter, the two could no longer communicate, and they parted in some embarrassment.

"Well?" Hennersdorff said to Duckwitz.

"I'm sorry!" Duckwitz said. "You'll have to forgive me. The business with the pudding at dinner was really stupid."

Hennersdorff laughed—the Frankfurt mailman he looked like had been a little shorter. Hennersdorff said it was incredible that the M.P. couldn't speak a word of English, let alone French.

"What were you talking about?" asked Duckwitz.

"Nothing," answered Hennersdorff.

For a while, the two of them stood there surveying the guests at a reception where nothing was happening, in a shoe box of a building that could have been located on the jagged coast of Dalmatia. "Vacancy." No style, no grace. Beautiful buildings always had a bloody history. Hennersdorff looked around and shook his head, saying that Duckwitz must have been crazy to give up his job as a lawyer. "For this!" he said with a certain bitterness. His wife was talking with the ambassador. Across the room, you could understand every word she said. It had been a particularly charming evening, she trumpeted. Duckwitz commented that, as a lawyer, he'd been forced to work too hard but had the feeling it was all for the birds. "This is for the birds, too," he said, gesturing toward the room, "but at least you don't have to do too much."

Hennersdorff said nothing. He did more. He had a sense of duty. He wanted to get ahead. He had to get ahead. And if you want to get ahead, you have to work at it.

"But you have to have something to do," he now said.

Duckwitz thought: if I were married to your wife, I'd sit in my office working all day, too.

"What do you do with your time?" asked Hennersdorff.

"I solve the riddles of existence," said Duckwitz. "To be more exact, I'm working toward solving the riddles of existence."

"For example?"

"For example, the German church tax."

"What? You mean, why you don't have to pay any church taxes while you're abroad?"

"No, I mean why I still pay church taxes when I'm at home."

"Because you're still a member of a church."

"And why am I a member of a church?"

"The usual insurance?"

"I beg your pardon!"

"Well, why then?"

"In order to pay church taxes."

"You're crazy! If that's what the answers to the riddles of existence look like," said Hennersdorff, "I'd rather sit in my office solving the riddles of the lost passports of German tourists in Africa."

Harry said the real joke was that he couldn't stand churches and didn't want to support them but that, unfortunately, church towers were important to him. He said that while he found the church as an institution intolerable and never attended a service, he did think it was right that in every sensible village there was a church with a tower you could see from a distance. The church was awful, but a village without a church tower was no village at all. And a drive through the countryside wouldn't be any fun if it weren't livened up by the church towers that punctuate the landscape like exclamation marks. By paying church taxes, he was making a contribution toward the preservation of church towers. "You're more impressive at spouting pudding than at spouting church tax philosophy," said Hennersdorff.

"When I was a lawyer, my head was so full of details, I never had time to think about stuff like that," said Duckwitz. "Just take the pyramids, for example. What nonsense! What megalomania! Nobody knows how cruel things really were back then. Who knows how cruel and humiliating slavery was in the ancient world? It's possible that more people died of the endless degradation and agony they suffered in building the pyramids than in the concentration camps."

"Careful," cautioned Hennersdorff.

"It could have been like that. Millions and millions of stone blocks, each of them weighing several tons, and they all had to be piled up by human hands. Today we stand there oohing and aahing and thinking, what would the desert be without the pyramids! Even my cigarette wrappers wouldn't be half as nice if it weren't for the pyramids," said Duckwitz, rolling himself a cigarette. The ambassador came over and joined them, an emphatic "Gentlemen!" on his lips. That was always appropriate. He watched Duckwitz roll his cigarette and said approvingly: "We used to do that, too."

As a diplomat, you could spit your pudding back onto your plate or roll your cigarettes like a student—the more out of line you got, the less likely you were to rub somebody the wrong way.

From across the room, Hennersdorff's wife called over to her husband—what choice did he have but to answer the call!

Duckwitz considered the idea of starting up a conversation with the literature professor and the Goethe woman about the relationship between splendor and brutality, between art and immorality. You had to be glad that, from time to time, there was someone you could talk to about these things. The other Germans who lived here and the ones who turned up occasionally at the embassy were about as humdrum as screw salesmen from Sindelfingen or automobile dealers from Wolfsburg. And the receptions they held in offices specially decked out for the purpose in this shoe box of an embassy were about as much fun as housewarming parties thrown by small-town mortgage company drudges.

The jeans-clad professor and the Goethe woman were talking with an awful character from Siemens. They probably wanted to hear whether Siemens was, in principle, willing to sponsor avant-garde art. The way Duckwitz judged this electronics wonder, he'd probably never even heard the English word "sponsoring" and thought it meant some new kind of electronic circuit. Actually, it did sound rather like that.

Duckwitz started to walk over to the Siemens/literary group but steered away before he ever got there. What did they know? What did they know about works of art and their origins in megalomania, about how the elevated originates in the low and mean and whether it still bears traces of its provenance? Harry wanted to keep the riddle to himself; he didn't want to let it be spoiled by some smart professor with a clever answer. There shouldn't be an answer for everything. That's why it was better to let your thoughts go blowing around in your own head than to talk to specialists who stop up all the chinks with their knowledge.

But he'd been ruminating a little too much recently. He'd been able to stand and sit and lie around, to let himself go and his thoughts wander. Tomorrow he'd work hard, because tomorrow there was something he wanted to do. At their regular morning briefing, he would hurl every bit of smut he could think of at the embassy's revolting military attaché. These idiotic officers had been told that freedom and democracy could only be preserved by their efforts; and in their stupid little officers' skulls, they actually believed it. They strutted around as if you owed them something.

Duckwitz looked at his watch. It was eleven o'clock. In just twelve hours he'd be flinging obscenities at the soul of an officer that lived inside this ludicrous monster. He was going to call soldiers pistol-polishers. He'd ask who was bribing him. What, no one is bribing you? Haven't you heard of the connections between the weapons industry and the Defense Ministry? Never heard of it? We know nothing. Aha! Duckwitz would then tell him the real reason he was in Cameroon: to set up weapons deals behind the back of the Foreign Office. What, that's not true? Pretty naive for a First Lieutenant. You don't say—you're a Lieutenant Colonel. Well excuse me, I'm not familiar with all that chicken shit on your shoulders! The real reason you're here is to circumvent the Law on the Control of Weapons of War, yes sir. You didn't know that? You merely pay friendly visits to the local troops with nothing improper in mind. You talk about weapons with those butchers you call colleagues, you invite one of the captain butchers and a colonel butcher to Germany, you show them a couple of nice military bases and a weapons factory. The weapons factory takes advantage of the occasion to offer a sample, a kind of grab bag: one hundred weapons at a special intro-ductory price—in the form of do-it-yourself kits, of course, since there are all those comical regulations in Germany. The barrels for the weapons are from England. Crazy, yes, yes, of course. And the magazines for the ammo are from Austria. All you have to do is put them together. We'll send along an assembly technician. Duckwitz would yell at the attaché: That's the way it's done! You're here to get around us and you don't even know it!

Duckwitz was looking forward to the next morning. It was going to be a pleasure. The ambassador would leave the room if it looked like things were getting too hot. The military attaché would go complain to the ambassador, who would answer, "Yes, yes, of course," but wouldn't report it any further. The ambassador had been an officer during the war and hadn't found it bad at all. But he didn't like the new army, and he liked the Defense Ministry even less. No one at the Foreign Office liked the Defense Ministry, and no one at the Defense Ministry thought very highly of the Foreign Office. They were both absolutely pitiful, and so they were constantly bad-mouthing each other.

In the afternoon, Duckwitz was going to turn to the road construction project and take a look at the bids made by German companies. He'd make use of his legal expertise to bring about exactly the opposite of what he was here to do, which was to look after the interests of German business. He would put every obstacle he could think of in the way of those thick-headed exporters of construction machinery, and the technicians, and all those airheads who go flying all over the world and don't understand a thing about how it all hangs together.

With a ridiculous bow, the Siemens man had just taken his leave of the two literary figures who were now moving toward Duckwitz with obvious relief. They were both a little smashed. Duckwitz was a little smashed himself. Suddenly, he couldn't remember what he'd had against the two of them. The jeans-clad professor was all right, though it was a bit much the way he'd just called himself a "radical demo-crat" in a conversation with a Swiss banker. And the Goethe woman's dress was no cause for alarm. In fact, it was sort of grotesquely funny. They had criticized his pudding number, but there was room for criticism there. Tomorrow he'd work hard. Tomorrow he'd do something sensible.

"How can you stand it here?" the Goethe woman asked in a friendly voice.

"You can stand it only if you're in love," answered Duckwitz.

"A diplomat in love," the professor said with an odd laugh. "Isn't that a bit trivial?"

"Rather trivial than radical!" Duckwitz replied.

"That's good, that's very good," said the professor. But there was something nagging about his approval. Duckwitz didn't like the way he was being graded.

"Apropos trivial!" said the Goethe woman. "The diplomatic service is on about the same level as the better sort of popular entertainment!"

Duckwitz couldn't let that one pass: "As far as I'm concerned, I say 'shit' so often, I couldn't provide the better sort of entertainment if I wanted to. What you have before you is a master of mockery, madam. Don't overlook my avant-gardist traits." Duckwitz left the reception and went to his office. He glanced at the telephone. Tomorrow he'd call Helen. He took down from a shelf a cigar box in which he kept his best ideas, written on slips of paper. He'd begun misusing the box for that purpose while at the diplomatic training center in Ippendorf. He'd put in slips with the titles of old jazz numbers that had saxophone solos he wanted to play on the trumpet someday. Might as well throw them away—it would never work. Below that layer there were a few leftovers from when he was a lawyer, usually written on the backs of bank statements. For example: "Clients are always at the pool." What was that supposed to mean? It had probably been the result of some summer frustration at the office. And then there were the slips of paper he'd saved from his student days, like: "Powerlessness ennobles—power demeans." Well, he wasn't so sure about that.

Harry tore two pages from a calendar note pad, November 1978, and began to write. *My favorite UPI report would be: UNESCO is examining whether it wouldn't be better to dismantle the pyramids. At the least, warning signs should be posted—it just isn't right that monuments of cruelty should be the subject of mindless admiration.* On the other slip of paper he wrote: *Rather trivial than radical, but better yet, banal.*

4 *How Duckwitz talks with an English-woman about folklore festivals and the Judgment of Paris beside a swimming pool in Yaunde, Cameroon. How he nevertheless does not fall in love with her but does send a letter that ends with a reference to marriage.*

Among Duckwitz's mail there was a letter from an English-woman who had spent fourteen days in Yaunde in the company of her husband and their two children. Elizabeth Peach, BBC Television. She'd been in Senegal first and then in Foumban in northwest Cameroon. Film and television people liked that town because it was the center of the still relatively intact kingdom of Bamum. Peach had been making a film called *African Woman*. Marked use of the singular. She hadn't been able to convince the BBC to call it *African Queen*. Duckwitz had first met her at the Italian embassy swimming pool. Theirs was the only embassy that had one, and diplomats in Yaunde spent a good deal of their leisure time beside its blue water.

Duckwitz had noticed Elizabeth Peach because she was wearing a large straw hat and sitting under an umbrella, filling up page after page of white paper with amazing speed. Occasionally, a breeze would ruffle the papers, carrying them farther and farther away each time. Harry was astonished at the woman's powers of concentration. She was writing so intently and so rapidly that she let the pages fall to the ground to be carried off by the breeze as if she were no longer the least bit interested in them. Duckwitz was impressed by her lack of concern for something she had produced with a fair amount of industriousness. Or did she know that she was being observed, and was she just waiting for him to bring her back the scattered sheets? That possibility could not be excluded. Her husband was standing blue-lipped in the pool, trying to teach their two daughters to swim. Duckwitz couldn't figure out why he didn't warn his wife to look out for her papers, since he was constantly looking her way. Was he near-sighted? Or could it be that he wanted her papers to fall in the water? Didn't he like her work? Or was she supposed to be punished for being so curiously engrossed?

Duckwitz told himself to stop fantasizing about the wiles of other people's marriages. That was something for writers, he thought, and he turned back to visible reality. He picked up the scattered sheets of paper and handed them to their author. "Oh, thank you!" she said. Without looking up or interrupting her writing for a moment, she took the pages with her free hand and laid them down on the ground, this time placing her foot on them. Duckwitz thought the way she disregarded the savior of her labors was magnificent. He sat down and tried to annoy her with his staring, but she simply ignored him. Since Duckwitz didn't want to be taken for a German, and since he wanted her to think, for a moment at least, that he was with the Italian embassy, he asked, "È poeta, signora?" "Non sono poeta," she said as she wrote, adding "unfortunately" in German. She obviously knew who he was. And she apparently knew all kinds of languages. As if to show off her polyglot talents, she said in English to the paper in front of her, but loudly enough for her husband to hear it in the pool: Don't forget the children have had colds and should get out of the water now. "Out of the water," she repeated and, as if that had been the last sentence she wrote, she made a period, pushed the paper aside, and turned to Duckwitz.

Harry introduced himself. She looked at him intently. That's the way she had always imagined diplomats, she said—standing around elegantly, engaging in charming conversation, and never working.

She had said it lightly and teasingly, but Harry was
hurt nevertheless. He didn't want to be elegant, he didn't
want to be charming, and he didn't want to conform to this
particular image of the diplomat. Of course he didn't work
too hard, but that's something you say to yourself. You don't
want someone else to say it for you—though it would have
been ludicrous to contradict her. Because he wasn't as inhibited as a lot of his diplomatic colleagues, he probably did
seem charming. And he couldn't stand the way white men
start wearing colonial-style khaki outfits the moment they
arrive in Africa, so he was wearing old-fashioned, dark
European slacks and a sports coat. It could be that he
looked rather elegant whether he wanted to or not.

These days diplomats were always trying to set themselves off from the clichéd image of the foreign service.
Some of them were even afraid to pick up a champagne
glass for fear they'd be considered useless, champagne-glass-
wielding diplomats. But since Duckwitz was concerned to set
himself off from his ridiculous colleagues, it didn't embarrass
him in the slightest to lounge around the pool, cocktail in
hand—even if it promptly made him look like a diplomat of
the old school. It was strange and a little tragic to be so
misunderstood by this Englishwoman.

"I am less a diplomat," he said with exaggerated bitterness, "than a cliché. One that is long out of date. I'm a
mere accomplice, milady." Elizabeth Peach didn't understand
the German word for accomplice.

"Untranslatable, inexplicable," said Duckwitz. "Terribly
German."

Nevertheless, Elizabeth Peach wanted to go on speaking German with him since she didn't get to do it very
often. "Duckwitz, Duckwitz," she said. "What an amusing
name!"

"I'm a new Disney character," said Harry, who found
her remark rather cheeky. He had planned to ask respectfully

about the reason for her curious writing frenzy, but now he said: "I think you look incredibly old-fashioned!" She was amazed at that. Her somewhat rigid air of concentration suddenly turned into lively interest. "What do you mean by that?" The name Brontë occurred to Harry from books he'd never read, films he could barely remember, and pictures in Rowohlt editions he may have seen in school. "I could imagine," he said, "that the Brontë sisters wrote their books with the same degree of intensity while wearing straw hats just like yours." Elizabeth Peach was obviously delighted. She liked the comparison. She wanted to know which of the Brontë sisters he meant. Duckwitz tried to remember: were there two or three of them? He'd never known their first names, never read a line they'd written. But then he thought of a film he'd seen on television with Helen, at the commune, at least twelve years ago. The *Wuthering Heights* one, he replied. Elizabeth Peach was speechless. "You are the one and only diplomat who ever read Emily Brontë!" she said.

From then on, every time Duckwitz came to the pool, Elizabeth Peach put away her papers so that she could talk with him—sometimes in English and sometimes in German, which she spoke extremely well, though she constantly insisted that she spoke it very poorly. "I can't express myself, Harry," she would say.

She called him Harry, but she didn't pronounce his name the way they do in English. As if to distinguish him from countless other, Anglo-American Harrys, she pronounced his name with a charmingly deep "a" and a throaty "r" that almost sounded like Berlin. "You're like those rich people who are constantly protesting that their fortune isn't all that large," said Harry. "My goodness, I'll really have to watch my step with you!" she replied. And for the first time it sounded, or was supposed to sound, as if Harry represented a threat to her marriage.

Her husband shouted from the pool that she should

look and see how well the children were swimming. He
called her "Betty." Without turning around, Betty shouted
back: "I'm talking just now." She said it without the least bit
of expression, right into Harry's face, the way she had once
spoken to her papers.

Harry said that people she wasn't paying any attention
to might find her a little preoccupied. Elizabeth Peach didn't
understand the German word for preoccupied and asked him
to translate. A little under the influence of her polyglot
conversation, Harry said boastfully in Spanish: "presente-
ausente." It was the title of a Latin American record album.
Elizabeth was quite taken. Her husband George, she said,
spoke English and nothing else. Harry was flattered on the
one hand but found her remark unseemly on the other. He
decided he'd go over to the edge of the pool later and,
taking Betty's place, talk with George about the progress the
children had made with their swimming.

After a week, Harry began to imagine what it would be
like if Elizabeth hadn't been married to this walrus of a
George but to him, to Harry. He imagined Betty figuring
out that he had never read a Brontë novel, that he couldn't
speak either Spanish or Italian but knew just a few phrases
—though they were good ones—in short, that he was an
impostor.

"Did you know that I'm an impostor?" he asked one
day. "That's why I like you," was Betty's answer. Clever
people are always impostors, she said. Her film about
women in Africa was pure posturing. She didn't know the
first thing about women in Africa. She had read two dozen
controversial books on the subject, had talked to the authors
of the books, and had spoken with several African women—
all of them atypical, of course, but adequate for a European
television documentary. And when the film was ready, she'd
be considered an expert on African women.

This was the way Harry felt about his own profession.

Diplomats distinguished themselves by not knowing a thing yet acting as if they knew it all. Betty told him that there was a series of books in England called *Bluff Your Way: Bluff Your Way Through Art, Bluff Your Way Through Business,* and so on. "*Bluff Your Way Through Sex?*" asked Harry. "Is there one about that, too?" This was supposed to be a hint that the lack of eroticism in his conversations with Elizabeth was beginning to bother him. After all, she was an attractive woman, and he wouldn't have minded seeing a few sparks fly. But Betty only said, yes, the series surely included a book on how to bluff your way through sex. She said it as if she were suddenly tired, and Harry felt irritated. This had all been about four weeks ago.

Now Harry tore open the letter from London and read: "Dear Harry, dear Duckwitz, dear accomplice, the days spent with you were infectious. Writing 'dear Duckwitz' sounds a little odd to me, though. Can a person named Duckwitz be dear at all? I mean your name, only your name, of course—it either puts one off or makes one laugh! And then you're a 'von' Duckwitz to boot. That is, with a monocle, very correct (forgive me, please forgive me!), not very *simpatico,* but nevertheless dear, even dearer, quite conceivably.... Though your 'vons' do always remind me of my father's favorite joke about German Tele-vons and Dis-counts! There you have it again—the notorious English mockery with which I sometimes dismantle that serious language of yours. Oh, I have a damned hard time with your language. It's a shame, Harry, that you didn't meet me in mine alone! But then you would have understood me completely, and I hate it when people understand me. Un po' di misterio, un po' di tiramisù, non è vero? Ironically enough, though, you are the one, the only one who knows me—my history as well as my future, about which I would like to know more. By the way, did you know that my namesake is not the queen but Elizabeth Barrett Browning?"

This was followed by a few comments on her job as a television producer, which she cursed. The letter ended: "Up with letters, down with the telephone, down with the boob tube, down with newspapers! Back to the last century when people were less well informed! With greetings from perfidious Albion, Your Elizabeth."

Harry read the letter three times but didn't understand everything even then. Elizabeth really was a little mysterious. What did that mean: the only one who knows me? He recalled another afternoon at the pool. Elizabeth was leafing through a huge art book, ten pounds worth at least. She'd dragged it all the way from London to Africa, she said, because she wanted to compare the graphic representation of women in European art with African likenesses of women. She turned the pages looking for something, then held up a picture for Harry's consideration. "Look!" It was a depiction of the Judgment of Paris. In the painting, Paris was leaning languidly against a tree, observing the three goddesses—three beautiful, slender, Renaissance fashion models, who were nonchalantly presenting themselves for the judge's consideration. "Would you like to be in his place?" Elizabeth asked. Harry sneered: "I'm not so sure." Elizabeth pointed to Paris's face: "He's magnificent in his indecision," she said.

Was she trying to introduce the neglected subject of sex into the conversation? The remark was strange in any case, and Duckwitz laughed out loud. For several seconds, George failed to accompany the strokes of their youngest child with his insistent "one-two-three." Elizabeth took a thick, felt-tipped pen and wrote across the illustration: "Make up your mind, dear sir!" Harry thought about what would happen if he suddenly took Betty in his arms.

Two days later, George and the children weren't at the pool. "They went to the folklore festival," said Betty. The inhabitants of Yaunde were celebrating some national holiday or other with dancing and parades. Since there wasn't much else to see in Yaunde, everyone at the foreign embassies, from the ambassadors to the secretaries and switchboard operators, was thronging to the festival. "Why aren't you there?" asked Elizabeth. "I can't stand these festivals," replied Harry. And since he meant it honestly, he made a face. "You can look so wonderfully disgusted," Elizabeth told him, tracing Harry's furrowed brows with her finger. Harry took her hand. Thinking it would be silly just to kiss the back of it, and because he wanted to be a little more passionate, he turned it over and kissed the palm—more embarrassed than bold. "Don't do that, Duckwitz," Betty said, and withdrew her hand. Harry felt like he was eighteen again. It had been a matter of duty then, too: every moment that allowed for an erotic advance had to be exploited to the fullest. It hadn't been any different this time. Just because no one was there, he'd thought he had to take her by storm. Yet since they weren't really in the mood for it, nothing had happened. He retreated to the safer ground of conversation: "I hate all those drums. These folk festivals always have a lot of drumming. Every time I hear drumming it makes me think of the Nazis. It's enough to make you puke."

"Oh, yes," said Elizabeth warmly, and Harry had the feeling he owed her fervent agreement to the fact that he hadn't made any further advances.

It was very quiet. They could hear the singsong of the dancers and the beating of drums from the different marketplaces in town. "What yowling!" said Harry. And then: "The supreme form of folk art is war."

"Exactly!" said Elizabeth. Then she looked at Harry almost ardently and wrote the sentence down on a sheet of paper: *The supreme form of folk art is war.* She handed it to Harry and said: "Save it. You can be proud of it."

●　　●　　●

Now Harry went over to his desk and took out the sheet of paper he had carefully laid away. He studied the sentence as if trying to unlock a secret. Six weeks after that stupid festival, the sentence Elizabeth had praised no longer had any real power. Now it was preparations for a trans-Cameroon rallye that was making his blood boil. Today it was a rallye that seemed like a simpler form of war.

He wasn't sure what to think of Elizabeth's letter. He felt as uncertain as he had the day he was alone with her and risked that abortive kiss on the palm of her hand. Her letter flattered him and made him feel a little in love with her. He was taken by the "ohs," the theatrical but somehow natural little "ohs" in her letter. But what tone should he use in his answer? He went into the conference room and got an encyclopedia to look up Elizabeth Barrett Browning. The compact Brockhaus from the fifties didn't have anything. He'd send an immediate request to the central office in Bonn for a decent encyclopedia. This cheap version, reeking of the fifties, was terrible! The budget directors at the central office would certainly get the point if he argued that reference books from the time of the Cold War were now totally out of place in an embassy of the Federal Republic of Germany.

Harry took pen and paper and went over to the British embassy, where he borrowed the relevant volume of the *Encyclopaedia Britannica*. Then he went on to the Italian embassy, sat down by the pool at the same spot where he and Elizabeth had sat, read the article in the encyclopedia, and wrote:

"Dear Elizabeth, don't worry, you're still mysterious, and more than 'un po.' But I'm afraid I'm duller and more wooden than you think. I hope you know that 'tiramisù' is not just a dessert but a delicious kind of love-making? Of course you know that. You shimmer so intriguingly. I'm so awkward and direct. You're better at my language than I am.

That's why I'm going to say, in English: *Bluffing your way through Browning.* That's what you're doing. You're bluffing, and that raises a question: how am I supposed to understand your saying that you feel a certain kinship with Elizabeth Barrett Browning? She sat mournfully at home, dreaming about the south, until her future husband carried her off to the country she had longed for—where she got well faster than you can count to three. Elizabeth! I beg your pardon! What is this supposed to mean? Shall I come and get you? I know, I know, abductors aren't supposed to ask permission beforehand. I always ruin things for myself. Mournfully yours, Harry."

He hesitated a moment, twirling his pen. Then he wrote:

"Do you remember the picture of Paris and the three chicks? 'Make up your mind, dear sir!' you wrote. I have made up my mind. I'm going to get married."

5 *How Rita Noorani-Kim enters Harry von Duckwitz's field of vision and soon loses a fingernail. Why Harry enters into a deal with her father, and how the ambassador gets a rare opportunity to play justice of the peace. How Harry, in spite of the joys of marriage, contacts his old friend Helen once again, and why he doesn't feel like lifting a finger for an imprisoned photographer. Also, a very sad encounter with his colleague Hennersdorff, and how Rita and Harry finally leave Africa.*

"Congratulations!" The ambassador shook Rita's hand, then Harry's. "I hope I did everything right," he said. It was the first wedding he'd ever performed as ambassador. "Short and painless," he added.

"What did he say?" Rita asked in English. She didn't speak a word of German. She looked eighteen today. She was twenty-four. Her mother was from Korea, her father from India, and she could look very different from one moment to the next. Harry had known Rita for six weeks. He thought she looked Korean in the morning, Indian in the dark and, strangely enough, French in the afternoon. Sometimes her giggles suddenly turned into laughter.

She took a quick look at their marriage certificate. "Dr. Harry Baron von Duckwitz, Lutheran, born in Berlin on October 18, 1945, currently residing in Yaunde, and Rita Noorani-Kim, Catholic, born in Bombay on August 24, 1955, currently residing in Yaunde, were married on November 8, 1979, in the Embassy of the Federal Republic of Germany in Yaunde, Cameroon." The phrase "Justice of the Peace" on the printed form had been crossed out and corrected by hand: "In lieu of a Justice of the Peace, the Ambassador."

"It was nice of you to spare us all the unctuous talk," said Duckwitz. People should only get married in embassies. Rita's father and Hennersdorff had served as witnesses. Rita was kissed, slyly by her father, shyly by Hennersdorff, and there was another handshake for the freshly married groom. "Don't forget this evening," said Duckwitz. "Big banquet at the hotel at seven."

Rita's father drove the couple home. Rita and Harry sat happily in the back of the old Citroën. Harry nibbled on Rita's earlobe.

He had moved out of his bachelor's quarters and into a somewhat larger house in the city's diplomatic quarter. The house had a small veranda. Compared with their shoebox of an embassy, it was passable. Mr. Noorani dropped the two of them off at the house. He was rather aloof and made no move to go inside. Rita was wearing her usual blue jeans and a plain white T-shirt. You could get married that way, too! They went right to the bedroom, getting undressed quickly and matter-of-factly. That's what they'd been missing. Both of them. Her and him. Rita and Harry. The whole time. They'd missed it today as well. And especially during the months before today. Even before they knew each other, it had been missing. Now it was there, and it formed a bond between them.

Everything had happened so fast. He'd noticed Rita about six weeks earlier at a reception hosted by the French embassy. Here in Yaunde, you couldn't pass up a reception—there wasn't anything else. The French embassy was several times larger than the embassy of the Federal Republic. Tens of thousands of French citizens lived in the country, thousands in Yaunde. The French, of course, called it Yaoundé.

Rita had been standing in front of a mirror in the

entryway, checking to see how her skirt looked. It was a silky skirt with slits in the sides. Yellow. She was speaking French with someone, and Harry took her to be French. Maybe one of her parents was Vietnamese. They smiled at each other in the mirror. She had a sweet smile. When she wasn't smiling, she wasn't the kind of woman to take your breath away. But the unabashed way she looked herself over in the mirror was breathtaking all right.

Later, Harry struck up a conversation with her. And suddenly she looked Indian. Her father was a local businessman. Her parents were divorced and her mother lived in Seoul. Rita was asked to play the piano. She didn't hesitate a moment. She played a few short pieces by Haydn and Beethoven and, at the special request of the French ambassador's wife, an awful piano version of "Mylord." Everyone applauded, and Harry was certain he had lost her to one of the 120 other guests; but Rita came back and picked up the conversation where they had left off.

He couldn't get Rita out of his head. When he saw her at another occasion two days later, he'd been hoping to see her again. They spent the entire evening together. Harry was crazy about her Indian accent. He saw her home, she saw him home, and since she couldn't go home alone in wildest Africa, she went into his bachelor quarters. For the sake of form, Harry poured two drinks to give them courage. One sip, and they were lying on the bed. If that was already the height of sensation, Rita's trembling, or rather quivering orgasm was the crowning touch. Harry had never known any woman who was electrified out of her senses the way Rita was. It couldn't be put on, impossible, it was real. Only a real one-hundred-and-fifty-percent orgasm could make a body vibrate that way.

The next morning there were two surprises. While Rita was in the bathroom, Harry noticed a drop of blood on the bed. It was a shock. Had this been, without his knowing it, the so-called "deflowering" of a virgin? The thing they say it takes years to prepare girls for in India, the thing men pay a fortune for—had that been resolved last night, not noise-lessly but normally, in a single drop of blood? Not a good feeling. Invasive. And Harry didn't want to be invasive. The drop of blood was incredibly thick. Indian virgin's blood. Or was Rita just having her period? But that looked different, as far as Harry could remember from his excesses with Helen.

There was definitely something strange about the drop of blood, and as he looked at it more closely, he realized that it was an artificial fingernail. The glue-on kind. As Rita came out of the bathroom, he noticed that she had very short fingernails. Probably she used to chew them. Perhaps she still did? She didn't look like she had hangups. Maybe her Korean mother had been one of those barbaric high-achievement types and had cut off her daughter's fingernails so she could play the piano better. He wouldn't have put it past an Asian—and not just that. Harry didn't mention the little blemish, and a few minutes later Rita had red cat's claws again.

As they were eating breakfast and their conversation began to go around in circles, a wildly gesticulating man suddenly appeared outside the house. What kind of an idiot was that? It turned out to be Rita's father. He was beside himself because Rita had spent the night there. Come home this minute! Harry had no choice but to put a manly arm around her. "She'll stay here!" he said in English. A simple matter of courtesy. "Thank you," said Rita.

For an entire week, Harry and Rita lived from one orgasm to the next. When it turned out that Rita had a motorcycle, and not just some squealing machine but a fat and shiny, sonorously gurgling motorcycle, the whole thing took on a different cast. It was like an omen. They began to feel they belonged together. They went for rides outside of town, and Harry thought about his rides with Helen on the ancient motorcycle that had belonged to Aunt Ursula's favorite boyfriend. It must still be in Frankfurt, like his trumpet. This was Rita's motorcycle. Harry tried it out, but Rita was the one who drove, with Harry riding in back. That was fine, because it was so different from the way it had been with Helen, and it was exciting to hold on to Rita's girlish body. A truly vital embrace.

Theirs was no grand passion, no blinding love. In fact, the word love wasn't mentioned at all. There were no tortured attacks of jealousy. None of those nagging doubts about how things should go on from here that often give lovemaking a little spice. There was never a hint of emptiness after they'd been in bed, just a feeling they'd been temporarily refreshed.

They spoke English with each other. Harry had to be on his toes in English, but at least he didn't run the risk of rambling on and on—his English wasn't good enough. The language they spoke in bed was French, but they did their screwing without commentary. They did, however, give it a name. They called it "une partie," and spoke of "playing parts." And just as an actor feels like playing a part on stage, they would feel like "playing parts" in bed—"faire une partie." And since "partie" could also mean a part of the body, Rita's small girlish breasts and her flat stomach and her butt were also called "parts." They played parts and they had parts. And once when Rita repeated the obscure maxim, "A woman should speak the language of her man," Harry could reassure her that she already knew the most important word, because "partie" means pretty much the same thing in German and is pronounced the same way. "Faire une partie," "faire l'amour"—make love—was there in the background, and so there was an echo of love, though it remained unspoken. It was part of the game. "Listen, Rita," said Harry. "The first lesson is: Love is a part of the game." And my part and your part, "ma partie" and "ta partie," those are the important parts of the body. "Comment va ta partie?" means "How's your willie or how's your vagina?"

Rita's father had not taken the theft of his daughter lightly. He'd gone to the ambassador and complained that a member of the German diplomatic mission had more or less abducted her. He wanted to talk to Herr von Duckwitz. This was already more polite than his performance that first morning. Duckwitz met with him. He was rather fat for an Indian, and there were no traces of character in the folds of his face.

"Mr. Noorani."

"Nice to meet you."

Harry didn't know why Rita's father wanted to have this talk. The man kept beating around the bush. Harry thought about his first night with Rita and about the drop of blood that wasn't one. Maybe this Mr. Noorani believed that his daughter was an Indian virgin and that Harry had violated her, that filing a complaint was in order. Rita's father talked the way all the mafiosi do, about a "tip" he wanted to give Harry. "I just want to warn you," he said, but without getting any more concrete. Was that supposed to mean: Hands off my daughter? It didn't sound as if Harry could expect a hail of bullets otherwise.

Rita's father finally indicated that he wouldn't have anything against a marriage. The whole thing was evidently an attempt to coerce Harry into marrying Rita.

"He's a fool," said Rita when Harry told her about it. But the word "marriage" had been introduced into the conversation by way of Rita's father, even if it was as a crazy idea, a "foolish thought."

Harry had never in his life given any consideration to getting married. While he was living with Helen, they'd never talked about it. Now the word had popped up all of a sudden. But since everything was so easy with Rita, even the idea of marriage didn't seem oppressive. In fact, it was fun to toy with the idea. Doing something you'd always considered the last thing you'd ever do! All of a sudden he felt like getting married—the same way someone else might feel like pulling a prank.

The most important thing was that he'd be able to move into a better house. Spacious quarters were important to Harry. Soon, time would be up for the current deputy chief of mission. Everyone was glad the jackass from Cultural Affairs was leaving. They hadn't seen much of him anyway. Normally his successor would move into his house, but if Duckwitz were married, he'd be first in line.

Other than that, the idea of marriage didn't take up too much room in his thoughts. It was rather like the idea of buying a new car. A new car is practical if you have the money for it; there are advantages. For old leftists, buying a new car is a clear sign of treason; it means you're giving in to the system. What's really important is going to bed, not getting married. Getting married's more like an absurd punch line.

He'd have to speak to Helen about it, Harry thought; so in order to give her a call in Frankfurt, he stayed at the embassy after everyone else had gone. Helen wasn't the least bit surprised, and that really bothered Harry. The first call in years, and Helen wasn't bowled over. "Just a second," she said, and turned down her TV.

"I'm calling from Africa," Harry said loudly.

That didn't impress Helen either. "Right," she said. Probably she'd heard from Fritz that Harry was in Africa. She was eating an apple.

"This is a long-distance call," said Harry.

"How late is it there?" asked Helen.

"We're in the same time zone," he answered. Harry was feeling very close to her.

Helen didn't seem to be impressed by this kind of

togetherness. In the background, Harry could hear the gong that announced the beginning of the eight o'clock news. Helen was still eating her apple. She said: "So tell me what's up." Harry thought it was great that she was so businesslike. He no longer felt like asking her what she thought about marriage, either in general or more specifically in the case of her old friend and lover Harry and another woman. Helen didn't sound like she would be able to contribute any important thoughts on the subject.

"Are you alone?" asked Harry.

"Yes, why?"

"It could have been that you weren't."

"Could have been," said Helen. Evidently she was listening to the news as their conversation traveled back and forth across thousands of kilometers, because suddenly she said: "You probably aren't interested in the pope's visit to Turkey, but maybe you'd like to know that the Greens have been elected to the city council in Bremen. It's the first time they've been voted in anywhere."

"I'm going to get married soon," said Harry.

That didn't shake her either. "A black mama?"

"No, an Indian virgin," said Harry.

After their conversation, he was bound and determined to get married. It was funny and crazy and to his advantage. It was a pact with life. What was the point of all this gabbing with Helen, of this affected flirtation with Elizabeth Peach? Life is a thing called Rita. It has its parts. Life has a silk skirt with slits. Life rides a motorcycle, has artificial fingernails, and plays the piano.

Rita kept giggling as he described in glowing terms his idea of getting married. They applied for the papers and Harry moved into the bigger house in the best of spirits.

Now Rita was lying next to him, asleep. And just as expected, the first "partie" as husband and wife hadn't been any different than all the ones that went before.

There had been a few nice little complications in the days before the wedding, though. Since Harry was dead set against having children, he had asked Rita outright, even before their first "partie" and while he still had some self-control, how things stood with birth control. "No problem," she had said, she was taking the pill. But it turned out that Rita wasn't taking the pill, didn't even have to. She'd had an abortion, and they'd removed her uterus. She'd never be able to have children. Harry thought this was wonderful and practical but that she should have told him before. It could well have been that he wanted nothing so much as a dozen children. It wasn't right. He swore, Rita cried, and he consoled her.

He went to Rita's father and complained: "And where am I supposed to get children now?"

Of course it was possible that the slippery Mr. Noorani hadn't known anything about it. A father isn't required to know everything about his adult daughter's belly. But he had known. "That's why I warned you," he said, grinning shamelessly. Harry couldn't exclude the possibility that he'd been the victim of a father-daughter conspiracy. Rita, who was doubly worthless by Indian standards—no hymen and no uterus—was to be married off. And Harry was a real catch. A German aristocrat. Rita, the fallen woman, would become Baroness von Duckwitz. If it really had been a conspiracy, then it was a damned good one, thought Harry. And it didn't take away from Rita's qualities—her quivering orgasm, her slit skirt, her motorcycle, her piano. And maybe her fingernails would grow back in the course of time. They weren't living in the nineteenth century. Thank God for that. Honor was just a joke. To hell with all the old values.

Still, Harry didn't let up on Rita's old man. At one time, there would have been a duel; nowadays you asked for damages. The wedding had been arranged but had not yet taken place. Harry was in a good position to threaten and negotiate. In just half an hour he had the slippery old fellow right where he wanted him—ready to sign. Rita's father promised in writing that even after her marriage, he'd contribute a certain amount of money to the support of his daughter as long as he lived. Harry thought about Rita's motorcycle, and in addition to the negotiated monthly payment, he had a clause added: "The amount shall never be less than the current cost of 1000 liters of gasoline." Mr. Noorani seemed to be half horrified and half delighted at the keen business sense shown by his future son-in-law.

• • •

The rainy season came, the rainy season went, but that was no substitute for the changing seasons near the Alps or in Grüneburg Park in Frankfurt. The ambassador fought indefatigably for more appropriate quarters. After all, an ambassador is addressed as "Excellency," and an Excellency lives in a Residence. But what if a Residence looked like a lousy youth hostel and had no air conditioning? When more than ten people stood around at a reception during the hot months, the temperature became unbearable. They often had to seek refuge in the embassy offices. Shameful state of affairs. On this point, Duckwitz was completely on the side of the suffering ambassador and his suffering wife: "They have enough money for their crappy NATO maneuvers but not enough for the rent on a decent house!" Unanimity. Those idiots in Bonn. We should let them have it. All of them!

One day Duckwitz finally had a decent case to deal with. He was, after all, the embassy's specialist for economic and legal affairs. He'd had it up to here with the economic side of things. Just recently he'd had to prevent a German company from palming off an auto inspection set-up to officials in Cameroon. Because when all is said and done, the most charming sights in Africa were the cars held together by baling wire and chewing gum!

This time the one seeking legal recourse wasn't a globetrotter who'd been robbed, but a photographer who'd been thrown in jail. Hennersdorff had put the case on his desk with a note: "Have fun!"

First, Duckwitz read a letter written by a high-ranking police officer and titular prison warden in Maroua, a provincial capital in the extreme northern part of the country. In perfect French he recounted the facts: the delinquent had been caught in Waza National Park, not too far from Maroua. He had violated two ordinances. First, he had left the prescribed route in the National Park without permission, and second, he had violated the prohibition against taking photographs in the area. He had been warned a few times, he had insulted the gamekeepers who warned him, and he had not desisted from taking photographs. The gamekeepers had waived their right to file a complaint against him for insulting them, but the minimum penalty for the other two violations was 23 days in prison.

Duckwitz looked at the calendar. June 11, 1980. He had to hurry. The deadline for filing an appeal would be up in just a few days. It was strange: while you react angrily to any kind of prohibition in Germany, especially if it's called to your attention by someone in uniform, such notification by the police here in Cameroon seemed downright good-natured. On the other hand, the Africans really do have a thing about prohibiting photography.

During the time Duckwitz had been there, nature photographers and filmmakers had repeatedly asked the embassy's help in securing various official permits. From time to time, Duckwitz had looked at the film material with fascination, because the huge telephoto lenses were able to show that even in the animal kingdom things can get rather gruesome. In one of the films, young lions creep up on a lioness playing with two cubs. Father lion is who knows where and hasn't the slightest interest in this family idyll. And then the following scene: the two young hooligans grab the cute little lion cubs, bite them in the neck, throw them in the air, and leave the two little creatures lying dead in the grass. The lioness doesn't just stand idly by, she turns her rear end rankly toward the murderers, who naturally get what they want.

Duckwitz had been beside himself. Fascism in the animal kingdom! The producer of the film saw things differently. A special case of natural selection.

Another filmmaker had filmed the life of the naked molerat in Tanzania. He had penetrated the animal's underground tunnels with special camera lenses. Naked molerats are not only the most unappetizing animals in the whole world, they also have an absolutely perverse hierarchy. Their skin looks like a plucked chicken's, and they actually eat their queen's crap after feeding her the tastiest of roots. The queen is the ugliest of all. She stays in one place her entire life and suffers only the presence of a court of so-called servant molerats that she marks with urine and excrement. "And they call that God's creation!" Harry had said in true despair. But the filmmaker told him not to look at it so narrowly.

People who provide the world with such priceless documents should not be thrown in prison just because they violate some ordinance or other about film or photography, thought Duckwitz, picking up the letter from the imprisoned photographer. But even if the man had been thrown into a dungeon, his handwriting would have been inexcusable. And the tone he took in the letter was even worse: indignant and insulted because blacks had dared to put him, the great artist, in jail. He expected the German embassy to take action immediately. In order to demonstrate his artistic merit, he enclosed a copy of a magazine containing a photo story he'd done in Kenya. Duckwitz leafed through it. The man had been in paradise. In the most beautiful parts of Kenya. Wildcats lounged about lazily, snakes coiled peacefully, and between them all, no less elegant, leaning against a tree, kneeling like a panther, stretching, lounging, sprawling, was a truly beautiful naked woman with incredibly long legs and the sort of small breasts Harry favored.

The police officer from Maroua had included a couple of rolls of film as evidence of the photographer's misdeeds. Harry took them to be developed and ordered large prints. Two days later, he had nearly 300 color photos lying on his desk. The French photo lab thanked him for his order and included a bill for 556,000 African francs, about 3,600 marks. That was going to cause trouble. This time the scene was Waza Park and the photos showed a naked model against a backdrop of buffalo; then snuggled against a cheetah that must have been given a tranquilizer; with hippopotamuses and giraffes looking on—an erotic blunder; with antelopes and gazelles; and then again wading in Lake Chad like Silvana Mangano in the waters of the Po, except that Mangano had been wearing something.

Harry took the photos home with him and invited Hennersdorff to come by. Unfortunately he came with his wife. After dinner, Harry passed the pictures around. "God," said Rita, "she is sexy, isn't she!"

"Awful!" said Hennersdorff, passing the photos.

It was Hennersdorff's wife's turn, and she said: "Fabulous, the way these pictures were taken!"

Three different opinions but no solution. The pictures were sexy, they were awful, and it was interesting the way the photographer had taken them. Harry tried to explain his position: on the one hand, he couldn't resist the erotic paradise, but on the other, he, too, found the pictures awful, so awful that he felt like leaving the photographer to stew for a while in that hole of a jail. Except that there were people who belonged in jail even more—chancellors, popes, arms dealers, presidents, soldiers, industrialists. Not photographers. "Arranging reality to suit you isn't a deadly sin," said Duckwitz, "it's just a lie."

"Would you please speak English!" said Rita.

The next day, Duckwitz called the police station in Maroua. He was finally able to reach the police officer in the afternoon. The man was drunk. He made it clear to Duckwitz right away that the law is the law, and for every day the photographer did not have to spend in jail, the price would be one digital watch. Not an LED but an LCD. That was the latest. They'd come out in Paris at the beginning of the year. No, he didn't accept normal wristwatches. As Duckwitz made a move to end the conversation, he started coming down on the price. Duckwitz finally agreed. Two days later, the photographer appeared at the embassy. He wasn't even grateful. In fact, he was insulted that it had taken so long and that no one from the embassy had been there to pick him up. He wanted to have his film back. He stared at the big pile of photos, then began stuffing the booty into his huge photo bag. "Stop!" said Duckwitz, showing him the bill. "Cash only."

"You're crazy!" said the photographer, calling Duckwitz a typical German bureaucrat. "Rather a German bureaucrat than a lousy photographer like you," said Duckwitz. He should have given the policeman some digital watches just to keep the photographer in jail a while longer.

A few days after these events, Duckwitz went to the office very early to avoid being disturbed while he called Helen in Frankfurt. The cleaning lady always left the doors to all the offices open when she went home, so that the stuffy air could circulate during the night. Hennersdorff's door was closed, which meant that he was already there. This early? Did he really have that much to do, or did he

too want to make a cheap, unregistered call to Germany?
Maybe he had an old girlfriend he could complain to about
his booming, Rugosa Rose of a wife. Or was he calling his
mother back home in Lüneburg or Uelzen? The walls in the
embassy building were thin, but he couldn't hear Hennersdorff. It could be that he was really working, looking at that
huge bill from the photo lab and wondering how to enter it
in the books. Actually, he was too correct to be using the
office phone for his own private purposes. Soon you
wouldn't be able to do that anyway. The central office had
already threatened to link every office phone to a computer
that would register the number dialed and the length of the
call.

Perhaps Hennersdorff wasn't there after all and the
door was closed for some other reason. Duckwitz got up and
went across the hall to Hennersdorff's office, knocked and
then opened the door. Well I'll be darned! Hennersdorff
taking a nap! Comes in here and gets his sleep at his desk.
It can't be very comfortable to sleep with your head on your
desk. Duckwitz whistled and twittered a bit, even went so
far as to crow like a rooster. Hennersdorff didn't react. It
was dreadful the way he was lying there. Duckwitz went
over to him and took his arm to shake him. But he wouldn't
be shaken. He was stiff. He was dead. Duckwitz wanted to
put his arm around him, wake him up, bring him back to
life, talk to him. But Hennersdorff was heavy, dead, alien,
gone. Still leaning over his desk. A glass of water and an
empty glass vial, the classical props of suicide, lying beside
the sink. It was too late. There was no hurry. Take your
time saying goodbye.

Harry closed the door and sat down. How rarely you
see dead people. When he was little, he'd seen his Aunt
Ursula dead. She died in her own room. During the last
weeks before she died, she didn't get out of bed. It was her
liver. "She drinks like a sailor," Aunt Huberta had always

said. She drank right up to the end because there was no point in not drinking. She made Harry an accomplice to her recklessness. She didn't think it was reckless. The doctor and his other aunts were the ones who talked about recklessness. She pointed to a chest of drawers. Her wallet was lying in the top drawer. "Beaujolais," she said, smiling sweetly. "And a carton of Nile cigarettes." Harry went to the Edeka market nearby and got her provisions. He was proud that she let him pull the cork. She was too weak now to do it herself. Aunt Ursula got thinner and weaker. She couldn't hold her wine glass anymore. One morning, Harry went into her room as usual. She'd never looked like this before. She didn't raise her head, but she did move her hand ever so slightly. "How are you this morning?" Harry asked, just as he did every morning. "Stupid question, fine, of course," she'd answered a few days earlier, giving Harry five marks. Today she didn't say anything. Her hand moved as if she were listening to music. "Oh, crap!" said Harry after a while. Aunt Ursula raised up in bed and said: "Crap! That's the word for it, all right!" She gave an exhausted smile and lay back down. That evening she died. Harry wasn't there. He saw her the next morning. He could still hear her last words. "Crap! That's the word for it!" It was a message, a legacy. You should never forget that everything is ultimately just crap. That is, you have to keep forgetting it—and you have to keep reminding yourself of it.

Crappy death. Crappy life. There was an open book lying beneath Hennersdorff's outstretched arm. Harry pulled it toward him. Hennersdorff's arm was heavy. A diary. The last entry was a week old. Then came yesterday's date, then nothing. He'd evidently come here yesterday evening to die.

Harry was shaken as he read the entries, where he found spare and unemotional confirmation of his frivolous hunch that Hennersdorff suffered under his wife. Not a single "crap" in the whole diary. Maybe Hennersdorff killed himself because he'd never been able to say "crap." "Rose has been terrible to the children." "Rose was impatient." Nothing about himself, only about his wife. "Rose was really nasty today." "Rose was being mean again." My God, Hennersdorff, is that any reason to kill yourself? "Rose as sweet as sugar to Duckwitz." Hennersdorff had noticed that too. Harry had always been afraid that she held him up to her husband as a model because of Harry's career in the senior diplomatic service and because of his university degree. She was capable of doing something like that. Thank God nothing like that was mentioned in the diary. All of a sudden, Harry noticed an entry under the date of his own wedding: "Witness for Duckwitz. Lucky man."

Harry took the diary. Yes, he could do that. As bad as she was, Rugosa Rose didn't need to read about it. Even if she did deserve to. Hennersdorff's death was punishment enough. Maybe she wouldn't even understand it. Duckwitz was afraid that was the case.

Harry put his hand on Hennersdorff's back. He didn't feel dead. "Farewell then. You were a good sort. I won't forget you," said Harry, his eyes growing damp. Then he went to his office and called Hennersdorff's wife. She was very businesslike and asked if there was any point in calling a doctor. No. She arrived at the embassy a short time later. Harry recognized her step. After a few minutes she came into his office.

"I'm sorry you were the one who found him," she said, as if she had to apologize for an imposition.

"I'm sorry he isn't still alive," said Duckwitz.

Hennersdorff's body was sent back to Germany for burial in the family plot, in a town on the Lüneburg heath. Hennersdorff's wife came back once after that to arrange the move back to the stock-stiff state of Lower Saxony.

When Aunt Ursula died back in Harry's Alpine days,

she left behind a few choice words that Harry came to understand only much later. "I don't think much of leave-taking," she'd said. "That's why I don't feel much like taking leave of life." But then, when things got serious and the formalities had to be discussed, she'd astonished his other aunts with her last request: "No funeral, girls," she'd said, "just a burneral!"

•   •   •

After spending nearly three years in Africa, Duckwitz had the growing suspicion that he was getting careless where politics was concerned. The more you know, the less you can do. Everyone who tries, makes mistakes. Everyone complains about the methods used in development aid, but no one can do it any better. Maybe, thought Duckwitz, maybe they needed to improve the not so ineffective system of corruption. Maybe that would be the place to start. If selflessness produces so much rubbish, maybe the cultivation of self-interest would be a better method. And as for spreading European culture in Africa, is that useless, harmful, ridiculous—or is there really a point to it after all? Three years of looking on and it was less clear to him than ever. In the beginning, he'd at least been against it; now it just didn't matter. It was a good thing he hadn't wound up in South Africa. With his wishy-washy conscience, he'd probably have been the sort to argue that he was against apartheid but that getting rid of it overnight would be a catastrophe for the entire continent.

He was going to miss the ambassador's wife. After all these years it was absolutely priceless how she still acted as if it were the fall of 1977 and the hijacking of that Lufthansa airliner to Somalia had taken place only yesterday. As if Mogadishu, 4000 kilometers away, was right next door, and as if everyone at the embassy had just barely escaped a terrorist attack. Just to make her angry, Harry had said early on that when he was a lawyer, he had devoted himself exclusively to defending terrorists. Since there was no East Germany in Africa for her to wish him to, the ambassador's wife had replied: "Go down to Angola or Mozambique. There you can have your precious terrorism!" She was right, but it would have been breaking the rules to admit it. So Duckwitz said: "For my next foreign assignment, I'll tell them I want to go to South Africa. But only after I've married a Hottentot."

He could be glad he hadn't been sent to the People's Republic of Mozambique. The thought of having to listen to all those slogans ten years after 1968 was simply awful. "Mobilize the masses!" "Carry on the class struggle!" The difference was that in Mozambique it was in earnest and not just commune chatter or demonstration ra-ra-ra. And then to see the way a native regime took on the noble task of getting rid of colonialism! It was obvious that diplomats from the West simply had to return home as staunch anti-Communists! At least he'd been spared that. Here in Cameroon there weren't any political leaders who'd been initiated into the secrets of Marxism-Leninism in Moscow in order to try them out on the African continent. At least Harry hadn't been forced to watch this kind of stuff and report it back to Bonn. Nevertheless he felt tired.

He couldn't talk about life's paradoxes with Rita, and that was a paradox in and of itself: regrettable on the one hand, but refreshing on the other. There was no point in constantly sticking your nose into misery. Especially since it isn't always so miserable. After all, people are happy to be alive in Cameroon, too, and probably even in South Africa.

After a first assignment abroad, a diplomat is usually assigned to a second foreign post immediately. Duckwitz had the feeling that his system of values was thoroughly confused. Three years somewhere else at this point and he wouldn't know which way was up. He'd rather watch other people do the rubbish than do the rubbish himself.

If he'd been single, it wouldn't have been easy to escape being sent God knows where. But now he could use Rita as an argument. "My wife has to learn to speak German properly," he'd said on the telephone to Bonn. "And she can't do that in Finland or Canada or anywhere else." The personnel division understood. But while Harry was thinking about preparations for a nest in Bonn, Rita was thinking of a visit to her far-flung family. Six weeks in Seoul with her mother's family, then another six weeks in India with relatives on her father's side. And before that a stopover in Uganda, where she had gone to school for a couple of years before going to boarding school in England.

Not a word from Rita about whether it was all right with Harry, about whether he could get along without her, or about their "parties." She gently confronted him with a fait accompli. Not a word of regret that they wouldn't see each other for months. Harry was delighted that Rita was so unsentimental. It hadn't been wrong to marry her. Rita asked him to see to it that the movers were careful with the piano. "And with the motorcycle," Harry added. "Oh, no, don't bother with the bike," said Rita. Harry was to sell the motorcycle.

"I certainly will not!" said Harry.

Rita called and made her reservations—Kampala, Seoul, Bombay, Bonn. As if it were the most normal thing in the world. As if she did it every day.

A week before Harry was to fly out of Cameroon on his way to Bonn, he took Rita to the airport in Yaunde. It was early May, and the rainy season would soon begin. They still had a little time when they got to the airport. These are the moments when you need a cigarette. They could see each other in the mirror behind the little airport bar. They were standing there together, smiling at each other. "I hope you'll come back to me," he said. Rita hadn't been giggling as much recently. She preferred to smile. She was 25 years old and didn't think a thing of flying halfway around the world alone. She didn't even need a drink. She had tomato juice. Harry needed a whisky. It was incredible the way she checked her luggage, wrote out checks; it was purely a matter of course. Harry was proud of her. He felt inexperienced and provincial by comparison. Rita was in good spirits and already a long way off in her thoughts.

While Rita went to the restroom, Harry bought himself a French magazine and an English news weekly. The U.S. Secretary of Defense favors stationing the neutron bomb in Europe, he read. John Lennon had been shot just a few weeks earlier. Why didn't they shoot the neutron-mongers? The President of the Federal Republic of Germany is paying a state visit to India. Unbelievable. It's a good thing that old Nazi never came to Cameroon. Passengers going to Kampala were being asked to board the plane. "Bye bye," said Rita. She shouldered her bag and then she was gone.

6 *How Harry von Duckwitz readjusts to*
Bonn after his years in Cameroon, while
his wife Rita attends to a number of things in
Africa and her home countries. In addition to
some comments on salad dressings, jukeboxes,
and the decline of pub culture. Also, how
Harry is once again plagued by indecision but
then does go out to dinner with Helen, and
what happens after that.

He hadn't seen her for three or four years. There had been
only a bit of telephone contact back and forth between
Cameroon and Frankfurt. Now she had called, and his
immediate pleasure was followed by the old irritation.
"Where should we go for dinner?" Harry had asked. Just as
in the old days when they were students, he didn't know
where he and Helen should go to eat. Her suggestion had
been so spontaneous. "Let's go out to eat somewhere," she'd
said. Why didn't she ask about Rita? She knew about her.
Rita isn't here yet—well, he didn't want to say that. It
would sound so ambiguous. Harry thought he remembered
Helen saying they could go to dinner "first." And then
possibly to bed? At least it wasn't out of the question.

Now Harry was annoyed because he hadn't been able
to come up with a restaurant where they could meet the day
after tomorrow at eight. He'd had to ask Helen to call back,
because try as he might, nothing occurred to him on the
spot. After all, he added in his defense, he'd been in Africa
for three years.

Because she had to call again, her completely unexpected entrance would lose some of its dramatic effect.
Harry thought he'd noticed that his indecisiveness was
making her nervous. His indecisiveness had been the reason

why his earlier relationship with Helen had come to nothing. And probably, it occurred to him, it was his indecisiveness that made him enter the diplomatic service—that idiotic refuge for helpless but immaculately dressed losers that he didn't want anything to do with.

Harry was waiting impatiently for Helen's call and didn't dare leave the telephone. That's what he got for his indecisiveness. His pleasure at the idea of seeing Helen again was so great and so confusing that he couldn't imagine a restaurant good enough to measure up to it.

When the telephone rang, Harry still hadn't come up with anything. He couldn't be undecided again. He grabbed the classified directory from the shelf and nervously flipped through the pages looking for the heading *Restaurants*. The telephone had already rung for a fifth time when he finally found a cross reference, *See eating establishments.* He gave up the search. He'd just have to face the music and counter Helen's mockery by pleading the case of helplessness. If there were more helplessness, there'd be less war. Decisiveness is a martial quality.

Harry picked up the receiver. It was his brother Fritz. He was having some kind of problem with his girlfriend.

She had two children and was in no way unhappily married, but she did think highly of poetry and therefore of Fritz the poet. In the meantime, Harry had found the entry for eating establishments. He listened to Fritz's rival-in-love worries with about as much concentration as he lavished on the phone book, jotting letters of the alphabet in the margins all the while. Gradually his calligraphic efforts produced a sentence: *Where am I headed?*

Suddenly he heard Fritz complaining that all he and his girlfriend ever did was go out to dinner. Harry asked immediately: "Where do you go?" Fritz didn't understand at first. "What do you mean, where?" Which restaurants do you go to, Harry naturally wanted to know. Fritz understood this even less. His problem wasn't the choice of restaurants but the fact that he could only meet his girlfriend, who was a doctor of some kind, in restaurants. Out of a mistaken sense of respect for her husband, she wouldn't go to Fritz's apartment. It was killing him. In spite of his feelings for her, it formed a sort of barrier. After all, they could hardly meet at her apartment. That's where her awful husband hung out while taking care of their children. Harry found the problem grotesque. All he wanted from Fritz was the name of a decent place to eat. But Fritz couldn't have cared less about that just now. He wanted to talk about how love was tearing him apart. Harry showed no mercy. "You as a writer," he said, knowing that Fritz liked being called a writer even when it was meant ironically, "you as a writer can't be indifferent to which pub you go to." But Fritz couldn't be softened up that way today. He didn't give one good goddamn which pub he went to with Inez. Harry was just giving him a hard time, he didn't understand anything about love, he was even less sensitive now than he had been before he became a diplomat. Harry, who didn't quite trust the writer's sensitivity so often conjured up by Fritz, quickly added that he found it quite sensitive of a person not to be able to bear a place that had a snooty menu, candles, and long-stemmed glasses. That put an end to the conversation. Harry hadn't made any progress.

It wasn't just the stupid candles that made him feel so wretched. He couldn't stand the new-fangled electronic chirping the cash registers made, either. And more and more often, waiters and waitresses were all decked out in uniforms, like hired help. They weren't very friendly, but they were so overworked you couldn't take their unfriendliness amiss. And they asked whether you wanted Italian or French "dressing" on your salad. Why don't they say "sauce" anymore, the way the French do? "Sauce" is a good word. It's a foreign word, too, but what a word! At least it still means something! It still has some pizzazz. You can still use it, at least in a metaphoric sense, for the indefinable glue that, like a mire, holds the things of life together. "Sauce" has something organic about it, makes you think about more or less successful stews, about juniper berries. But "dressing," that's just some artificial stuff they dab on salads. There's a capitalist sauce and a socialist sauce into which the West and the East have been dunked, but there's no capitalist or socialist dressing. That's all we need! Someday Porsche drivers will probably advertise themselves in the personals with either a progressive or a conservative dressing. Seasoned with ready-to-use world-views. At least that would be the next logical step. In "new German," everyone was already talking about how something "dresses up a meal." Harry von Duckwitz found the expression pitiful from the moment he first heard it. Anyone who "dresses up a meal" turns himself into a cabbage, once and for all!

Harry's mood grew darker and darker. All the good old pubs had long since been ruined. This awful country and all the other awful industrialized countries were getting uglier and uglier. When you're sent to work in some far-off corner of the world, you at least don't have to watch the decline that passes itself off as innovation. Every few years you come back to a fait accompli. That keeps your senses sharpened. You notice the changes right away. Three years ago there hadn't been any automatic teller machines. Now you were constantly seeing people, half brazen, half embarrassed, take their money from a machine as if it were some obscene donation. Harry had moved heaven and earth to be able to spend the next three years in Bonn. Now he'd been here a couple of weeks and he was already longing for his next foreign assignment. All he wanted to do was get away. If he was lucky, he'd be sent to Buenos Aires. There were probably enough pubs for him and Helen there. If she came for a visit, that is. It was much less complicated to go out to dinner with Rita.

It used to be that he and Helen hadn't cared one way or the other about how well and what they ate, the main thing was the atmosphere. As long as the sun slanted in through the windows, they'd been willing to put up with the reactionary chatter of workers and pensioners just a few tables away. Besides, the chatter could easily be drowned out with an Elvis Presley number from an old jukebox—"one night with you," how convincingly he growled and purred that magnificently fraudulent wish. Elvis followed by "The Emperor Waltz," and the riddles of existence were solved for the rest of the day.

There weren't any pubs like that now. The jukeboxes had all been moved to the hallways of elegant old apartment buildings, and the pubs had been taken over by restaurant chains. They'd been like meeting halls. Their roominess was the only really generous and elevating thing about them, but it evidently didn't suit those new interior decorators, the pinheads. In consultation with marketing psychologists, they put their money on close and cozy, lowering the ceilings and dividing up the rooms into booths and cubbyholes. Success proved them right: places that had been half empty were now full of people. Man is an animal, most comfortable in a stall.

Harry had to be careful not to be too harsh, because his misanthropic attacks left their traces at the corners of his mouth, even after they'd passed. In any case, Helen had always been able to tell at a glance. Harry's total contempt for the rest of the world had been a thorn in Helen's leftist side. Now that their reunion had already begun with Harry's old indecisiveness, he didn't want to remind her of his equally old peevishness.

Of course, it occurred to him, we could drive to Cologne and go to one of those chic pubs run by those

impenetrably nice young people. With the unfailing self-
assurance of the sleepwalker, they'd gone straight for the
latest trend, trading the old pubs' Teutonic, canteen-like
furnishings for French bistro chairs. They'd put white tablecloths on the tables and added a few tasty Italian specialties
to the menu. Since there weren't enough places like that
around, they were always full and you always had to wait for
an empty table. You bumped into people, got crushed in the
crowd, but somehow everyone was in a good mood. Being in
a crowd evidently makes people feel they belong. But after
recently being in one of these pubs with a colleague for the
first and last time, and after eating his mozzarella baguette
standing up, Harry had asked himself whether man was
meant to hang around in clusters. He could live without this
kind of belonging. It wasn't a stall, but you did stand
crowded around the bar as if you'd come down to the watering hole. Going with Helen to one of these "in places,"
where the people who belong to the so-called "scene"
sharpen their claws on one another, was out of the question.
The idea of mingling with a crowd of people enjoying life at
the top of their lungs was disgusting.

With a mixture of exaggerated snobbism and despair,
he decided he'd rather take Helen to a Wienerwald restaurant than to one of those places. Wienerwald was like being
in a stall, too, but it had already become such a symbol of
low-class taste that even people with the worst of taste were
free to pick on it. You could see that they were a sign of
decline; that's what gave them a trace of dignity.

One of the "better restaurants" was also out of the
question. Harry hated "better restaurants" with a passion.
The whole business of gourmet cooking was just a pitiful
form of vicarious pleasure—something for the lonely, the
unhappy, the impotent. Harry, in love and happy as he was
from time to time, had never been able to combine love and
food. Love stilled his hunger. The way to a man's heart is

through his stomach—that's one of those obnoxious and completely wrongheaded old adages. Who thought that one up? Women who were tied to their stove, in order to keep a grip on their husbands? Or some fat—or skinny—supermother who didn't want to let her kids go and who tried to tempt them into staying with some good home cooking? It's a poor excuse for love that can be bought with a meal!

In their prime, Harry and Helen often sat in front of a plate of spaghetti without any appetite at all, eating each other up with their eyes. As if to seal an agreement, Helen had always tapped Harry's foot with her own, parting her lips slightly at the same time. It drove Harry wild. He'd take off one of his shoes and rub his foot along the inside of Helen's thigh. Helen used to wear those tight, smooth leather pants. Without a sound, his wool sock would slide up her thigh to her lap. Helen would take Harry's foot and press it to her even harder. Their dark caresses were discreetly hidden under the tablecloth.

The memory of this lust-filled ritual reinforced Harry's distaste for the fuss about eating that was spreading through the Foreign Office. People were being wangled into buying the most revoltingly sweet aperitifs just because they were in fashion. As if there weren't already enough fads, there had to be fads in eating and drinking, too. Like fashion designers searching frantically for new styles, chefs were constantly searching for new dishes. And diners nodded and tasted, cocked their heads and made pleased little noises with closed mouths, poking their forks into tiny little heaps of food on huge plates, and not even noticing that, with the gullibility of the layman, they were falling for the grotesque perversities of unscrupulous experts.

The only tolerable refuge, Harry now thought, was the foreign workers' pub, just as foreign workers were the only ones who made life in this stupid, squeaky clean country halfway bearable. Harry felt a link with the foreignness of the Italians, Greeks, Spanish, Turks, and Yugoslavs. But you had to make sure it was a *Gastarbeiter* pub where there were no Germans sitting around, trying out on the waiter their vacation knowledge of Mediterranean languages.

All of a sudden Harry decided to go to the Greek restaurant just around the corner, where he'd recently wrecked his stomach on the gyros. At least it had the right kind of atmosphere, he thought. Every bit as uninviting as an old train station restaurant. The Greeks gave an irritated glance to any non-Greek who set foot on their territory, but that was better than having some waiter fawn all over you, then dictate where you should sit. Harry always felt like an intruder at the Greek place, the way he had felt in Africa. But at least the feeling of desolation was familiar. Every-thing was filled with longing, including the music. The Greeks longed for home—and Harry longed to be someplace else.

This time it wasn't the telephone that was ringing but the doorbell. This time it was Helen. She looked great, but she was wearing the most impossible clothes. Were they modern or old-fashioned? Harry could see that their game of footsy was in jeopardy because of an awful pair of pants that looked more like a wrap-around skirt.

Following their old familiar greeting, Helen said she was hungry and had to get something into her stomach right away, no matter where. She saw the open phone book: "Where am I headed?" she read out loud. "Sounds good," she said, "really poetic." She asked if Harry wanted to be a poet now too, like his brother. Then her finger stopped at a specialty fish restaurant. "Come on!" she said. Harry didn't have a chance to recommend the Greek. She was just dying to have some of that muck from the bottom of the ocean, could have pulled the mussels from their shells with her teeth! And the way she said it was complete compensation for her billowing wrap-around. Without hesitating, Helen dialed the number and reserved a table. Harry freed himself from the past and got moving. He searched the whole house for his checkbook, then remembered the long tablecloths in fine restaurants and put on a clean pair of socks, just in case.

•   •   •

How could he have had any doubts! Of course Helen came back with him after dinner. Of course they wound up in bed.

"Will you tell her?"

Harry laughed: "The way you say that!"

"I want to meet her."

"Good. Very good," said Harry.

"But only if she knows."

Harry thought about Rita, heard her giggle, and realized that he was suddenly giggling just the way she did. "I can tell her, or not. Whatever you want. It doesn't make any difference to me, and probably not to Rita either."

"That's what you think!" said Helen.

"You're right," said Harry. "What do we know?"

Helen suddenly grew stern. Harry shouldn't be so high-handed. She could just imagine how he lorded it over poor Rita.

"Finally," said Harry, "finally you're showing some female solidarity. High time."

Helen bit him in the calf. She'd clear things up with Rita one of these days.

"What do you mean? There's nothing to clear up," said Harry.

That was her business, said Helen. In any case, she didn't feel like being a cheat.

Harry turned soft and tender. He wanted to know if

Helen always had such reservations when she slept with a married man.

She gave him a little punch: "That's none of your business!"

Harry stroked her. "It does you credit, but it's completely uncalled-for. In any case in this case."

Helen laughed and repeated what he'd said: in any case in this case. There was something to that, illogical as it was. Harry was still in pretty good form where paradoxical quips were concerned. Harry sat up: "Only as far as my quips are concerned?"

Helen looked Harry up and down. On the outside, he was still in pretty good shape. "How old are you?" she asked.

"Oh, come on!"

Helen swore she didn't know.

Harry groaned. His age kept changing all the time—he was born in 1945. Now it was 1981. If he were to look at Helen's body as skeptically as she looked at his, she'd call him a macho meat inspector, wouldn't she?

Helen nodded. "That's right."

Harry found that women got away with being a lot more brazen than men. "At any rate," he said, "your nose hasn't grown any shorter."

"How's your relationship with Rita?" asked Helen.

Harry stared at the ceiling. "I don't know. I really don't know. It's an old-fashioned relationship, I think. Yes, that's it. An old-fashioned relationship. We're friendly to each other, but we're strangers. And somehow that's just fine."

"The opposite of us, in other words," said Helen.

"That's right," said Harry. "Just the opposite. Our relationship is modern. We're unfriendly to each other." He pulled Helen to him and panted in her ear: "We belong together."

"Somehow that's true," said Helen, turning surprisingly serious.

"And how's the screwing?" she asked after a short silence.

"The screwing?"

Helen pretended she was jealous. She shook him and screeched: "She's younger, prettier, better in bed! Oh, how I hate you!"

Harry laughed. She's tighter, he thought, but he didn't say it. He didn't say those male things. What did it mean, anyway? Nothing. Tighter, looser—they had their advantages and disadvantages. "Unproblematic," he said. "It's completely unproblematic with Rita." Helen was lying next to him, and Harry wanted to show her what it was like with Rita. "I stroke her shoulders and then her ass," he said, stroking Helen. "Then I sniff her hair. . . ."

"Like a dog," said Helen, laughing. "You're still at it— that ridiculous and completely unerotic sniffing."

"That's the difference between you and Rita," said Harry, interrupting his demonstration. "She doesn't think my sniffing is ridiculous."

"Or she doesn't say so," said Helen. "She doesn't dare to tell her hero that his sniffing is ridiculous. She tolerates it, poor thing." Helen threatened him: she was going to meet Rita and help her obtain her rights and teach her how to defend herself against sniffing husbands.

Harry noticed that his own smile was a little forced. "You have no idea," he said. "You're not an animal." And since he wanted to provoke her, he added: "You wouldn't believe the way black women sniff and pant."

"Hear, hear!" said Helen. "The man of the world speaking!"

Harry had gone to hookers a number of times in Yaunde. Not so much because he had to as because you couldn't pass it up once you were in Africa. The black women hadn't panted at all. They were extremely quiet. But it had been really good. Black skin is just more beautiful.

Heavy or thin, fat butt or hanging breasts, black always looks good. And just as Harry was sometimes envied for his not very dark but nevertheless exotic Rita, he sometimes envied the colleagues who had, in effect, made the more rigorously logical decision and brought a coal-black beauty back to Bonn with them.

"And this other business?" asked Helen.

"Which business?"

"With the motorcycle. On a motorcycle."

"Oh, that."

"Did you? Did the two of you?"

Harry was still a little embarrassed about the letter he'd written to Helen from Yaunde. In order to make her jealous, he'd described the pleasure he got from sitting behind Rita on the motorcycle while she drove him around.

Helen didn't let up: "Well, did you or didn't you?"

Harry shook his head.

"Loser!"

Harry nodded.

Helen knelt above him: "I'd imagined it very clearly."

"And?"

"What do you mean 'and'—isn't that enough?"

Harry pulled her to him. "You're even better than an animal," he said, and he tried to keep his breathing from sounding the least bit like a sniff.

•   •   •

Helen wanted him to wake her up at seven in the morning. Her train was leaving around ten. At breakfast he was going to give her a short report about his three years as a diplomat in Africa. Harry was curious to hear her opinion. About questions of power and powerlessness, Third World policy, the mood among intellectuals in Germany. He was about to

begin as he was cooking eggs the next morning, when Helen
came into the kitchen and started brushing her mop of dark
hair, ignoring the loose hairs that fell to the floor. Harry
should stop talking nonsense, she said. Politics, his career,
nothing but compromises. Who was interested in that? She
buttered her toast and said: "Tell me instead how you met
Rita."

7 *How Duckwitz is less moved by the change of government in the fall of 1982 than by the sight of his wife outside a supermarket. In addition, a few remarks about Rita's skin color and Helen's background, about small talk and coming to terms with the past. Also, why Duckwitz no longer wears his light summer suit, and how he works on suggestions for improvements at the Foreign Office.*

October 1982 did not leave the Foreign Office totally untouched. Televisions were turned on first thing in the morning. A "constructive vote of no confidence" had resulted in a change of government. As chairman of the Liberal Party, the head of the Foreign Office was a key figure in the coup. He kept his job as Foreign Minister. He had to fight the Judas image for a while. That is, he didn't fight, he simply didn't do anything at all, merely waited till the affair had been forgotten. Somehow he succeeded in keeping the smell of the treason he'd spread from clinging to him. The Defense Ministry, which was always causing trouble, got a new boss, this time not just a dud but a conceited ape as well. Worst of all was the Interior Minister. The world hadn't seen the likes of him before. And they called this the "Turning Point."

It was less a turning point than a changeover in faces and tone. The previous cabinet had been regarded with the usual mixture of annoyance and amusement; now disgust and contempt were added as new categories in civics. Before, a venomous little man had done a passable rhetorical job of enunciating his rigid policies; now a mighty oaf stood there helplessly flailing his arms. For decades people had been used to the idea that Bonn was a stage on which rotten actors performed rotten plays. You could laugh at them and boo at them. But you didn't even feel like criticizing the new cast. The Turning Point wasn't a change, but a decline in the level of performance on the public stage. The entertainment value of politics was now less than nil. But it was no catastrophe, it didn't touch people to the quick.

Duckwitz himself was moved one morning by the sight of Rita. He went to the office early, had his coffee there, then got in the car again to drive home. Near their duplex, between Bonn and Bad Godesberg, there was one of those cheap chain supermarkets that kept changing its name. Right now it was called "Aldi." Harry had bought peanuts there once while he was at the diplomatic training center in nearby Ippendorf. As far as he could remember, the chain had been called "Albrecht" then. These were the kinds of changes that might be more decisive than the change in government. This was the more interesting turning point: the trend toward diminishing things. Everything had to have some playful name that made it sound like a chocolate bar—everything, that is, but existence. Those stupid Americans already gave nicknames to hurricanes. Missiles had nicknames. Wars absolutely had to have them, too.

It was just before nine, and the store wasn't open yet. A few people stood outside the door, waiting. One of them was Rita. Harry was so startled that he hit the gas. She hadn't seen him. It was a boring, gray morning, and the day wasn't going to be any different. Rita didn't belong here. Not in this wretched residential area on the wretched edge of wretched Bonn. Her beautiful yellow skin had already turned pallid in the months she'd spent in Germany. He shouldn't have married her and dragged her to this part of the world. Already her glow had disappeared. What did she think about all day? What did she do when she wasn't playing the piano? Hadn't her cute little quivering orgasm grown less joyful? You don't come from Korea and India, grow up in Africa and England, just to stand outside some miserable store, in some barren suburb, waiting for it to open.

Harry didn't drive home. He couldn't bear to see Rita in her wretchedness again. All he'd wanted to do was pick up the new issue of *Der Spiegel* so that he could read it in peace at the office.

What a miserable, gray town. Who invented the fairy tale that Bonn was a hothouse? If only it were! It's nothing but a gray, endless weekend when time stands still, you can't think of anything to do, there are no good movies showing, and there's no one to talk to.

The coast of Cameroon, now that was a hothouse. Duala. Rita hadn't looked foreign in Cameroon, although she was foreign there, too. Harry had to think about how, during his time in Cameroon, he was always looking for excuses to pay a visit to the embassy's branch office in Duala, the country's busiest commercial center. It was blazing hot there. No one wanted to go. Whenever there was something that had to be done in Duala, Duckwitz volunteered. No, it wasn't too much for him. No, they didn't need to be grateful to him. In Duala, he did what he had to do as quickly as possible, then drove out of town, past the harbor, past the recently built and already crumbling high-rise hotels where no tourist wanted to stay. Beyond them was a picture-perfect beach. There was no one there in the heat of the African afternoon. Harry put on his swimming trunks, ran down to the water, where the sand was firm and moist, looked around, then took off his trunks and ran along the beach stark naked, holding his trunks in his hand. He wanted to be brown all over. He didn't want to impose a white man's body, and certainly not a white behind, on beautiful Rita. Rita was beautiful, and he wanted to be beautiful, too. It's not only ridiculous, it's crazy, if not fatal, to lie broiling in the African sun. But you can run in the sun. The air by the ocean is cooler. If fate had already made him a white man, he at least wanted to be off-white. But it shouldn't look too much like he'd recently come back from vacation. He could get just the right shade by going about these odd errands in Duala from time to time. Duckwitz didn't like athletic men with deep tans. Occasionally, when he went to the pool at the Italian embassy with Rita, he was happy that his skin was a sort of yellowish brown, that it looked almost as Indian as Rita's. Your skin is enough to make a person jealous, Hennersdorff's snow-white wife, of all people, had said to him once. Duckwitz had shaken his head. Really? You think so? No, I don't go in for sports. I don't go out in the sun.

This damned Bonn had made them both pale. The place turned you into a maggot. Harry and Rita von Duckwitz. A childless, row-house couple. He's the kind who snaps up an exotic woman and then lets her go sour. Once in a while he sleeps with his old girlfriend. One of those.

In the seventies you could lie around naked in the parks of all the bigger cities in West Germany. And they had, he and Helen. Associate-at-law Duckwitz lay stark naked next to Helen Grünberg in Grüneburg Park in Frankfurt. You couldn't even imagine doing that any longer. It had been the height of uninhibitedness then. Soon it became embarrassing, ugly, silly. The naked human being just doesn't belong out in the open. It was the same with a child's upbringing—it wasn't supposed to be antiauthoritarian. All of it had been a mistake. But at least they hadn't had ugly white butts.

Helen Grünberg. As he was driving along Godesberger Allee toward the government quarter, he remembered that at first he'd thought Helen was Jewish. Grünberg, that was a Jewish name. Harry rejected the assertion that you could recognize Jews and Jewesses by their appearance. That, by the way, had been one of the few points of disagreement between Harry and his aunts. From time to time his aunts

would say that one person or the other looked Jewish. Harry
would fly off the handle. What kind of nonsense is that!
"Don't get your dander up!" Aunt Frieda would say. "A lot
of Amis look like Amis, and a lot of Germans look like
Germans. Experts can already tell West Germans from East
Germans, and so Jews look Jewish, that's normal." Later, he
found out from Aunt Huberta that Aunt Frieda's great flame
in old Berlin had been a Jewish nightclub emcee who died
in a concentration camp. No one had hated the Nazis like
Aunt Frieda. In spite of the explanation, Harry still thought
the idea that somebody could look Jewish was just stupid
talk. Sure, there are Middle Eastern faces, but Egyptians,
Palestinians, and Israelis look just as much alike as the
Dutch, Belgians, and Germans. The only difference is that
Middle Easterners are much better looking.

Helen had been good looking, dark, and not a single
gray hair. Harry secretly thought she was Jewish, and somehow he was glad. It was like fulfilling a dream of reconcili-
ation. To his surprise, though, Helen called her father a
"stupid army type." It was really confusing. How could her
Jewish father—Harry always imagined him as a pious man
who observed the sabbath—how could he have been a
soldier? Or had Helen been traumatized? Was she suppress-
ing something terrible? Had her father been a victim of the
Nazis and did she simply not want to believe it? Was the
Nazi terror affecting even Helen's post-war soul? Then one
day as they were lying naked in Grüneburg Park and Harry
was explaining the advantages of his circumcised willie, he
discovered that Grünberg was an absolutely normal German
name and that Helen's father really had been an officer in
the war. No trauma—but the dream was over. Harry
couldn't hide his disappointment. "I'm sorry I can't be your
woman for all reparations," Helen had said.

He shouldn't keep thinking about Helen, he should
think about Rita. Rita was the present. He had to take care

of Rita. He had to make her glow again. Flowers would be too much; Harry couldn't bring himself to do that. He wouldn't let things go that far. Leave the office and go home with a bouquet of flowers for his wife—no! It was bad enough that he was married, but that would be playing too much the husband. During his lunch break, Harry drove into town and bought a recording of Mozart piano sonatas for fortepiano and a coffee-table Mozart biography. In the back of his mind he was thinking that this might encourage Rita to play more Mozart. Lately she'd been doing an awful lot of plinking around in the chaste works of Bach.

He asked Rita whether she felt comfortable in Bonn. Her "absolutely" was quite convincing, and she was dutifully pleased about the record and the book.

After dinner, Harry helped Rita with her German, the way he always did. Rita repeated in German after Harry: "This is a plate. That is a table. We live in a duplex. My husband is a diplomat. He is crazy. Normal people do not go to work for the Foreign Office. I am his wife. Unfortunately, I married this man. Unfortunately, he is a dirty rat. I am sorry I married him. This is an apple. I am going to throw the apple at his head. My name is Rita. I am much too good for him. I can play the piano. I have a motorcycle. I come from far away. I don't know what I have lost by coming to Bonn. My name is now Duckwitz. I weigh 50 kilograms. That is a chair. That is a fork. That is the floor. The floor is covered with wall-to-wall carpeting. The carpet is enough to make you puke. I will be happy when I no longer have to look at it. What will become of us? Where do things go from here? Questions and more questions. I am not happy. I am very lonely."

Rita tossed Harry an apple. "This is an apple," she said, "but I am not lonely." She beamed. Their word games were fun. Harry enjoyed having a chance to call things by their real names. "That is a table"—a sentence like that was such a relief. It was the truth. "I am not lonely"—a clear statement. A lot of diplomats had foreign wives. They got together, had tea, and organized flea markets to get rid of the junk they accumulated. There was a German course for them. "It's not as funny as it is with you," Rita told Harry, "but I learn more."

Harry's colleague Sachtleben lived just a few streets away. He had a sensible wife. She played the flute but looked absolutely awful when she did. She and Rita played Schubert's "Der Hirt auf dem Felsen," and it sounded pretty good. But the fact that Rita refused to be talked into trying her hand at boogie woogie was sheer orneriness.

Frau Sachtleben was always cursing about the diplomat's profession. It was no job for a decent man, she said one time when she was visiting Duckwitz with her husband. She was absolutely right about that, but somehow she provoked Harry into contradiction. Strange, he didn't want to hear it from her.

"What's your problem?" said Harry. "A diplomat is typical of the human species—cowardly, false, cautious, powerless, and idle, with a limited mental horizon. What do you want! Rather a diplomat than a decorator." Frau Sachtleben didn't give up; she said that the only thing diplomats knew inside out was small talk. "What do you have against small talk?" asked Duckwitz. There's nothing better than casual, aimless conversation, than a noncommittal chat. Filling up the silence with the patter of unimportant words. Just standing in a room, killing time by talking about the weather—that too is a kind of truth. What is it people have against a conversation like, "It's turned cooler, hasn't it?" "Yes, you're right, it is cooler, we should go inside." There isn't anything more profound than a dialogue like that. "You have a lovely place." "You think so?" Or simply, "How are you?" "Fine, thanks." Question and answer, a throwaway question and a throwaway answer. But what warmth such a dialogue can convey! What a relief it had always been after a fight with Helen when one of them would ask the other as they were reading the newspaper: "What's new?" A peace offering. That was life. That was love. No need to prove anything or swear any oaths. No confessions. No reproaches. No poking around in old wounds. Just the gentle, conciliatory question: "What's new?" Some diplomats of the old school were still masters at this way of saying everything and nothing. Younger diplomats thought well-mannered chatter was a put-on. They wanted to be doers and didn't realize that they could do precious little. They talked about the challenges of the profession and couldn't see that the challenges didn't exist.

After the Sachtlebens had gone home, Harry took out the cigar box with his good ideas. Where eighty Brazilian cigars with discolored wrappers had once rested, there was a growing number of messy notes. In Cameroon, he'd pasted on a label from a school notebook and had written in his best high-school-teacher hand: *Continuing Education.* That was the great thing about Third World countries—they still had notebook labels of the kind that had been eradicated in a fit of innovative fury in the central Europe of the late fifties. Harry wrote: *In praise of small talk. The truth of small talk. Examine the question of whether a conversation about the weather isn't worth more than Kant's* Critique of Pure Reason.

"What are you doing?" asked Rita. She was tired and didn't want to speak German anymore. So in English Harry tried to explain his defense of small talk, but he wasn't sure she understood.

The next morning, Rita asked him why he didn't wear that light summer suit, the beautiful, elegantly sloppy linen one from Cameroon. "Isn't it a little snobbish?" asked Harry. And then he drove off to the office.

Of course the color of the suit was too pale for Bonn. Not so light that Duckwitz would have been encouraged to leave the foreign service if he'd insisted on wearing it to the office, but it was off the mark for a dark-gray diplomatic mouse. Though it wasn't a suit for a dandy, either. As a matter of fact, it wasn't very stylish, and it looked a little dirty even when it had just come from the cleaners. There was a reason why he hadn't taken it out of his closet lately.

In the summer of 1981, before Rita arrived in Bonn, Harry had taken a trip to Paris with Helen, and he had naturally worn the light-colored suit from Cameroon. In Paris, one of the movie theaters was showing a German film about Hitler that was several hours long. The film was already a couple of years old, and it wasn't shown very often. It lasted almost all night. Intellectuals from the American Left came to Paris from New York just to see this masterly example of "coming to terms with the past." Harry thought it was going too far to sacrifice one of their three nights of lovemaking in Paris to a movie, but he couldn't say anything against coming to terms with the past. The director was in the audience. "Look!" Helen had said. The director was wearing a suit just like Harry's. The movie started. "This is just burning incense before the altar of that damned Nazi shit!" Harry said loudly in the direction of the screen half an hour into the film. And then all he wanted to do was get out. If this was coming to terms with the past, then he'd rather suppress it. This was a disgusting show of empathy for the kitschy mentality of the Nazis. A revolting piece of work. Helen joined Harry at the hotel three and a half hours later, when the show was still only half over. How could she have stood that glitzy rubbish so long? Harry was furious. They had argued all night, but soon after came to agree about the movie. Harry hadn't worn the suit since.

Harry von Duckwitz, who was soon to be promoted from Counsellor of the Legation to Counsellor of the Legation First Class, drove to his office—which was actually a cubicle. Like all cubicles, it was so small that the armrest of his desk chair made a nick in the wall. Harry worked in Political Divison 3, in the Office of African Affairs. At the moment, he was preparing material for a Commission for the Reform of the Foreign Service. He was examining the usefulness of all the embassy reports that reached the central office, the ones that usually disappeared unread into the files. He even looked at the reports he'd written himself while he was in Cameroon. Awfully brash, with all those references to French companies that "controlled" the market and German companies that were seeking "market control." The ambassador hadn't liked terms like that.

The best part was reading the reports by Members of Parliament. On their horizon-broadening trips around the world, they were sure to visit the German embassies, and they couldn't get out of writing a report. That's the way the iron rules of parliament would have it. Every last one of those reports was the charming height of naiveté.

A couple of offices down the hall, Frau Huber was working on reports from Latin America for the same commission. She'd been a Counsellor at the embassy in Buenos Aires. She was a clever, energetic person who contradicted all the rules of the Foreign Office: she was a woman, she was not an aristocrat, and she hadn't studied law. Yet if she was lucky, in just six months she'd be named ambassador to one of the bigger embassies in Europe. They were talking about Madrid. A pleasant colleague. No erotic temptation there. She loved Latin America and supplied Duckwitz with Latin American records and tapes. She and Duckwitz enjoyed showing each other the finest examples they stumbled on in their research. Today, Frau Huber came to Duckwitz's office with a report by three M.P.s. One was a Social Democrat, one a Liberal, and one a Christian Democrat. It was a joint report. Laziness unites.

"In the afternoon, we accepted an invitation to an *estancia*," the report began. "There we saw an exhibition of various cattle breeds. This was followed by a 'maté' tea hour and by one of the highly popular barbecues called an 'asada.'"

"They can't even get that right," said Frau Huber, "even though there's an Asado Steak House here on every streetcorner!" The report continued:

"Met with the usual warmth, like everywhere in Argentina. Discussions with leading figures from business and politics. Huge bowls of salad served. The opinion that peace and quiet must return to the country was heard repeatedly. After three weeks of exhausting travel and many new impressions, we were happy to return home. Germany truly is wonderful."

Duckwitz and Frau Huber laughed. "And boneheads like this are members of the Bundestag!"

"Wait just a minute," said Harry, looking for a report from Amnesty International that described in quite different terms the situation in Argentina at the time of that trip: "In the early morning hours, the dismembered bodies of four men and a woman were found on the outskirts of Buenos Aires. They could not be identified. They were probably the members of the outlawed CGT Union abducted three years ago. In the course of the day, it was determined, twenty-three people were abducted in the city."

Without a word, Frau Huber put on Duckwitz's desk a supplementary report to the central office from a member of the German embassy: "The Honorable Members of Parliament drove out into the country to gather their impressions. Their openness to political issues is to be welcomed. For the Embassy, such visits always raise questions about personnel and financing. Since two members of the intermediate-level staff are currently on home leave, an Argentine chauffeur had to be hired. The petty cash fund we have frequently requested is urgently advised. In addition, binding instructions should be issued on whether the consumption of meals in public establishments is to be paid for by the Embassy or out of the expense accounts of the Members of Parliament themselves. It would also be advisable to inform the M.P.s before the beginning of such a fact-finding trip that the Embassies cannot always arrange the desired talks with cabinet ministers and presidents and that recourse must frequently be made to those officials' representatives. During the trip, damage was done to wheel bearings in rough terrain. In this context, urgent attention must be called to the fact that the acquisition of spare parts for the Embassy's vehicles represents a significant problem."

Duckwitz pictured those odd tourists in Africa who, with a reproachful grin, were always asking for the assistance of the embassy, whether with money, visas, or telephone calls. One of them had driven all over Africa in an old Hanomag truck, and at the end of his trip he'd sold the rusty crate for 9000 dollars in bitterly poor Sudan. A year earlier, he'd paid just 2000 marks for it in Hanover.

The commission immediately recognized the seriousness of the situation and was prepared to make the "Procurement of Official Replacement Vehicles" an extra category on their list of suggestions for improvement, though the formulation did sound as if they'd been offended: "While for years it has been within the purview of the Federal Ministers of the Interior and Defense to decide on procurements for the replacement of department vehicles, each individual case involving Foreign Office vehicles must be submitted to the Federal Minister of Finance." Following a long passage on the extreme difficulty of acquiring spare parts such as knuckle bolts, air filters, and clutch plates, and on the susceptibility of vehicles to breakdown on bumpy Third World roads, it was recommended that no repairs be under-taken. Broken-down embassy cars should be sold for good money and new ones purchased: "The Foreign Office should therefore seek a solution in cooperation with the Federal

Minister of Finance, if necessary seeking a change in any contrary budget regulations in order to make possible the rapid and unbureaucratic disposal of the foreign missions' official vehicles and their replacement with new vehicles."

Duckwitz went to a copying machine two stories down. It was usually out of order, but today it did produce barely readable copies. He photocopied the commission's statement. He would read it to Rita that evening and ask if she didn't want to drop the whole idea of trying to learn German.

8 How anecdotal diplomats get on Duck-witz's nerves, how and where to get a beer in Moscow, on German culture abroad and, above all, on how life sometimes seems like a film, along with Harry and Helen's reflections on what that means. In addition, a diatribe against simulation.

Duckwitz absolutely loved it when someone said the meals at the Foreign Office cafeteria were first rate. Still, on occasion he'd be overpowered, shortly before noon, by a longing for the unpleasant smell of the canteen and the constant bitching about the food. His colleagues would bewail the fact that diplomats were nothing but common civil servants these days. What none of them understood was that belly-aching like a civil servant made you one all the more.

Duckwitz sat down at a table with Sachtleben and the chinless Count Waldburg. Sachtleben had been in Moscow for two years and was still full of stories about it. The crazi-est part was the evening movies at the embassy. Since there weren't any Goethe Institutes in communist countries, he'd had to go to a lot of trouble to supply the Ivans with German culture. Showing films was the best solution. The embassy always tried to get the director to come along with the reels of film. That way, people would have something to get their hands on. It usually turned out to be rather embar-rassing. The director would be prepared to answer the tons of questions a Soviet audience would direct at him, and then no one would say a word. The Russians came only for the alcohol, so the embassy staff would have to come up with a few questions to keep the silence from growing oppressive.

Sachtleben was probably right, but he told the story in such a condescending way that Duckwitz felt compelled to object: "Alcohol my foot! Everybody knows the Russians are just dying to know about Western culture!"

So who was in Moscow, you or me? Sachtleben positively glowed with a sense of his own superiority. There wasn't a thing to drink in Moscow, not a drop. Soviet citizens were dying first and foremost for a drink; secondly for a drink; and way behind that, maybe, for Western culture. And they had a right to, or didn't Duckwitz think so? The embassy had taken all of this into account. Cultural Affairs offices were stuffed with cartons of beer—ordinary beer in cans, and bottles of Beck's for finer occasions. When they showed films, they always served drinks both before and after. Naturally their modest drinking bouts hadn't been open to just any old Muscovite. In order to get to the fountainhead, the thirsty public had to make the Russian guards outside the embassy believe they were interested in German culture. Sachtleben had even heard of Russians who took German at language schools and universities just so they could get into the cultural events and grab a few beers and a sip of whisky. Absolutely terrible conditions.

The others at the table hung on Sachtleben's every word. Duckwitz was annoyed. It could be that conditions in Moscow were terrible. But they were terrible in Africa as well, and he couldn't stand it when people talked about terrible conditions in that slyly triumphant tone of voice that was a mixture of true gloating and false sympathy. There was no stopping Sachtleben: you actually had to twist the glasses out of the Russians' hands and turn out the lights in the reception room in order to get them to take their seats for the movie; you had to tell them there would, of course, be more to drink after the showing. What you didn't do was call the thing by its real name. Instead you spoke of it as a "social gathering."

Once, and this was really just too much, the head of Cultural Affairs had ordered a film by that genius of a

Bavarian, a real original.... His name had slipped Sachtleben's mind. One of those bearish, rough-hewn types. Had been involved in a legal battle with the Interior Minister over some film subsidy or other. He was the kind of director—what was his name, anyway?—who made movies people found so anarchistic that the Goethe Institutes had been instructed by headquarters—Sachtleben pointed to his tray—not to use them as examples of German culture, at least for the time being. That's probably what had made it so enticing to the head of Cultural Affairs.

"Brilliant!" said the chinless Count Waldburg. "Splendid, an excellent man!" No one at the Foreign Office could stand the Interior Minister. He should keep his nose out of other people's business. They all agreed on that. It was absolutely right for the head of Cultural Affairs at the embassy in Moscow to circumvent the man's instructions. "Impeccable!" added the chinless Count Waldburg. There were smart-asses like Waldburg all over the Foreign Office. No matter what they were talking about or what they said, it always sounded unbearably snooty. Of course the Interior Minister was a monstrosity. Any passionate moralist would consider him a bastard. But if his critics here didn't seem quite as nasty, they were still unpleasant enough in their own right.

Sachtleben went on. He wasn't a bad storyteller; Duckwitz had to admit that. Everyone was sitting at the table, waiting for the next laugh. Incredibly enough, the film by this ingenious Bavarian—he'd think of the name in just a second—was about guzzling beer.

The plot was totally confusing. Someone in a policeman's uniform, probably the director himself, went swaying drunkenly through a crowd at the Oktoberfest in Munich, gulping beer from the steins of complete strangers. Just imagine that! squawked Sachtleben, and all of it in Moscow! Eighty or ninety Muscovites, dying for the movie to be over so they could crowd around a makeshift bar to get a stingy drink, and they had to watch not only the mystifying protagonist but tents full of people as they downed huge quantities of beer. Duckwitz laughed in spite of himself. He was the only one who did. The others still seemed to be waiting for the punch line. Most diplomats don't even register the grotesque things that go on all around them; Sachtleben was an exception. He wasn't such a bad sort. The others at the table evidently couldn't see how crazy the whole thing was.

The chinless Count Waldburg and the colorless woman sitting next to him bent over their trays and began shoveling in the mashed potatoes. Sachtleben, a little subdued now without an audience, turned to Duckwitz. The crazy thing was that this torturous evening at the movies wasn't over yet. To the relief of the Russians, the director himself wasn't there. At least they might be able to get a sip of beer immediately after the film, without the usual excruciating discussion! But then something even worse happened. An extremely well-known film historian had come along, maybe for safety's sake, in case Bonn heard about the embassy's brazen decision to show the film. This way they could fall back on an authority whose opinion was above question. To the dismay of the thirsty Russians and the now very thirsty but duty-bound members of the embassy staff, the historian launched into unflagging praise of this film about beer-boozing. It was incredibly avant-garde, a masterpiece whose timeless validity went far beyond the limits of the Oktoberfest and the borders of the country. It could be that his praise was especially thorough because he felt he had to earn his speaker's fee. He just couldn't be stopped. Some of the Russians were already asleep and snoring, others fearfully contemplated missing the last subway home and having to undertake a march of thirty kilometers—all for the sake of three glasses of beer and an incomprehensible film about people guzzling hectoliters of the stuff! Maybe the film critic thought he had to counter the philistinism of the Interior Minister by bestowing high praise on something the Minister wanted to send to eternal damnation. Duckwitz shook with delight, expressing his complete sympathy: what a dreadful evening! No, the German embassy in Moscow certainly wasn't the right place for some long-winded proof of the stupidity of the Interior Minister, that old toad. That was going too far. Not at the cost of thirsty Russians!

The chinless Count Waldburg nibbled at his breaded perch. When he was chewing, his lower jaw slid even further back. From his hairline to the tip of his nose, in profile, he simply looked rich and stupid. He said he didn't have much to do with that cultural crap in India. God knows they've got other problems there. The misery is inconceivable. People die like dogs, right in the street. And you have no idea of the brutality of the Indian police. Journalists here only set their sights on the human rights violations of Latin America and the Middle East. People think of India as a dependable Third World country where German industry can invest without a qualm. They think the unending misery is merely passive. The active cruelty that takes place there is hardly registered.

That was an amazingly sensible statement for a man with a profile like that, thought Duckwitz. This was apparently a day for true confessions. Was Waldburg, who'd always seemed such a dumb snob, going to turn out to be a politically sensible person? Had Duckwitz judged him falsely? Had the degenerate count undergone rarefaction in India? Or was he just mindlessly repeating what he'd heard some clever journalist say? On the other hand, isn't clever analysis of terrible conditions usually just mindless chatter? What was the difference, Duckwitz thought with sudden apprehension, between these other diplomats and himself, if even the biggest conformists knew what was going on behind the scenes, understood where the misery came from, and griped about the politicians in power—at least in the cafeteria? Going to the cafeteria was dangerous. He'd have to avoid eating lunch here in the future. It made his colleagues look like thinking beings instead of the functioning weenies they actually were, here in their tiny little offices. Or the tough men of action they pretended to be, out in the foreign embassies. Especially now that the image of the diplomat as some high-class tiger on the dance floor was past saving.

An anecdote being told for all it was worth was sheer torture to Duckwitz, even if there wasn't really anything objectionable about it. There should be something cozy about people sitting around telling what they've done and what they've seen. Like in old adventure novels. These people simply lacked the necessary stature. Besides, the atmosphere in the cafeteria didn't bear much resemblance to a fireside. And instead of resembling thick tweed, the way they should, these voices were loud and boastful. There were no Münchhausens in diplomacy anymore—though Münchhausen wouldn't be a bad name for a diplomat. Duckwitz decided to ask the personnel department whether there was a Münchhausen among the more than 6000 embassy employees and, if so, what his first name was. It would be a good way to kill time on a dreary afternoon.

Duckwitz could have contributed a few amusing adventures. But not here, not for people who were at best not intolerable but not one jot better than that. And he needed to have a woman in his audience. In any case, he didn't consider that faded wapiti cow sitting next to chinless Waldburg a woman. She was the last person who could have stimulated Duckwitz to a display of eloquence, let alone anything else. She reminded him of Hennersdorff's wife, may he rest in peace, the way she was just bursting with self-confidence. This woman probably thought she was charming. She even seemed to have a husband; at least she had one of those ridiculous hyphenated names that was

probably the result of a marriage: Kretschmann-Häusermann
or something like that. Duckwitz had an urge to call her
Frau Hyphenation. Astonishingly enough, she'd already been
promoted to the rank of Minister Counsellor. What a
strange sign of emancipation—to attach your maiden name
to your husband's name. After some delay, the custom had
begun to spread through the Foreign Office; brash women
M.P.s, progressive women journalists, and women professors
with no sense of style had already been decorating themselves with hyphens for years.

The woman with the unbearable name had an intractable self-assurance and the voice to go with it: cutting,
raspy, trembling, and Hanoverian. The voice suddenly rose
to say: you just can't imagine what goes on in the delegations to international organizations. A beehive is absolutely
nothing by comparison. Referring to Sachtleben's beer-and-
film anecdote, she said that as a German diplomat at one of
those missions, you might not have anything to do with
showing films, yet the whole thing was like a film. There
was no other way to put it. The goings on, the hectic pace,
the confusion, the turmoil, the topsy-turviness, the intrigues
—you often had the feeling you were watching a movie.

Her description fell completely flat, and no one wanted
to ask for details about the hectic pace at the German U.N.
mission. The hyphenated diplomat wasn't the least bit
perturbed and stolidly continued spooning up her plum
compote.

•   •   •

Nowadays you often heard people say, *It's just like in the
movies.* The less people were able to express themselves, the
more they maintained that things were *just like in the movies.*
This was especially true of diplomats assigned to an area of

political crisis. Whether it was Mozambique or Lebanon, Guatemala or Pakistan, it was *just like in the movies.* Corruption, sneak attacks, blows with the butt of a rifle, *it's just like in the movies.* By seeing, or pretending to see reality as if it were a film, you turn yourself into a spectator. You may be horrified, but you can't do anything about it. If the chaotic voices in the German U.N. mission in New York seemed to this hyphenated woman to be something out of a movie, it just showed she was incapable of taking action, of doing anything about it. You had to pass your exams with very high marks and do extremely well during diplomatic training to get one of those highly desirable jobs with an international delegation in Brussels, Geneva, or New York. But this woman had already lost her sense of perspective. Otherwise what went on at the U.N. wouldn't seem unreal—like a movie—but real. Maybe she got the job because she had connections. Surely it wasn't because of a lover? But then, there might be someone who thinks she's charming, with her voice like a rusty saw and her skin like gorgonzola.

Duckwitz was irritated by his own laziness, his reserve, annoyed by his tact, his sympathy, his disdain, his cowardice. Instead of entertaining venomous thoughts about this hyphenated diplomat, he should be asking about the hectic sexual pace among the people at the U.N. He should be asking about the fucking around which, according to the stories, completely overshadowed all the politicking. He wondered whether her gorgonzola skin could blush. Probably not.

From a reliable source, Duckwitz had learned some of the details about the fucking around. Right up into the beds of French government ministers. There's only one subject of conversation in Geneva, Brussels, and New York: *Who is fuckable?* In the remote embassies, on the other hand, where diplomats get to know each other well, things are as chaste as at a Catholic missionary station. At best there's a kind of repressed desire. Life there isn't a movie, it's a more or less terrible but, above all, a real joke.

Duckwitz came to life, the way he always did when he was pursuing great thoughts. He cheerfully went back to the office he despised. He wasn't going to waste his time inquiring in the personnel division about a possible Münchhausen. He wanted to be with Helen. Thinking alone isn't any fun. He could get hold of his thoughts better when he was with her. He wanted to get out of Bonn, sit around in Frankfurt with Helen. He called her up. It had been too brief the last time, to be honest with you, said Harry. Dinner was too long, the night was too short. They'd screwed too much and talked too little. Helen laughed. Is Rita still away? "Far enough away," said Harry.

"Oh, Harry!" said Helen. Had she sighed? Had she fluttered? It could have meant anything. Harry was terribly bourgeois, calling his old girlfriend when his wife wasn't home! "You've got it," said Harry, "and on an official phone. Long distance from the office." That really did him good. Too bad Helen wasn't abroad anymore. Long distance calls were the only way to get back some of his tax money.

"Office!" Helen exclaimed. Harry had turned into a real office stud. He shouldn't keep talking about the "office," it sounded so slick.

He said he'd rather be slick and say "office" than trendy and say "headquarters," the way his younger colleagues did. And it was certainly better than speaking dustily of the "bureau," like some graying undersecretary. No, it was a good thing Helen wasn't abroad right now but in Frankfurt. How long does it take to get from Bonn to Frankfurt by train? What time is it now? Do you have anything better to do this evening? He just wanted to gab. Not screw, just gab.

"Why no screwing?" asked Helen.

Harry thought that the last time had been mere duty

for Helen, that he was the only one who thought it was great. But now he kept this to himself. He simply had to be past the age when a thought like that was torture.

"What about Rita?" asked Helen.

Rita was at a piano competition in Copenhagen, said Harry, but he swore his call didn't have anything to do with Rita. Helen said Harry should decide on a train and then call back. No, said Harry, the room might be tiny, but he did have two telephones. He didn't want to disconnect her while he checked on train schedules. Besides, the point was to drive up costs with his private calls while blocking the lines for official business.

Harry put through a call to one of the secretaries in the administrative office and asked her for information about the next train to Frankfurt.

"Business or pleasure?" she asked while she was checking.

"What difference does that make?" asked Harry.

If it was official business, she could get a first-class ticket for Herr von Duckwitz right away, said the voice. Harry was holding a receiver to each ear.

"Did you hear that?" he asked Helen. "Is my visit going to be business or pleasure?"

"You're turning me into an accessory," said Helen.

He wasn't bourgeois after all, said Harry. He didn't do everything in secret.

"On the contrary," said Helen. If someone is really bourgeois, the secretary is always in on it. Yuk!

"Have you decided?" asked the voice politely.

"Oh God, another decision!" groaned Harry. "Can't you make it for me, Helen?"

"Herr von Duckwitz would like a round-trip ticket to Frankfurt, business, but second class."

Harry was holding the two receivers together. "Did you hear that?" he asked the secretary.

"You can't travel second class," said the secretary, completely unmoved. The Foreign Office has an agreement with the travel agency, she said. However, Herr von Duckwitz could sit in a second-class compartment once he got on the train.

●   ●   ●

Helen's apartment smelled just like her old quarters in the commune, but here chaos had more room for expansion. There were open books lying face down everywhere, and her desk was unmistakably a shrine to labor. The first thing they did was not to have tea together, but to have a good romp in bed. That is, on a big mattress on the floor. With Helen this was no silly relic of old student days, it was a solemn relic. Harry told her so.

They were sitting next to each other, not too close, not too far apart, their backs to the wall, their knees drawn up under a warm blanket. The classic pose. Harry lit a cigarette. "Just to make it even more classic," he said.

"Early Godard, absolutely," said Helen, and then she corrected herself: No, actually, it was Chabrol, considering the fact that Harry was a married man. An adulterer! But even if he was a member of the bourgeois establishment, he wasn't old enough or fat enough for Chabrol, said Helen as she played cat woman, purring and pinching Harry's flat stomach. "Truffaut!" she said, just the way they do in Truffaut films.

Harry told her about having lunch at the cafeteria that day, about the woman with the ridiculous hyphenated name and how she said everything was just like in the movies. Everyone was starting to say that; he thought it was a sign of increasing stupidity and sloppy thinking. He saw the comparison of reality and scenes from movies as a sign of people's inability to comprehend reality. People who aren't willing or able to understand reality, whether it's strange, touching, or cruel, see it as a film, as something unreal. That way they can comfortably avoid the obligation of having to do anything about it. If something is like a film, it can't be changed, it can only be observed in amazement, amusement, or horror. This was the attitude of a lot of diplomats.

"Aha!" Helen asked Harry whether he planned to write a Philosophy of Diplomacy—what he'd said sounded pretty good! Harry thought his intellectual gymnastics had been rather successful. And just as he had expected, Helen now exercised her own ideas on the subject. Above all, she said, it was a problem of simulation. The way she kept using the word *simulation* made it sound like a new theoretical term. Duckwitz must have missed the boat where simulation was concerned, probably while he was in Africa. It didn't matter, though, because in seven years at the latest it would have lost its meaning. That good old pair of terms, *real* and *unreal*, on the other hand, would still be good for getting a grip on things in a hundred years.

"That's all just hot air!" said Harry. All the talk about simulation is absolute nonsense. Helen should keep her feet firmly on the ground. Where was the empiricism in all of this?

Just as they had discussed the exploitation of the working class in the old days, Harry and Helen now gave rein to their ideas on the perception of reality as film. It used to be that a film pretended to be life, said Harry, now life pretends to be a film.

"But that's simulation!" said Helen excitedly. Harry should read Baudrillard!

"The devil I will!" Harry said loudly. It's all nonsense, academic bullshit. He took back what he had said: it sounded good but it didn't mean a thing. In reality, no one was pretending anything. No one really thought life was a film, not even diplomats were that dumb. It was merely a comparison. There's just a mania for comparing things, no grand deception. You shouldn't demonize sloppy thinking just because it's trendy. Besides, they'd ignored the psychological aspects, and that's what was really interesting about it—the fact that the supposed perception of reality as film is a form of escape and that it provides you with a great excuse: in the role of the powerless spectator, you bear absolutely no responsibility.

Helen said that Harry could sure as hell identify with that role, it happened to be his as well, right? The whole thing was really his own problem, and he was simply projecting it onto the profession of the diplomat. That's what it seemed like to her.

Harry denied it emphatically. He hadn't started the whole business of comparing things to movies, he'd merely observed it. As he had a moment ago with Helen and her Truffaut comparison.

"Right now, you seem more like one of those babblers from an early Rohmer movie," said Helen.

They both laughed and remembered the one they'd seen together years before, though they couldn't remember the title or what it was about. All they remembered was the pretentious but somehow refreshing babble. They agreed that it was one thing to perceive reality as a film, vaguely and without imagination, and quite another to be reminded of a certain film by reality. The way Helen had just been reminded of a Truffaut or Rohmer movie, or at least scenes from them, by the fact that they were sitting together in bed. That was anything but simulation, deception, faulty perception, loss of a sense of reality, a sign of sloppy thinking, or lethargy. It was, rather, a spirited and telling association or, as Helen once again cleverly put it: by remembering or alluding to a film, two initiates can make use of a code to clarify a particular aspect of reality and give it an ironic twist. That's a sign of intelligence, education, agility. It's witty and lively and can enrich a description. It's the exact opposite of a dry assertion—for instance, that the arrest of demonstrators who are hustled into cars by police on the streets of Paraguay is a scene that unfolds just like in the movies, or that the turmoil in U.N. delegations is like a film. Helen was therefore the exact opposite of that broad with the grotesquely hyphenated name.

Harry shouldn't get so hung up on insignificant things, Helen told him. An odd hyphenated name is hardly worth mentioning. And besides, she wouldn't want her name to be Helen Duckwitz. She wouldn't give up the wonderful name of Grünberg for Harry's sake. She'd call herself Grünberg-Duckwitz, even if it did sound ridiculous. Thanks to Rita, though, that was no longer a problem. "Right," said Harry, and by the way Rita had a hyphenated Korean-Indian maiden name, Noorani-Kim. Though she didn't look at all like her namesake Rita Hayworth, her father's movie idol.

They were back to comparisons and films, and they agreed that there are situations you can only describe as Buñuel-like. There are Fellini types, there's a nervousness that's peculiar to Woody Allen, and for certain kinds of hopelessness, only the word Bergmanesque will do. Movies and directors provide an ideal kind of shorthand for naming certain situations.

Then Helen started talking about the "creation of trivial myths" and about "archetypes," and Harry said: "All that talk about archetypes is rubbish!" Helen replied that Harry had always had such a convincing way of saying "rubbish!" They agreed that one point of art could be its usefulness in making a more exact description of reality. Not only in films. There's also the Chekhovian woman who looks into the distance with a particular mixture of hope and despair, for example, and there's the path through a summer meadow that's a touch too idyllic, just like in paintings by Hans Thoma.

Harry enjoyed the conversation. He felt at home here. It had been crazy to marry Rita. He told an elaborate story about how he had come to marry Rita, about how her Indian father had commended her to him as a virgin, and about how Rita—by saying she was on the pill—had disguised the infertility that had been caused by an abortion. He told Helen how he, Harry, had found out and how easy it had been to blackmail Rita after that. Occasionally he would take advantage of it and ask her to put on the unbelievably sexy skirt she'd been wearing when they met, to stand in front of a mirror just as smugly as she had when the spark was ignited. He told Helen that Rita didn't understand a single one of his jokes but fulfilled every abstruse wish, that it aroused him, that he had a guilty conscience about exploiting Rita for this strange ritual, but that his horniness stifled his guilty conscience. . . .

"Cut it out!" said Helen. She was beginning to feel lecherous just listening to him! No, he wasn't going to stop, said Harry, because he was coming back to the subject of film: every time Rita put on her oriental skirt and posed as he wished in front of the mirror, it made him think of an old Hitchcock movie. In the film, an obsessed American tries to deck out his new girlfriend to look like his supposedly dead lover.

Vertigo, said Helen, wonderful, with Kim Novak and James Stewart.

Right, said Harry. But Kim Novak was a busty, platinum blonde whereas Rita, thank God, had small breasts and dark hair. And he hoped he didn't have that false, watery-blue look in his eyes like James Stewart. Still, when he walked over to Rita and stood behind her in front of the mirror, when they gave each other the eye and things ran their lascivious course, he couldn't help but think of James

Stewart's glassy-eyed look of obsession and the way Kim
Novak silently endured the insane ritual. Although it was the
cheapest kind of American pop psychology, the memory of
that movie interfered with his pleasure.

Helen said it sounded so enchanting that she envied
Harry, and Rita even more. She was positively jealous! She
could feel the tickling between her legs just listening to him
talk about it. Go on!

Harry said the sad thing was that associations like this
weren't available to Rita. Even though she'd seen the
Hitchcock movie, he couldn't use "Kim Novak" and "James
Stewart" as code words to designate and expose the absurdity
of the situation.

Harry should be glad the situation couldn't be desig-
nated with a code word from the Hollywood dream factory,
Helen said unexpectedly. There was something to be said for
that. It had the authenticity an intellectual in the middle of
Europe could only dream about. Comparisons with films,
playfully seeing yourself reflected in the products of culture,
may be a pleasant way to pass the time, but it's refreshingly
natural if the code isn't available to you, if you have to
depend on yourself alone, if you aren't constantly and almost
compulsively reminded of a Woody Allen character, or a
figure from a soap opera. If the figure doesn't remind you of
Hitchcock, the New German cinema, or *Casablanca.* Or
even, and especially, if the *verismo* quality of a passion
doesn't remind you of Visconti's *Ossessione,* a fat freak of
Fellini, a braggart of James Dean, and an earlobe-puller of
Humphrey Bogart. Or if, aside from film, not every fanatic's
glance reminds you of Dostoyevsky, not every quirky person
you meet is like a character out of Gogol, the poppy fields
you drive by aren't like Monet, and the landscape in the
Lake District doesn't look like Claude Lorrain. It certainly
can't hurt if everything is the way it actually is—enigmatic,
not decoded.

It was unbelievable: Helen was lying there naked using words like "decoded." Harry told her he thought it was ludicrous. And besides, he was surprised at Helen. He'd been prepared to listen to her reproach him for exploiting poor Rita, for being an oppressor, and instead she thought the story was sexy and authentic and that it undermined their newly invented theory of the associational value of film and other works of art.

"The times they are a changin'," said Helen, trying to remember the Bob Dylan melody. Besides, Rita didn't seem to have anything against Harry's ritualized foreplay.

"I'm not so sure about that," said Harry.

"That's her problem," said Helen. Harry thought that sounded pretty harsh. Helen had grown hard. She used to react like a fury to even the slightest hint of oppression. And now this. Harry found her new hardness a little scary, yet it appealed to him. Rita should defend herself if she didn't like it, Helen said cheekily, showing no mercy. What should she take amiss? It was a delicious game! She, Helen, thought it was absolutely enviable.

"You'd say thanks but no thanks!" said Harry. He reminded her how he'd protested against her frumpy sack dresses, how in desperation he'd said they made her look like a grouse, or a quail; how she'd called him a lecherous chauvinist and had irritated him by wearing clothes that concealed any hint of erotic charm. He reminded her how he'd vexed her by raving about other women's asses and by scraping together his last penny as a student to buy her a coal-black, skintight pair of leather pants. He reminded her how she'd yelled "Yuck! I'll never wear those," only to put them on a few weeks later; how he'd said: "I like you this way," at which she would take them off because, at the time, the last thing a woman wanted to be was a sex object.

"Cut it out!" said Helen. That was all past. That's the way things were then. Besides, she'd worn the pants after all.

Had Harry forgotten how he ran his stocking feet up her leg at the pub? He'd look at her, glassy-eyed, and say: "It just slides right up, right up!" Had he forgotten that?

Remembering their old desire rekindled their hunger, and they went at it again. It was so good afterward not to have to retreat silently into their own private thoughts, to return to the tried and tested Truffaut film position. "I just have to meet your Rita," said Helen.

And then they rambled on again about perception and reality, and it occurred to them that they'd forgotten to make television images partly responsible for the rupture in the perception of reality. Harry maintained that there was a dialectical process at work: reality determines what film is about, and film influences our image of reality. Strangely enough, Helen no longer used the term "dialectical." It used to be that she saw the dialectical process everywhere: theory and practice, abstract and concrete—everything was immensely dialectical. Using the term now, Harry noticed what an outmoded tool it had become. It was as if he'd suddenly put on a shirt with a shark-fin collar. Where had he missed the boat? While he was a lawyer? While he was in training to be a diplomat? During the years he spent in Africa? Wherever he was, it wasn't so bad to have missed the boat. You notice the changes even more that way.

They talked about progress and wondered whether the Baroque concept of the world as a stage and life as a dream didn't render superfluous all of yesterday's blather about reality and all of today's bunk about simulation.

They recalled an old hit song, though they couldn't remember who sang it—a woman, late fifties or early sixties they supposed. Unspeakably bad, but priceless. The singer was scoffing at her admirer because he'd been imitating silver-screen heroes. "From Gary Cooper you got your gait," Helen sang, and Harry remembered the next line: "That's the way you ambulate." Of all the stars he was just a "bad copy," which rhymed in the song with "mon ami." From someone he got his haircut, too. Who was it, Marlon Brando? No, it must have been Elvis Presley. They weren't sure anymore. It was good to be the same age, to be from the same country, and to have the same memories. Helen ran her fingers through Harry's hair: "From Charlie Chaplin you got your hair, from there, from there, but only your hair."

9 *Why Harry is sent to the embassy in Quito, Ecuador, and how he has problems adjusting to life there, whereas Rita learns from the Indians how to make pottery. About an election campaign, the deficit crisis, and the impossibility of recognizing the truth up close. As well as a look back at Harry and Rita's wedding, and all kinds of information about his birthday wishes and Latin American music.*

Even on his arrival in Ecuador's capital city of Quito it was clear to Harry that he wasn't going to like it there. Even as he left the airplane. He made an effort to hide his disappointment from Rita. A first impression isn't very important. You can get used to a place.

It was really his own fault. He wouldn't be averse to a Latin American country, he'd told the people in Personnel when his tour at the home office was coming to an end and his next foreign appointment drew closer. Except, if at all possible, for Brazil and Chile, Duckwitz had said. With all due respect to diplomatic impotence, he didn't want to go to a country with a terrorist regime like the one in Chile. Not that. He didn't want to meet constantly with people who should be shot on the spot. And as far as Brazil was concerned, he didn't like Carnival or the mushy sound of Portuguese, and he certainly didn't want to live in a capital that had been built overnight and had no old buildings. Especially one with a name as synthetic as Brasilia. "Pretty choosy, dear Baron," the personnel man had said, but not unsympathetically, it seemed to Harry.

You couldn't avoid the problems of the Third World entirely, as Harry had admitted to himself in an upwelling of moral sentiment. India and Korea were out of the question,

however, since they were Rita's homelands. It wasn't at all
rare that a diplomat abroad would succumb to the charms of
an exotic woman and marry her. In such cases, the Foreign
Office avoided posting them to the wife's home country in
order to keep the dutiful representative of the Federal
Republic from becoming ensnared in a sinister web of
dependency. That would jeopardize his neutrality. Colleagues
who complained that their wives would like to spend some
time at home were reminded that the foreign ministries of
most other countries didn't even permit their diplomats to
marry foreigners, or threatened them with immediate dis-
missal if they did. Harry recalled the smart, young French
cultural attaché in Yaunde who fell in love with an
Ethiopian. Ethiopians are a handsome people to begin with,
and of all of them this Ethiopian was the most beautiful.
Duckwitz was already married to Rita at the time, but his
first sordid thought upon seeing the woman had been: why
couldn't I have waited for one like that? If you're going to
marry someone exotic, do it right. The French attaché was
in a state of utter dismay. For him it was an either/or
question: if he married her, he'd have to leave the diplomatic
service. The Germans weren't that cruel.

Rita didn't have anything against Latin America. She'd
been brought up, or was structured in such a way that she
would follow her husband wherever he went. Unfortunately.
Harry would have appreciated a little resistance. He didn't
want to get his way all the time. Compared with that
Ethiopian, that princess, Rita seemed like a schoolgirl. If it
hadn't been for the refreshing screwing parties and Rita's
quivering orgasm, he could sometimes have thought of her
as a daughter. Harry, of all people, the man who didn't want
to have children, felt like a father. When, after a short time,
the piano arrived in Quito and they'd found a good place for
it in their roomy house, Rita, at least, seemed to be completely content.

The fact that they landed in Latin America was largely owing to Duckwitz's colleague Huber, a Latin America specialist who was constantly supplying him with Latin American folk music while they were at the home office in Bonn. There were songs from the Andes whose mournful exuberance reminded him of melodies he'd heard on some kind of holiday during his childhood near the Alps. He'd even done some investigating and found that in the nineteenth century, emigrant pastors from Bohemia and monks from Tyrol had taken the mazurka, the polka, and a shoe-slapping Bavarian folk dance to the Andes with them. The rhythms had combined to produce a singsong quality familiar to European ears: "Según es favor del viento, me voy, me voy": I drift at the pleasure of the wind, away, away. The melody was ingeniously simple, and it was sung in a grating but vivid voice by a woman named Violeta Parra, a Chilean who killed herself in 1967. Not for political reasons but for love, which didn't quite suit the record companies. "Despierte el hombre, despierte, despierte por un momento, despierte toda la patria antes que venga el trueno furioso y barra los ministerios": If only people would awaken, awaken for a moment, if only the whole country would awaken, she sang, adding softly but maliciously: before the furious thunder sweeps away the government's ministries! Songs like this had attracted Harry to the part of the world they came from. He'd begun to learn Spanish. He learned it quickly and easily, but only up to a point. He'd never be able to speak a foreign language perfectly. But it sounded good. Harry could bluff. His English was still imperfect after three years in Cameroon, but he had less of an accent, he was told, than did Rita. She spoke perfect English but had a charming Indian lilt to her speech, even though she'd attended boarding school in England.

But he'd been familiar with the music, not the country. The location of the embassy was the worst part. It was in a modern office building that belonged to a German company. Foreign policy the tenant of business—at least that made clear where the power lay. The big slab belonged to the Hoechst Company, someone had said. It didn't make any difference. It was all the same trash. At any rate there were art calendars with the Hoechst logo all over the embassy. May 1984. The calendar had a landscape by Claude Lorrain. It was the only bright spot in Harry's office. If that little group of figures weren't dancing around so ridiculously in the foreground, it would be even better. There were mountains in the background that reminded him of the Alps. The caption said that the painting portrayed an ideal landscape.

He went over to the window and looked up at the massive slopes and foolishly high peaks of the Andes. How much more beautiful was the artist's ideal landscape. Looking at a reproduction of a 300-year-old painting in a complimentary calendar from Hoechst was more satisfying than a glance out his window. That's why you hang art on your walls. Art is always a pin-up. A pin-up girl is more perfectly formed than the real thing. Beauty is only real if it's conjured up. If Harry remembered correctly the feeble-minded stuff art critics had been writing in the papers for years, then modern art had been waging a decades-long campaign against the traditional function of art, which was to help make life more beautiful. Supposedly, modern art wants to make visible the fears and terrors of man. Not for me, thought Harry. Rather a diplomat than a modern artist!

However, it was a bitter fate to have to sit around in this damned high-rise instead of a decent old palace with huge rooms, plaster peeling off the walls, and a fan revolving slowly on the ceiling. In this case, too, reality did not measure up to the imagination. Though a fan would be nonsense in Quito. The city might be located directly on the equator, but at nearly 3000 meters, it was never unpleasantly hot.

When Harry went out to eat with Rita, she read the

menu as intently as if it were a wild sonata by Franz Liszt.
Rita gave him something he could hold on to. She liked
Quito. She noticed the beautiful old houses. Harry noticed
the ugly new ones.

You didn't see really serious misery here. And since you
couldn't see it, you had to remind yourself what was actually
going on. In that sense, the naive reports of traveling M.P.s
were understandable. Where, if you please, are the kidnap-
pings, the human rights violations, the torture? Always
somewhere else. Same as in Cameroon. He always wound up
in a moderate country. As if he was supposed to be spared
the serious horrors. Cameroon was known as the Switzerland
of Africa. Ecuador was the Switzerland of Latin America.
You can recognize the Third World's problems most clearly
while lying on a sofa in Europe, reading about them.

The closer you get to injustice, the more your sense of
it slackens. You pass on the news with a shrug of your
shoulders. Journalists operate the same way. They uncover
the abuses but leave the outrage to somebody else. Oil flows,
its price falls, the national debt grows. Nine billion dollars.
You can't get rid of the debt by exporting a few Panama
hats made in Ecuador.

The Third World is actually renting space within its
own borders. Harry asked himself whether there were certain
advantages to that. After all, what does national dignity
really mean? As a tenant, you don't have to bother about
anything. That's not so bad. But what a reprehensible
thought! In Bonn, everything had been clear. Here everything was murky.

Harry and Rita went to Quito in April of 1984, and
that summer there was a presidential election. The candidate
of the democratic left and the candidate of the Christian-
democratic right accused each other of the worst possible
crimes. And they did it in such a way that even as great an
admirer of the disparaging remark as Duckwitz didn't like

what he heard. Please, abuse only from the bottom to the top. The powerless against the powerful, the demonstrator against the politician—not the other way around! And definitely not one politician against another. But here the presidential candidates called each other drug addicts, atheists, communists, fascists. After the elections it turned out that, before the voting, both candidates distributed coupons that could supposedly be turned in by the poor at specially created offices in exchange for membership in an agricultural cooperative in the event the candidate won. After the election, the offices closed, never to reopen. Was that a crime, or an operetta? Duckwitz couldn't decide. Rita couldn't decide. Helen might have been able to decide. Duckwitz wrote it up in a report, which no one would ever read.

Months passed. Just as Harry thought he was slowly getting used to Quito and Ecuador and the Andes, he realized that he'd been homesick the entire time. In order to keep from thinking about it, he'd gone to the other embassies regularly, visited the Italians and the French, and had milk in his tea with the British.

East Germany also had an embassy in Quito. Why they were there, no one knew. It was hard to imagine that communism could regain the ground it had lost in Latin America. West Germans had no contact with the East Germans, who were as wary as hedgehogs. In Yaunde it had been the same. It was the same everywhere. If East Germans showed up, they didn't say a word. But once in a while, somewhere in the world, someone from an East German embassy would seek asylum in the embassy of his free West German colleagues.

In contrast to the awful quarters of West German diplomats, the East German embassy was located in a building that wasn't bad at all. Once, Duckwitz had been in a good mood and had knocked on the door of the East German embassy as he was taking a walk through the city.

"What do you want?" asked the man who let him in. Why is it that these people are always from Saxony? thought Duckwitz.

"I'd like to meet the ambassador," he said, and at least for a moment he meant it seriously.

The Saxon vanished, leaving Duckwitz to wait. When the ambassador finally appeared, the first thing he did was ask Duckwitz: "Who sent you?"

"I'll tell you only if this room is really bugged," said Duckwitz.

The East German ambassador didn't know what to make of the remark. "What's that supposed to mean?"

"I was sent by the head of your government, the Chairman of the Council of State himself," said Duckwitz.

"Nonsense! What do you want?"

"Well, I certainly don't want to subject myself to an interrogation," said Duckwitz, and he turned on his heel and left.

"Watch it, Mister!" the East German ambassador called after him.

In October Harry turned 39. One of his birthday wishes was that Rita pick him up at the office on her motorcycle. Rita shook her head in disbelief, gave him an indulgent smile, and promised that she would.

Rita's beautiful motorcycle, which had been shipped with her piano, was standing in the garage. It was a shame she took it out so seldom. She looked like a heavenly courier when she rode it. The bringer of the very best of news. She sat, proud and upright, on the heavy machine whose motor rumbled solidly and dependably. That's how he'd fallen in love with her. A rather romantic picture. Rita's transformations had always impressed him: from a slit-skirt Suzie Wong to an angel on a motorcycle to a daughter from the best of families, practicing the classics on her piano with iron determination.

Even in Bonn, her motorcycle usually just stood around. He'd had the same birthday wish there. "You have simple wishes," she'd said, and picked him up at the office. Like an emissary from another world, she waited for him in the Foreign Office parking lot, leaning casually on the tilted machine. A divine picture. As his colleagues crawled into their cars, Harry swung himself onto the seat behind Rita and off they roared in the direction of Bad Godesberg. Ten minutes of pure happiness. Past Schaumburg Palace, past that monstrosity of a monument to Adenauer, past that chicken coop of a Chancellor's office, past the Press Office. Past the Ministries of Education, Justice, Research and Technology. Leaving everything behind and thundering along with Rita. Vamos, vamos, mi compañera, let us sweep away the ministries, barramos los ministerios, me voy, me voy.

•   •   •

The wife of a Swiss diplomat had organized a ceramics class, and Rita joined it. Two local Indian women taught a dozen diplomats' wives how to make pottery. They made huge bowls. No one knew what they were supposed to put in them. They painted Indian ornaments on tiles. They were going to use them to tile their bathrooms back in Germany, they said. Back home, Harry would have made fun of pottery-making women. That was another one of the differences between Quito and Bonn: something that was a silly group-therapy or creativity-training fad there made amiable good sense here.

On Duckwitz's desk there were letters from the West German companies MAN, Hoechst, VW, Krauss-Maffei, Bayer-Leverkusen, Daimler-Benz, Siemens, and still others that were less well known. They were all interested in investments, financing, exporting, importing, rescheduling of debt, relieving of debt, creating debt. Their unspeakable representatives would actually appear in the flesh from time to time, wanting you to establish some sort of contacts for them. Duckwitz couldn't figure out whether the whole thing was a sell-out of the Third World or its salvation, or whether the sell-out meant salvation or ruin. There was talk of "second-hand" loans, debt bought and sold; they worked on the restructuring of so-called problem loans; they measured the value of a country by the percentage that creditors might possibly recover: 30 percent in Mexico, 45 percent in Ecuador, where the situation was comparatively stable. Bankers and company representatives were constantly talking about "debt-equity swaps" and "macho provisioning." These were the latest expressions for a credit maneuver that helped hide the insolvency of Third World countries. The embassy looked on helplessly.

Duckwitz watched with a certain amount of glee as a whole group of briefcase-carrying executives descended like vultures to try and sell the Ecuadoran airline a few Airbuses, the pride of the European airplane industry. For some reason, they weren't getting anywhere. Then all of a sudden it became apparent that the U.S. ambassador, who was a particularly nasty piece of work, had ruined the deal by alerting Boeing. Boeing promised a free jet if the Ecuadorans closed the deal, and so Boeing got the contract. The Airbus people flew off so bitterly disappointed that Duckwitz almost felt sorry for them.

He was in possession of a letter written by the U.S. ambassador that made it clear there was both a legal and a shady side to the deal. Duckwitz played it over the head of the Foreign Office into the hands of the German press, which reported on it at length in the business pages. But the business journalists did not ask the fundamental question: should such accursed investments be tolerated or prevented—

or should they be promoted, which was the task of the foreign service.

There was a story making the rounds about two former policemen from Lima, in neighboring Peru. The law was after them, and they requested asylum in the Swedish embassy. The ambassador himself had driven them to the airport, hidden in the trunk of his official limousine, and put them on a plane for Stockholm. That was apparently the only kind of heroism a diplomat could indulge in these days. Harry, too, would rather have helped a few victims of political persecution out of a tight spot than watch more or less helplessly as unsavory white-collar criminals snatched away each other's choicest morsels. Naturally, though, no persecuted heroes had knocked on his door to ask for help. Just suspicious characters you could picture to yourself as having shot a couple of poor farmers out in the fields in the name of world revolution.

"Maldigo la cordillera de los Andes y la costa," the great Violeta had sung—damned be the *cordillera* of the Andes and the coasts. In her anger, she had even damned the deceits of summer and winter, the twittering of canaries, and the bishops. She even damned the stars in the high heavens with their twinkling: "Maldigo del alto cielo la estrella con su reflejo."

That was one side of things; the other was love. Did he love Rita? Sometimes. No one can love more than just sometimes. And Helen? He loved her too. Sometimes. Still.

At one of those countless festivals with music and dancing celebrated in the streets of the old city, Harry once heard a singer from El Salvador do a charming song he couldn't get out of his head. The time had come to sing it to Rita.

"Do you remember that funny wedding of ours?" he asked Rita.

"Of course, and the old ambassador who married us."

"He forgot to ask us whether we wanted to be man and wife. We signed our names, but we didn't say yes." Harry had somehow been quite satisfied at the time not to have to stand there and be a yes-man. Rita hadn't noticed.

"Are you trying to tell me," asked Rita, "that you regret it, or what? Do you want to make up for it and say yes now, or no? Do you want a divorce?"

"I want to make up for it," said Harry, "but I want to sing it." It's better if you sing an odd little word like "yes." "A song," he said. "But I didn't write it. I'm just going to sing it. As a P.S. to our German lessons: 'Yes, yes en mal inglés / piano piano en italiano / yo te amo en castellano.'"

10 *How the West German embassy in Quito awaits a high-ranking visitor from Bonn and Harry von Duckwitz once again thinks he has to be offensive. How he then, under the influence of real suffering, shows remorse and writes a letter to Helen. In addition, some information about the correct designation of Latin American slums, about a Brazilian named Marida Böckle, and about Harry's assertiveness training under a eucalyptus tree.*

Never heard of him in my life! And neither had anyone else at the embassy. Supposedly he was the closest adviser to the new undersecretary. But they didn't know much about the new undersecretary, either. Only that he was a nothing. But then, almost everyone in Bonn was a nothing. As adviser to the new, young undersecretary, they'd probably chosen some older man whose personal ambitions had long since died but who did have a lot of experience. Someone who was as modest as he was pompous and would wear the title "closest adviser" like a halo.

The Foreign Office had announced that the unknown adviser would make a fact-finding tour to Ecuador. Since the ambassador was on home leave, Harry von Duckwitz, chargé d'affaires in the ambassador's absence, would have to look after the guest when he arrived in Quito.

Duckwitz hated visits like this one. "I didn't become a diplomat just to play seeing-eye dog to some fellow countryman who has to go groping around in every corner of the world," he'd said at their morning briefing. Everyone nodded. Once again Herr von Duckwitz told it like it is. If the ambassador had been there, he'd have nodded, too. Though it might have been in embarrassment, the way you

do when you don't want to agree to the truth out loud. A
conspiratorial glance shows you're of the same opinion.
D'accord.

Duckwitz immediately regretted his offhand remark.
He kept making the same mistake: whenever he cussed,
bitched, or jeered, whenever he made fun of politicians or
the diplomatic service, they agreed with him. That is, the
wrong people agreed with him. Or should he try to convince
himself that if a person agreed with him, he was on the
right side? But which side was the right one?

"Just a minute," said Duckwitz, and he disappeared into
the men's room. He had to concentrate. Who you are
doesn't make any difference, and wanting to find yourself is
ridiculous. But you could try to find out what kind of an
effect you have on people, and what kind of people they are.
That's already something.

Agreement from people you're leery of is suspect, that
much was clear. He had to think it through as quickly as
possible. He didn't want to be in here forever; the others
would think he had diarrhea or was constipated. It shouldn't
make any difference, thought Duckwitz, whether his
colleagues were interested in his digestive tract or not. But it
did. And it was all related to the question: how do I come
across, what do people think of me? Duckwitz flushed the
toilet to speed up his thinking on the subject. The problem
was the applause from the wrong side, that's what was bothering him. Bothering him? He found it intriguing. In fact,
he found it so intriguing that it had made him interrupt
their morning briefing, the most important part of an
embassy's day.

He'd only just begun to pick on those monkeys from
Bonn, to gripe about having to look after them, and already
he'd felt the others' solidarity. You're right, their faces said,
who are we to knock ourselves out for those halfwits!
Evidently they thought they were a cut above the others and

were reassured by Duckwitz's outburst. But Duckwitz didn't want to be a cut above everyone else, and he couldn't stand people who thought they were.

There must be something misleading about what he did, he reflected; it was always the wrong people who sided with him. If he took a dig at somebody, if he insulted or damned someone, it wasn't because he looked down on them. He was just taking potshots. Okay, okay, he did come forward and take a stand. You had to stand up if you were going to hit your mark. But a churlish remark was still a churlish remark, and it didn't make you any better than the rest. You were still a churl. The only thing that makes it okay to go around damning everything in sight is the fact that you're powerless. Only if you're powerless can you afford to be arrogant. The arrogance of power, on the other hand, is absolutely contemptible.

Duckwitz washed his hands. Things were clearer to him now: the conservatives among them, the ones who suffered from a fixation on authority, thought it was great when he got up and started ranting. The others, the ones who leaned more to the left, considered his behavior arrogant. The left misunderstood him, the right misunderstood him. Or was it just the middle-class mentality in all of them that misunderstood him? That question would have to wait until later, he didn't have time for it right now. He'd have to clear it up with Helen. On his next home leave. By then, however, all of these complicated reflections would have slipped his mind.

Duckwitz looked at himself in the mirror above the sink and thought: "No one understands me. I don't fit in anywhere." A fit of laughter overcame him as he imagined one of his colleagues overhearing his confession.

The cramped secretary, the only one who thought those cramped characters from the East German embassy were normal human beings, was the only one who hadn't smiled in agreement. Could it be that rejection was even more unpleasant than false approval? She'd looked past Duckwitz in anger and disapproval, looked as if her name were Gertrude or, even better, Hiltrude. Looked as if she were debating whether to tell Herr von Duckwitz what she thought, which was that Herr von Duckwitz was describing diplomats here as a class of people who were above the everyday grind. That was the way she looked. And she was right, whether she misunderstood him or not. What was the point of all this barking? Still, it had to be. Dogs bark. Barking is one of the privileges of canine existence. The secretary was probably the only one who knew who the adviser was. Maybe he was an especially liberal Liberal, the kind from whom you could seriously expect political improvement. And Duckwitz, that ignorant loudmouth, Duckwitz with his barefaced mockery, was boycotting every Liberal, maybe even every Social Democratic effort toward improvement before it got off the ground.

When Harry came back to the conference room, the meeting had already broken up. He could imagine his enemy, Gertrude/Hiltrude, glancing impatiently at her watch and then, a look of reproach on her face, heading for her office, where all kinds of allegedly important work was waiting for her.

The switchboard operator was talking to the Third Secretary. Harry had time to recall his grand performance in Cameroon, the one where he spit out his pudding in such disgust. The leftist literature professor and that leftist old maid from the Goethe Institute thought it was just the snobbish behavior of a jaded aristocrat. In their eyes, that kind of protest was tolerable only if it called itself art. Feeble-minded artists could call slaughtering pigs and wallowing in their entrails a work of art. That was progressive. But while it may not have been exactly heroic for Duckwitz to dribble dessert onto his plate in that illustrious company, it was more artistic and more progressive than splashing mystically around in pig's blood, damn it! Unfortunately, this fine argument hadn't occurred to him at the time. While conservatives winked in agreement with his anarchistic outbursts, progressives turned away in annoyance. Yet he felt much closer to their way of thinking. Or was he really a conservative who mistakenly thought of himself as a leftist? Nonsense. He simply had to talk this over with Helen.

Harry took a slip of paper and wrote *left-right* on it. He dropped it into the cigar box, that accommodating coffin for all his ideas and questions. "Left-right"—tomorrow he wouldn't know what that meant. He took out the slip again and added: *Supposedly there are people who don't want to believe they're gay. Question for Helen: are there, by analogy, leftists who don't want to believe they're conservative?* Good question. Though it was nonsense to be dividing the world up into right and left all the time. Maybe understanding and misunderstanding didn't have anything to do with right and left.

"Closest adviser. Sounds obscene," Duckwitz said scornfully to the switchboard operator, who'd finally rid herself of the Third Secretary. "He might be bringing his wife along," the operator said with a laugh; that was the only thing the secretary had let slip. In that case, said Duckwitz, the hotel should draw up an extra bill. He couldn't stand it when politicians took their wives along for a cheap vacation. All some of them could think of was how to get their wives' trips paid for. The Federal Republic, thought Harry, that wretched country whose wretched representative he was, should only be cheated by people who were really against it.

•   •   •

The day the adviser arrived, Duckwitz dressed more casually than usual and made an appointment for a supposedly important meeting with the agriculture minister. The man just happened to be one of Duckwitz's bridge partners. The chauffeur was to go alone to the airport to pick up the uninvited guest from Germany. No, the car didn't have to be washed before he went. "No, do not wash it, please!" said Duckwitz.

Besides the agriculture minister and a stony-faced colonel, Duckwitz's bridge group included the American ambassador. Before they started to play, he handed Duckwitz the latest issue of the *Washington Post*. "You're an Amnesty freak, aren't you?" he asked with a laugh, pointing to an article on human rights violations in Latin America. He thought the report was exaggerated. The colonel, as soon as he picked up the word "amnesty," looked the ambassador in the eye, leaned over to Duckwitz, and said: "Es un cagaleche!"—he's an absolute shitheels! The American ambassador didn't speak a word of Spanish. Duckwitz replied in German, which nobody understood, "Bunch of degenerate scum!" And then they began to play cards.

At about five o'clock, someone from the embassy called the bridge club to say that the adviser had been waiting for two hours. As if he were all dressed up with no place to go.

"I'm on my way," Harry said into the telephone. It was time to leave. He had his reasons for playing bridge with these people; it had certain advantages. It was one way to get information. Still, he'd have to give the reasons a going over before too long. Sitting at the same table with this bunch was going too far.

Harry went back to the card table and invited the three dubious characters to a reception at the embassy at eight that evening. An influential confidante of the Chancellor was there for a visit. Harry made the sign for money with his thumb and index finger and was amused by the light in the eyes of the colonel and the agriculture minister. "Hasta luego, conquistadores malditos," he said, and as he left he could hear them laughing like a band of thieves.

The adviser turned out not to be one of those older men with a lot of experience. He might have been in his mid-thirties, evidently an expert on something or other. You only rose that quickly if you had a certain amount of expertise. He didn't take it amiss that Duckwitz had kept him waiting so long. "Not at all," he said when he heard about the talk with the agriculture minister. "Everyday business comes first!"

He had actually brought his wife. Frau von Duckwitz had very kindly shown her Quito's market. "Your wife is enchanting," he said. How often Duckwitz had been told Rita was enchanting! But what else was she? She was exotic. At first, Harry had found Rita incredibly attractive; now, after three, nearly four years of marriage, he still found her mysterious. She was musically gifted. But even her musicality was mysterious. All of it just wasn't enough over the long haul. She was also Catholic. Duckwitz would never understand how this woman could disappear every Sunday into some dark church.

Rita had taken the adviser's wife home with her, and Duckwitz had no choice but to invite the man to tea. Duckwitz wondered what kind of person the adviser might be. He evidently was not one of those politicians journalists refer to as "blockheads." "Blockhead"—it was an insult you could still use in the living room or on the air, a word television commentators could use without fear of penalty in order to underscore their indignation at a political adversary's lack of insight. The adviser, who was sitting unpleasantly close to Duckwitz in the car, gave the impression of being flexible, artificially flexible. Duckwitz decided that the adviser was made of some sort of synthetic fiber. A member of the new generation of silicone politicians. He was in fact a financial expert and had connections to the Chancellor's office, which was worth a lot. He was here to feel out the Ecuadorans on the subject of future loan policies.

The adviser's wife was also enchanting in her way. Unfortunately. The fact that he found her attractive was painful to Duckwitz. Once again it brought home the senselessness of his marriage to Rita. Maybe it would be better to be unhappy with an adviser-type wife like this one than with the Eastern and completely incomprehensible Rita, who was now smiling silently as she showed the adviser's wife ponchos made of llama wool from her native crafts collection.

For that evening, Duckwitz had invited to the embassy all the people who could be of importance to the adviser. He'd succeeded in getting three government ministers and the American ambassador, as well as that ghastly colonel. You couldn't get around inviting him to receptions like this one. The adviser was very impressed with Duckwitz's good contacts. "Well, I'll be damned!" he said, and it was supposed to sound like he'd tell the Foreign Minister—if not the Chancellor himself—that there was a diplomat in Ecuador who might be very unconventional but did have excellent contacts. Duckwitz didn't at all like the idea of this prospective recommendation. He could see the adviser during a break in a meeting, whispering into the Chancellor's ear, and the Chancellor nodding his bloated skull in response.

There were still two hours until the evening reception. They had tea, and Duckwitz found that the time had come for a little provocation. He made sure the adviser's wife was within earshot and then said during a break in the conversation: "How's our S.O.B. of a Chancellor?" He'd already put a number of M.P.s on the spot by saying things like that. Most of them didn't react at first, so Duckwitz had to repeat the insult. The women always started to giggle, loosening up the suddenly frozen atmosphere. M.P.s put to the test this way took advantage of the relaxed atmosphere to rip into the political intrigues back home. They always drank too much. Duckwitz drank, too, and insisted that everyone in power was a crook. His plastered guests would nod and say "exactly," but they either didn't understand what he meant or they understood it quite differently. And it was so unusual to hear a diplomat talk that way that by the next morning everything was forgotten. Duckwitz had never so much as been given a hint of a warning about his outbursts.

This adviser, though, was a cut above the ordinary. While his wife turned toward Duckwitz as if she'd been bitten by a tarantula—immediately forfeiting Duckwitz's sympathies—the adviser was in complete command of the situation. He acted as if he heard things like this every day. He grinned at Duckwitz and said: "You've grown accustomed to a pretty rough manner of speaking out here on the prairie!" He was also evidently an expert at warding off provocation. Probably the result of a weekend training session. Or had he come prepared? Did he know something? Could he really be here to find out if that wild Duckwitz was still acceptable to the Foreign Office? If that's why he was here, he'd get the surprise of his life. Duckwitz hadn't wanted to be acceptable for a long time! Duckwitz didn't give in: "Just looking at the man has to make you sick!" he added. The adviser laughed. "You're not the only one who doesn't like him," he said in a friendly and almost understanding tone. Duckwitz was shaken. If this was the new line in Bonn, he might as well pack it in.

Duckwitz had arranged for an interpreter to come for the evening. He didn't want to be forced to translate all the financial garbage the adviser would be exchanging with Ecuador's debtors. The adviser's wife, having been unmasked as a reactionary, a mere fool's-gold angel, was clearly avoiding Duckwitz. She was talking with the wife of the American ambassador, now that there was nothing more to be said to Rita.

The adviser was in his element. He talked constantly about interest rates and the possibility of an Argentine credit lever. Credit lever—an expression that was apparently of his own expert invention. His principal victim was the finance minister. He nodded the whole time the adviser was speaking, even before the interpreter said a word. The adviser wasn't going to go as far in politics as he'd first thought, Duckwitz decided with satisfaction: he couldn't tell whether someone was listening to him or not.

Duckwitz, on the other hand, had the pleasant feeling that he was superfluous at this gathering. He disappeared into the cozy sitting room next door. Rita had also retreated into one of the adjoining rooms. She was practicing an early Mozart sonata. Duckwitz opened up the *Washington Post* to read the story the American ambassador had called to his attention. It was one of the worst reports on torture he'd ever read. Told by a woman who was a member of the Chilean resistance, the horror of her testimony was given added weight by the incredible sobriety with which it was narrated. They'd put rats in her vagina. "The poor animals always try to find some way out," she explained. One of her sons had been set on fire. The military officers in charge had laughed as the boy tried to run from the flames. They went to trial and were acquitted.

Duckwitz put down the newspaper. Why didn't he break out in a sweat? Why didn't his heart beat faster? How could the American ambassador have mentioned the article in jest? That's how things really were: you had to read a newspaper from the United States, of all places, to remind yourself what was really happening here. Everyone knew it, but nobody cared. Interest rates, loans, exports—they were all more important. And the Counsellor to the Legation, Harry von Duckwitz, thought it was more important to call the Chancellor an S.O.B. just to annoy some silly career politician. Why didn't he smash everything to bits?

Harry took a deep breath. Light a fuse and blow up the whole damned globe? A world that produced this sort of thing, that allowed it to happen, deserved destruction. Without question. Without mercy. No long debates about who was responsible. Away with it. Away with the U.S. ambassador, with the Ecuadoran colonel. Do them in. What a touching dolt the German Chancellor was in contrast to these sinister characters.

Today the description of torture had touched him to the quick. Today he hadn't succeeded in looking away or closing his eyes after a dutiful glance at the paper. Duckwitz had forced himself to read the report from beginning to end. The dispassionate and seemingly indifferent language of the American reporter was almost unbearable. The reporter had grown rather hard himself. But maybe his tone was exactly what got to the reader.

Suddenly, Duckwitz was asking himself anxiously whether he wasn't more affected by his own sense of powerlessness than by compassion. The sense of hatred, horror, and sadness, the desire for revenge made it impossible to distinguish even between your own feelings. Torture was so perverse that it made you perverse, too. Because it was definitely perverse to ask yourself if you were sufficiently capable of suffering. And the worst thing was that you knew all about it. You could read about it in every Amnesty International report—except that you usually didn't because you didn't want to be ripped apart.

There were people who were constantly talking about the cruelty of the Nazis, which also ripped you apart. And that was the past. This was happening now. Thousands of people die on the roads of Europe every year, but what a well-looked-after and well-mourned death. No grounds for despair about mankind. As an on-looker to a fifty-car pileup, you can shake your head regretfully, but it doesn't throw you completely off balance. You simply make a resolution to drive more carefully—after all, there's something to be learned from every accident. But torture leads only to despair. It leaves no room for hope. You must think about it, but you can't let yourself think about it very often. And not in too much detail. Otherwise hate can lead to endless fantasizing about violence, to a longing to be in the right place at the right time.

Duckwitz hated his childish desire for revenge. For a long time now, American presidents had seemed like such dangerous and unpredictable idiots. They stirred up crises by sending aircraft carriers into areas of conflict, they made threats—but not one had pressed the famous red button. They were evidently more reasonable and had more self-control than some people thought. That wasn't a very pleasant realization, either. Some people might have blown things up already.

Others had experienced torture; the gentlemanly Harry von Duckwitz was beside himself just reading about it. Totally out of proportion. He knew people who had been tortured. He treated them like saints. A lot of them made no more of an impression on you than a European who's been in a serious automobile accident. They wore it like a medal, with a sort of pride at having survived hell. That too was incomprehensible. They played down the pain almost boastfully, maybe to protect themselves, to be able to bear the memory of it better. You never heard from the ones who didn't survive it emotionally, only from the ones who seemed to have survived intact. Some of them shrugged their shoulders as if it were all a game—a game of life and death, but a game nevertheless.

Duckwitz had never met anyone who'd been tortured that swore to take revenge. Incredibly enough, they remained cool-headed. And Duckwitz? No one had ever so much as touched a hair on his head, and yet just the thought of cruelty aroused in him a cruel desire for annihilation. Such reports made a person a reactionary; for hours they turned Duckwitz into an advocate of the death penalty. The awful feelings they aroused turned back in on him and on the idiotic and somehow criminal profession he'd chosen. What you did as a diplomat was turn yourself into an accessory to genocide. Instead of helping some jerk establish a business or a subsidiary or a branch office, you should steadfastly boycott and blockade. The West German government had to be forced to put pressure on Third World countries. To try blackmail! You could blackmail them into observing human rights the same way you could blackmail them into buying your machinery. Maybe the day would come when military dictators in Latin America could be forced to stop trampling roughshod over the bodies of their opponents. The only thing was, the Third World wasn't all that lucrative any-more. And above all, whispered the true economic experts, it would be the poor people in the Third World who would suffer economically.

That's the way it was. You couldn't and didn't want to hear any more about torture and exploitation. You had your fill of such crimes. You listened, then you stopped listening, and this too was a crime. Or should you help one of those underground organizations that shoots down a drug baron in Colombia from time to time and thinks it's doing the world a favor? The brutishness of the world turns you into a brute. You try to protect yourself. But occasionally something gets through and you become totally confused. That's something at least.

Harry poured himself a big shot of whisky. Since he didn't like it without ice, he went into the kitchen. He could hear the babble of voices at the reception and Rita playing on and on. There wasn't anyone in this house, in this city, in this country that he could talk to. He sat down at the desk in the sitting room, took out a sheet of paper, and began to write hastily: "Dear Helen, I've just read a report about people who have been tortured in the most horrible ways. And I need a drink. I not only need a drink, I need an ice cube to go with it. What has to happen to keep me from thinking about ice cubes? I find myself disgusting. I'm an S.O.B. I play bridge with murderers and their accomplices."

Harry thought again about the tortured Chilean woman. She could just as well have been from Ecuador, from Argentina, or from neighboring Peru. The thought of her pain reawakened his desire for revenge, and he wrote: "I'm too spineless to react politically to reports of such atrocities. What could I do about it anyway? I haven't the slightest idea. I don't even break out in a sweat, just blood-thirsty fantasies, that's all." Harry let himself go and wrote about how he longed to empty the ammunition from all those hated weapons into the hated bodies of all the uniformed and ununiformed criminals. "I'm a thoroughly laughable character," he continued. "I'm a fellow traveler. I thought I was subversive because I didn't hesitate to call the Chancellor an S.O.B. and the Foreign Minister a jellyfish. But I'm just a political clown, Helen, someone who's rubbed the wrong way by comparatively harmless democrats but plays cards with putschists. Maybe I'm just one of them, firing off insults instead of bullets." Duckwitz read the last sentence and was shaken by his insight into himself. It all sounded plausible, but hopefully it wasn't true.

Rita was still playing Mozart. She came from Korea and played a two-hundred-year-old sonata so that it brought Mozart back to life. How could that be? How could it be that the teenaged Mozart came up with compositions that permanently embodied all the mature feelings of the world? And then there was that colonel next door. How could it be that this man—who wasn't totally lacking in wit—probably wouldn't hesitate a second before giving orders with the most dreadful consequences? Everywhere you looked there were things you couldn't believe people would do. Even his letter to Helen was somehow too honest for comfort.

He longed for Helen and her political common sense and the way she sometimes unexpectedly stuck her tongue in his mouth. Harry threw himself on one of the sofas, moaning the name "Helen" into the cushions. Only when he remembered that abandoned women in American movies act that way did he stand up and go back to his letter. Something about it was right, and something about it wasn't. He'd leave it to Helen to find out for herself. He wrote: "I'm married to a woman with whom I can't discuss a thing. I miss you. I need you. Your Harry. Your hypocrite. Your S.O.B."

He felt better somehow. He folded up the letter. Tomorrow he'd put it in the spinach-green plastic tray for outgoing mail. It was time to leave this place.

Duckwitz went back to the reception. Compared with the official residence of the ambassador in Cameroon, this was almost feudal splendor. Miserable bunch, they were half plastered now. Miserable piano in a room that looked like a church recreation hall. Rita was still playing. She had started looking at the notes on the page in that aggressive way she once had, as if they were her enemy. As if she wanted to show them who was boss. Maybe that explained why people from the East played Western music so perfectly: they couldn't stand it and wanted to destroy it with their perfect mastery. Rita saw Harry waiting at the door. "You go home, Harry," she said. "I would like to finish this piece. I am sure the American ambassador will be kind enough to take me home in his automobile." Rita's German had become perfect in the meantime, that is, if you could call it perfect when a sentence sounded like an echo of the nineteenth century.

Good. All right. Harry left the car at the embassy and went home on foot. Nights in Quito were all more or less the same. There were no mild summer evenings like the ones that made up for a lot of other things at home. Just like Cameroon, there was no real twilight because they were so close to the damned equator. At six o'clock the sun went down and night began. And in the morning it was as if some unfriendly neighbor turned on the light. Always the same old thing. This was all wrong. No short winter afternoons, no long summer evenings. There was no time of day for genteel melancholy. However, there was plenty of wind and rain—sudden and brief and surprisingly like weather in the middle of Europe. The kind that invigorates you, the way it did when you were seventeen or eighteen, that grand existentialist time of life when you turned up your collar, put on your Camus face, and braved the gusts of being.

He'd been in Quito for a year now, and he'd have to spend another two years here. Unless he could get a doctor to attest that the high elevation, the nightly fits. . . . But then they'd send him somewhere else, and somewhere else wasn't any better than here. It wasn't any better in Bonn, either. Maybe it was better in the Bavarian Alps. Harry decided to take a trip to the mountains in Bavaria during his next home leave, to revisit the places where he'd spent his childhood. These damned Andes were a stupid, senseless bunch of mountains. Much too big, much too high, much too long, much too bare. One big slag heap. Since Harry had the peaks of the Andes constantly before his eyes, they were a constant source of irritation. You should feel unchanging anger at the unchangeable. And yet he could be glad that he worked at the embassy in Quito and not in La Paz. La Paz was even higher, even more barren; everything was even more senseless. There was more violence, more misery, the Indians were even more wizened, and the middle class was even more arrogant, even more proud that not a drop of Indian blood flowed in its veins. The fires in the streets at night, where the poorest of the poor burned trash to keep themselves warm and to boil their soup, were even eerier.

It was absurd. As a student in the late sixties, you'd found it unbearable that workers in industrialized countries had to put in eight-hour days at the factory. Fifteen years later you were living in a Latin American capital where the majority of the population was worse off than the most unbearably exploited worker in the nineteenth century. And you didn't even find it particularly bothersome. Maybe it really was less terrible to sit and vegetate all day than to work yourself to death in a factory. Suffering can't be quantified.

The best thing to do was not to talk about it. You saw it, you swallowed hard, and you kept quiet. Complaining would be mere hypocrisy. Then there were the ones who didn't complain but referred to the slums, in German, as "slöms," the way the ambassador's wife did. She was one of those ladies who, for some unknown reason, pronounced the English word "butter" as if it were spelled "bötter," called a tropical storm a "hörricane," and abbreviated the cutaway in their husband's diplomatic wardrobe to a "cöt." At the card table and in the kitchen, the German umlaut, which can't quite be taken seriously, had taken over completely: "cörry," for "curry," and "blöff" for "bluff." The absolute epitome of this new Great Vowel Shift was calling slums "slöms." The pseudo-genteel pronunciation of the word automatically carried with it the image of a nose turned up at the stench.

But it was more odd than it was cynical. It was too stupid to be cynical. Cynical is calling the slums in big Latin American cities by their particular names: the "favelas" in Rio, the "chacaritas" in Asunción, the "barriadas" in Lima and Bogotá. That's the way Latin America experts talk. It's supposed to demonstrate their expertise, but it merely shows their lack of taste. It sounds as if they're talking about some tortilla dish from Mexico or some dance like the *milonga*

from Montevideo or the *cueca* from Santiago. It doesn't help
to call misery by its real name; that's presumptuous. People
who are ethnologically interested or travelers who are critical
of the social conditions in these countries show a greater
lack of tact than the diplomats and their wives. They, at
least, are merely blind to reality.

Duckwitz had passed through the heart of town. He
was walking uphill now, approaching the area where the
well-to-do lived. He tried to suppress his thoughts of the
incredibly deep, dark eyes of the wife of a Swiss businessman, of Marida Böckle from Brazil. She called him
"Duckwitz" but used the familiar "you." "You can come any
time, Duckwitz," she had said, even before the first time
they'd screwed. Her uncomplicated willingness had seemed
wild and tempting at first. Duckwitz had given in to his
desire a few times, if only because he would have found it
too chaste to resist. But then he realized that it was simply
too uncomplicated. Marida didn't know about anything but
love. She liked to play the role of the love goddess. Love
was the most important and the most beautiful thing in life,
she cooed, as if it were an insight only she was privy to. She
celebrated love. If your attention wandered away from her
very beautiful body for even a moment, she asked you what
was wrong. She could really knock the love right out of you
with her raptures about love.

You looked out of Señora Böckle's bedroom window
and remembered how often you'd said that love is beautiful,
that nothing is more beautiful, that love is the most important thing there is, and so on and so forth. You sat there
with this truly red-hot Brazilian who'd managed to fall into
the hands of a constantly absent Swiss businessman—
according to her, someone she really loved—and the splendid
female purred silkily on the bed and was concerned about
doing right by you. She wanted top grades in love, she
wanted to hear how good she was in bed, and she wanted to

tell you that you were, too. Duckwitz couldn't listen to it anymore. It was his misfortune that he'd been an untiring lover the first time he'd given in to Marida's deep, dark eyes. He'd tumbled around all night, her eyes drove him so wild. Since then, she'd called him the best of all possible lovers, even when his love-making had been absent-minded and cursory and totally lacking in passion.

Duckwitz walked past Marida's house. Desire pounded away, but this time he didn't give in—even if it was silly not to let desire have its way. But not now, not after writing that letter to Helen, not after the way he felt reading that terrible story about torture. The fact that he could even think about love and sex made him unpleasant to himself. It would be in bad taste to take a tumble with Marida Böckle right now, forgetting all the rest. It would definitely be in bad taste where Helen was concerned. Where his wife Rita was concerned, it wouldn't be a matter of bad taste, thought Harry. No business of hers—just as her going to church was no business of his.

The worst thing about Marida Böckle was that her submissiveness made you inconsiderate. By telling you constantly that you were different from other men, that you were more affectionate and better in bed, that it was great you weren't constantly thinking about your job the way all the other men did, she turned you into exactly the kind of man she pretended to abhor. "You're different from all the others"—what a line for a pop song! How Duckwitz would have liked to hear a line like that when he was 18 or 20. How hollow and wrong and dumb it sounded now. Marida chattered so much about the importance of love and the unimportance of men's jobs that Duckwitz soon wished his was an important one. How he used to look down on men who had no time for love! The other attorneys at the firm where he worked would rather have missed a rendezvous with a lover than an appointment with a client. Love and your private life had to have top priority. That was Harry's motto. Now he thought life might be more interesting if he were a journalist or a businessman. Then he'd have good reason to look at his watch and escape Marida's chatter after the screwing. Then she'd say: "You're just like all the rest," but he'd be able to escape the clutches of her passion until his next attack of horniness. If making a deal or writing an article really mattered to him, love wouldn't be so inordinately important. Probably it had been the biggest mistake of his life to throw in the towel as a lawyer. You weren't born just to loll around in bed, raving about love. It wasn't any better than talking about food the whole time you were eating.

Marida was from the Brazilian upper class. She called herself an Indian, but she was proud of her light skin. When she talked about the "favelas," it was like the crack of a whip. "The people there are lazy and degenerate," she said. Her comment was every bit as reactionary as it was correct. Of course the people who live in slums are lazy and degenerate. Of course nothing can be done about it. Of course it's hypocritical to promise change. Even sympathy is hypocritical. And it's hypocritical to ask rhetorical questions about why they're lazy and degenerate simply to show how knowledgeable you are about social conditions. Still, hypocrisy is a more sympathetic reaction than coolly shrugging your shoulders.

Desire had stopped pounding, and Harry went home with a new purity and determination. Rita was already in bed. He lay down beside her. She didn't wake up. Marida would have purred and pressed her ass against him. You read more and more about AIDS lately. The wife of a diplomat at the French embassy had joked that in Brazil there were so many women with AIDS, even the planes pulled in their tails when they flew over. Marida Böckle hadn't told him that one.

• • •

The next morning, Duckwitz did not go to the embassy. Rita prevented him from mulling things over with her good cheer and her questions about what he wanted for dinner. He felt he'd been pretty shabby and gave her a hug. While she was out shopping, Harry tried to make sense of his violent fantasies. He hated violence, and he hated fantasies about violence, and that's why he wanted to clear up some things about himself. He came to the conclusion that his had been counter-violent fantasies. That was reassuring. Except that people who commit violence always pass it off as counter-violence: if I hesitate to use torture to secure the names of communists, the communists will come to power and destroy everything, thinks the torturer. Or isn't that what he thinks? Does he think torturing people is fun?

One thing was certain—at the slightest thought of torture, a jarring mixture of blind hatred, powerlessness, and despair welled up inside Harry, an almost hungry desire to destroy the bosses, the men behind the scenes. It was comforting that even in his imagination, he didn't have any desire to torture the torturers. In even the most harmless people, the longing for counter-violence expresses itself in the form of terrible obscenities and curses: Skin him alive! Boil him in oil! At least Harry didn't want that. Yesterday he'd pictured to himself what a relief it would be to gun down the people who'd tortured that poor Chilean woman. Today, even that seemed horrible to him. The only thing left was a desire to sweep people like that from the face of the earth, like dirt. To fell the riff-raff with a blow from a giant, godly paw, then sweep them off the edge of the world. All this crap had begun with the fact that the earth isn't flat, isn't a plate with a rim from which you can dump all the rubbish once and for all. The globe is faultily constructed. It turns on its own axis. How ridiculous. Nothing sensible can ever come of it. The rational and the irrational form a vicious circle. That's why the torturers shouldn't be tortured. At the least you have to try to slow down the turning. They weren't supposed to suffer. He didn't want to revel in their fear. Just get them away from here!

And yet Duckwitz wasn't even capable of emptying his glass in the face of some brazenly glib colonel. At the least he should have done that. It still wasn't too late. There would be a new opportunity every week. You were always running into those dirty bastards somewhere, and they were constantly saying something that was incredibly base and mean and deserving of a public dousing. But how do you do it? It has to be done with flair. It requires practice. It would be a terrible disgrace not to hit them square in the middle of their rotten faces.

Harry filled a pitcher with water, picked up a glass, and went out into the backyard. There was a eucalyptus tree with a knothole at eye level, just the thing for target practice. Harry stood in front of the tree, filled the glass with water, said to the eucalyptus tree: "You bastard!" and emptied his glass in the direction of the knothole. Too low. Good thing he'd thought to practice. "Lárguese!" Get lost! he yelled at the tree, and he threw another glass of water at it. This time he came closer. He refilled the glass. One more time: "Siento náuseas al verle, animal asqueroso!" It makes me sick just to look at you, you disgusting animal!

He heard noises in the house. Apparently Rita had come back from shopping. What if she'd been watching him the whole time? Or the housekeeper: Señor Duckwitz has flipped his lid! You'd never find out what Rita was thinking. Harry put down the pitcher and the glass. Helen would be here soon. He'd gladly have let Helen watch him. It wouldn't have been embarrassing to stand there in all his foolishness in front of *her.*

Six weeks later, Harry picked her up at the airport. "I'm coming!" she'd said in a telegram. "Depart Rotterdam February 3."

"An old friend of mine is coming for a visit," Harry told Rita. Unfortunately, she was rehearsing a boring sonata by Schumann. "Lovely," Rita said, without looking up from her music. She'd been saying that a lot lately. In Bonn, Harry had discovered to his dismay that Rita didn't know anything about the Beatles' Sergeant Pepper album. Her name was Rita and she'd never heard of lovely Rita, the metermaid. Okay, okay, in 1967 she was only twelve years old. Harry went right out and bought her the album. Sadly enough, the half-Indian Rita couldn't make heads or tails of the half-Indian songs the Beatles had recorded. Harry had hoped to open up the pleasures of pop music to her, but the only thing she got out of it was the word *lovely.* She said it as if to compensate Harry for his efforts.

As Harry drove to the airport, he began to feel uneasy. What's that supposed to mean, anyway: I'm coming. What an offhand way to announce a visit! At the airport, he saw Helen before she saw him. She looked pale and drawn. It was winter in Germany. A single strand of gray hair gave Harry a quick pang. They embraced, almost in embarrassment. Then Helen said: "You're not that way at all!" And Harry forgot all his shameful thoughts.

11 *How Harry and Rita get along with Helen as a long-term guest, and how, for one night and a day, Harry is the happiest man in the world. What high society in Ecuador thinks of Harry, how he has his first opportunity to intervene in world affairs, and how, with a good deal of hesitation, he makes use of that opportunity. In addition to some information about a zoologist, a deaf artillery colonel, and a large landowner named Eduardo Dünnbier.*

Helen made no move to leave. Harry was delighted. The house was big enough.

When you're a guest, you make yourself useful by helping around the house. That's the way it's always been. Here that wasn't possible. This was a problem for Helen. There were servants who wouldn't let you take their work away from them. They cooked and did the laundry, and you had to beg to be allowed to make your own tea once in a while. The cook and the maid didn't want to be sent home, because it was nicer here. Maybe they also thought it was amusing to work for people who were constantly saying thank you and telling you what things you didn't need to do. Rita, who turned 30 that summer of 1985, was the only one who was comfortable with servants. She allowed them to wait on her, just as she was supposed to, and she didn't take the tray out of their hands the way Helen did. Harry had to let himself be told by Helen that he shouldn't be so un-friendly to the servants. They had their first argument when Harry couldn't admit what Helen's criticism made obvious. Rita watched the two intently. She and Harry had never had a disagreement about the servants. But then, she never would have noticed that Harry's embarrassment might be regarded as unfriendliness by the cook or the maid.

Helen went on trips and excursions; sometimes she took Rita along. Harry noticed that Rita had apparently been missing such a change of pace. So when Helen asked them, after a while, to let her know if she was driving them up the wall, the question seemed merely rhetorical. Rita had become fluent in German in the meantime, but she didn't know what "driving someone up the wall" meant. She laughed when Harry explained and gave Helen a sisterly hug. Sometimes Harry wondered whether good old honest Helen might have told Rita that he'd gone to bed with her a couple of times in Germany while Rita was away. It didn't matter. That couldn't possibly be a problem. Since Helen had been in Quito, Harry took special pleasure in sleeping with Rita. He was absolutely wild in bed. Let Helen hear it! If she hadn't gone off in a huff to northern England then— ten years ago—everything would be different now. So he had a right, Harry decided, to provoke Helen a little. At least he didn't have to give up his pleasurable groaning in bed. It was bad enough that the servants were always slinking around the house.

A couple of weeks had passed since Helen's arrival when one night the door to the bedroom suddenly opened and Helen slipped into bed with them. It was as if it had to be that way, as if it never could have been any other way. All night long, Harry was the happiest man in the world. This must be the beginning of life in paradise.

He had been similarly happy after his first kiss, long ago, in the Alpine foothills, when he was surprised by the strange feeling of Regina's tongue moving around in his mouth, ushering in a new age. And then the first time he screwed a girl. As imperfect as it had been, it did prove that it worked. Not only by hand but in a vagina; in fact, it worked much better. And now there were two vaginas, and

178 Joseph von Westphalen

it worked not only not imperfectly, but without the least bit
of discord. Each one of them knew what to do, as if there
were an invisible director on the scene. Now Helen was no
longer a guest, now she belonged here. This was progress,
liberation, the end of darkness. It was absolutely the only
way of life. Completely overcome by an approaching lifetime
of happiness, Harry suddenly found room in his heart for
even that mousy woman at the embassy, the secretary who
might as well have come from East Germany. And just look
at that: the moment he smiled at her, she smiled back, still
a little suspiciously, but that would change. People are good,
and beautiful, and capable of learning.

But the next evening nothing happened. Harry tried to
get rid of the servants as early as possible. Desire made him
impatient; his tone of voice was harsh. He was irritated
because neither Rita nor Helen would help him drive them
off. That was evidently men's work. But why did they inter-
fere by discussing with the cook and the maid what they
should shop for the next day? As if that's what it was really
all about!

When they were finally alone, Harry had to face the
fact that Rita and Helen weren't interested. The night before
hadn't been embarrassing to them, but they didn't want to
be reminded of it.

"Don't talk everything to death!"

"I don't want to talk, I want to. . . ."

"Well, what?" asked Helen. "What is it you want?"

What could you call it? The thing didn't have a
sensible name yet.

"I want a repeat performance," said Harry.

"That's not very original," Helen told him.

Rita giggled shamelessly. There was nothing to be
done. For days Harry tried his luck as a seducer—in vain.
And how could it have been otherwise? It was difficult
enough to bring one woman to the melting point; it was

apparently doubly difficult to succeed with two women at the same time.

Harry shouldn't be such a pest, said Helen. After all, life didn't consist of tumbling around in bed, three at a time. It was fine once in a while, no problem, but not all the time. And the way he went on about it was enough to ruin your appetite anyway!

When nothing happened for three long weeks, Harry visited Marida Böckle again. She'd heard that a woman, a long-term visitor, had set up quarters at Harry's. If she were Harry's wife, she said, she'd have killed the "other woman" long ago. "There's nothing going on between us," said Harry. Marida Böckle didn't believe him. She thought Harry was a glutton, and she liked the idea that she was apparently the only one who could satisfy his hunger. Harry went home feeling absolutely awful. There's no point in getting your kicks if there's no love in it. He wrote a letter to Elizabeth Peach in London and told her everything. Her answer wasn't long in coming: "When you exposed less, I liked you more!"

Rita and Helen seemed to be quite content. Harry was on the watch for any signs of lesbian love—nothing. Unfortunately.

Instead, a warm friendship developed between Rita and Helen. They were like sisters. After a while he was sometimes able to go to bed with Rita, sometimes with Helen, carefully, politely, shyly, quietly. Harry couldn't rid himself of the suspicion that it was all just meant to keep him in a good mood. Suddenly, about six months later, there ensued another of those performances in bed featuring the entire cast. Harry hadn't seen it coming, and he temporarily gave up thinking about his love life. Shacking up with Rita and Helen was not the epitome of happiness, was not heaven on earth, but it was more lively and more stimulating than living with Rita alone.

"You're my acupuncture needle," Harry said to Helen,

poking his finger into her calf. Instead of a guest, she'd become a significant other, and they were living in a commune again.

In October 1985, Harry turned 40. Helen was 38, Rita 30. That same month, the president of Ecuador broke off diplomatic relations with Nicaragua. "That fascist pig!" said Helen. She said it with almost as much zest as in the good old days. Harry had fallen in love with Helen in 1968, when she called some professor a "fascist pig" at a student meeting. No one could trumpet it out as magnificently as Helen. She was beautiful in her righteous wrath.

"For my birthday, I wish for it to happen again," said Harry. But they all got so drunk that no one gave it another thought.

Rita had been playing more Chopin than Mozart recently. Unfortunately. Although Chopin was damned good. She played the Funeral March the way it might have been conceived: to bring the dead to life in their graves. Enter a voice like a trumpet, turning the music into a little piece about resurrection, then a sudden shift from a minor to a major key, and off it goes, tearing along so fast it makes the bones clatter! Helen reminded Harry that his trumpet had been lying on top of her wardrobe in Frankfurt since 1968.

Sometimes they all went out together, sometimes they invited people over. The Germans weren't all as bad as Harry had portrayed them. And Helen even managed to locate some pleasant Americans. No one took offense at their little triangle. What a shame, thought Harry. He would like the ambassador to have asked him whether he thought it was proper, as a representative of the Federal Republic of Germany, to be romping about with two women. But the man didn't ask. He wouldn't consider asking.

Duckwitz was not a Don Juan who stood Quito's nightlife on its head with his two women. There was no nightlife. At least not for Duckwitz. Harry, Rita, and Helen were paragons of domesticity. Reading and music. "I feel like a Mormon," said Harry. "A polygamist, but middle class through and through." Helen discovered Latin American novels and caught up on her reading. She recommended books to Harry and Rita, but without success. "I don't like myths," said Harry after reading a blurb on a dust jacket that said the book "wove a colorful mythic tapestry." Novels with historical themes didn't interest him. And he found anything mystical even worse than the mythical, so he also refused to read Borges, whom Helen had warmly recommended. Harry thought the man's work was too far-fetched, too erudite. The only book that found Harry's favor was a short novel by an author from Uruguay; it was in the form of a diary written by an office worker who puts the make on some woman. Nothing more. "Pretty banal," Helen said about the book. "Exactly," replied Harry.

He remembered a discussion he'd had in Cameroon with the leftist literature professor, and he started rummaging around in his cigar box. There it was: *Rather trivial than radical, but better yet, banal.* Helen studied the slip of paper as if it bore a secret message, then put it down again. "Well, okay."

"I'm interested only in the everyday," said Harry, "not its glorification. I'd rather read a newspaper."

Once, Helen fell in love with an English zoologist. He was doing field work on the Galápagos Islands, but he was based in Quito. Harry wouldn't have thought a zoologist could be a chain smoker. He was one of those closemouthed types. Looked like a badger. Rita found Harry's comments out of place. The situation was more serious than he thought. Would it be all the same to Harry if Helen went off with the gentleman? It would make a difference to her. Harry said: "If Helen leaves us for him, then we aren't worth much anyway." Rita said: "You never learned how to fight for something." Suddenly she sounded like she was doing public relations work for a Korean electronics company.

Helen loved and suffered, because the man didn't love her enough and wasn't there enough. Then suddenly he was gone, and Helen suffered even more. Rita and Harry's joint efforts to cure her malady were apparently so comical that her pain dissolved into thin air one evening during a drinking bout. And a few days later, it happened again.

Helen had books sent to her from Europe and she translated them from French into German. Things like *Patronage of the Arts in the Early Italian Renaissance*. "Whose work is more pointless, yours or mine?" Harry wanted to know.

Once, Helen handed Rita and Harry a paperback. "Here, for Mr. and Mrs. Duckwitz!" It was a German translation of a novel by Simone de Beauvoir. They had a good laugh over the German title: *Sie kam und blieb*, She Came to Stay. It was about a couple that lived peacefully together until they were suddenly joined by a second woman. Rita read the book without comment. Harry leafed through it and said: "It ends with a murder!" Murder is a cheap solution. He wasn't going to read it: "Absolument pas!" He reminded Helen that they had seen an interview with Simone de Beauvoir on television in the early seventies when they were living in the commune. When asked if she and Sartre had ever thought about having children, this personification of the liberated woman hurled an indignant "Absolument pas!" at the woman interviewer. Harry and Helen had adopted her half-foolish, half-convincing exclamation as their own. Children were out of the question for them, too. "Absolument pas!"

Now Beauvoir was dead, and Harry said he thought she had probably been pretty unbearable, a witch eaten up with ambition. Helen didn't contradict him. It wouldn't surprise him a bit, Harry said, if that exemplary leftist marriage with Sartre had actually been the pits. Rubbish and posturing, right down to their rejection of children. "I'll bet we're more liberal than that horrid pair."

The only ones who paid any attention to Duckwitz's unofficial family status were the criminals who were part of the Ecuadoran oligarchy. The corrupt, landowning string-pullers Duckwitz more or less had to deal with in his capacity as Counsellor for Economic Affairs. They had not remained blind to the fact that Primer Consejero Duckwitz of the West German embassy was living outside the bounds of law and civil order. Duckwitz was no wimp, no sissy, no *cretino,* he was their peer. You could depend on a man who had two women. A lot of men in the upper classes of Latin American society had a mistress who in time became a kind of second wife. It wasn't a secret, but it did require two houses at a goodly distance from one another. It involved two completely different circles that were never allowed to intersect. Latinos found the fact that Duckwitz lived under one roof with two women in part impressive, in part regrettable. Duckwitz remained stony-faced. He didn't have anything against impressing these bums, but he didn't want to get into a discussion with them about women. One plantation owner said he bet that one of these days Primer Consejero Duckwitz would need a second house he could get away to.

Sometimes Duckwitz took a certain pleasure in knocking around in upper-class circles. He enjoyed being able to see through and despise people he didn't think could see through him. He felt like a secret agent. Here in the feudal urban mansions of Quito and the country houses outside of town, he picked up political information no one else at the German embassy knew anything about. He found out, for example, how realistic the chance of a putsch by airforce generals really was. The rumors had been increasing of late. Here there were signs that the corrupt military didn't have a chance against the corrupt civilian government. The thoroughly depraved president of the country was regarded as the United States' most dependable guarantor in Latin America, and so a military putsch that wasn't supported by the U.S. didn't have the slightest chance of success. American companies had their fingers too deep in the country's oil business for that.

All of this was perfectly clear, and then again it wasn't. What wasn't perfectly clear was the answer to the human riddle that posed itself in every corner of Latin America: why aren't repulsive characters always repulsive? Maybe there had been enough time for depravity to take on a certain cultivation on this continent, to develop a certain style—in contrast to Africa, where the ruling class, caught off guard by decolonization, tended toward confusion. For it was a fact: the worst villains, a hundred times as corrupt and depraved as the people who pulled the political and economic strings in old Europe, the people who were truly dangerous and who wouldn't shrink from murder, behaved like harmless oddballs in some stage play. That was the problem. They were criminals, but they were comical. For instance, at a reception for high-placed guests at an aristocratic hacienda, one general bellowed his opinion of the civilian government in Ecuador into the stone-deaf ear of an artillery colonel: "Ellos no entienden nada de la vida!" They don't understand anything about life! You could go up to a man like that and yell in his ear: "Pero ustedes entienden todo de la muerte!" But you understand everything about death! Though it was better to let it be; he would probably just give an enthusiastic nod.

At another reception at a showy country house, a large landowner with the wonderful name Eduardo Dünnbier came up to Duckwitz and said, "Entre hombres," man to man, he was also one of those who had two women. "You understand!" In Quito he lived with his family. He pointed out an elegant woman—his wife. And there were his two daughters. All of them beautiful and slender, with black hair. He had given his second woman a house in the country, on the road that leads down to the Pacific Ocean, where it stops being bare and cool and mountainous but is not yet humid and tropical. Where the climate and the landscape are best, right there. A refuge. A paradise. A beautiful house in a valley, remote, but only about ten kilometers from the road between Quito and Esmeraldas. But here was his problem: a road was to be built through that valley to link the interior with the oil-producing coast and to make it easier to transport the timber that was being felled in the rain forest on the Colombian border. The paradise his second woman lived in would disappear. Eduardo Dünnbier, he said, is an influential man, he can do a lot, he can prevent a lot; he knows all the ministers in the cabinet. But with this project he has come up against his limits. Primer Consejero Duckwitz, economic expert at the German embassy, is his last chance.

Incredible. Harry kept him dangling for a while: where did he get that peculiar name, Dünnbier? Eduardo Dünnbier told him readily that his family had emigrated to Ecuador from Nuremberg-Fürth in 1848. Then he got back to business. *Entre hombres.* Man to man. He knew something Harry should have known as well, but of course it had again gone right past the Foreign Office—a West German construction equipment company was negotiating directly with the government of Ecuador. There was a prospect of delivering 150 road construction machines, possibly even of establishing a subsidiary for producing additional equipment in the country. A fat egg. And about as close to illegality as you could get.

Duckwitz listened to everything the man had to say. It was wonderful the way Eduardo Dünnbier used only the argument of his second woman and his hacienda. Man to man. He didn't give a damn how many roads were built through the rain forest, how many trees were cut down. He was the sort who has a laughing fit when you mention the ecological consequences of clearing the rain forest. He evidently knew nothing about Harry's ecological morals, only about his two women. And so he appealed to him man to man, bastard to bastard, Dünnbier to Duckwitz.

Harry displayed his heartfelt understanding, and he didn't even have to pretend. It was completely legitimate not to want your love nest disturbed by months of construction work and an ugly highway. Obviously, Dünnbier's affections were intimately bound up with this unspoiled landscape. He had enough money to buy his second woman a hacienda somewhere else. It was touching how desperately this scoundrel clung to his bit of earth. There was something refreshing about Eduardo Dünnbier's egocentrism.

Duckwitz didn't tell him that he'd always had a singular aversion to construction sites and heavy equipment and that this bit of information was most welcome to him. There were enough roads in this world. They should stop destroying the last oases of undisturbed nature with all this road building.

Harry knew that, as a diplomat, he couldn't do anything about it. He could write in his reports that the export of German road-building equipment was good for the German economy but disastrous for the rain forest and the last of the Indians, but that would be mere sentimentality. What could he do? He could warn of a global climatic disaster, the way Helen did, but that wouldn't bother anyone because everyone already knew about it. The only thing left was the aesthetic argument—pointing to forest that had already been destroyed and saying: "Now doesn't that look terrible!"

Harry finally had a concrete opportunity to prevent something—not just to talk and to write, but to take action. And it was certainly in keeping with the grand irony of existence that he should exploit the personal interests of a crook for his own purposes—to block an irresponsible road construction project. It was a promising symbiosis.

Eduardo Dünnbier, his atrocious crony, insisted on showing Duckwitz his wonderful hacienda and his second woman, otherwise the Primer Consejero wouldn't know what it was all about. And a couple of days later the two actually did go for a drive. An hour and a half out of Quito, a valley opened up on their left. They turned off, and a few kilometers further on they came to the hacienda—a large, garish pseudo-hacienda. A fat woman was sitting on the terrace, and Señor Dünnbier went up and took her blissfully in his arms.

"I understand," said Duckwitz on the drive back to town. "I understand what you mean."

Then he tried to make it clear to Eduardo Dünnbier that he didn't want any money if he succeeded in keeping the road from being built. Before he went into action, however, he expected Señor Dünnbier's help in another matter that had come to his attention. It was a delicate business in which German companies were negotiating with representatives from various Ecuadoran government ministries over the delivery of 5000 cylinders for the production of munitions. "This deal simply must fall through," said Duckwitz. He told Dünnbier he should come up with something.

Señor Dünnbier was suspicious. He'd have preferred that Duckwitz ask for money. Idealists had to be handled with kid gloves. Duckwitz could see that Dünnbier was struggling with himself.

"Or are you involved in the deal?" he asked.

"No, no!"

"Your business is riskier for me than you think," said Duckwitz.

That convinced Señor Dünnbier. Without a word he

steered his luxurious American car up into the Andes in the direction of Quito. They emerged from the pleasant green of the subtropics and things turned desolate once more.

"Do you think these high, bare mountains have had an influence on the character of the people here?" asked Duckwitz. Living hundreds of years on a giant slag heap just couldn't leave people completely untouched. Could it be that the brutality of human rights violations was one of the consequences of a brutal landscape that made people seem small and human life appear worthless?

Eduardo Dünnbier shrugged his shoulders. After a time he said: In Germany the landscape is gentle, but to the best of his knowledge, just a few decades ago the country had been subject to a violence that made Latin American violence look like a joke.

They fell silent again and drove on. Harry wondered what it was that had formed his own character. One characteristic he had turned into a profession was his tendency to play things down, to smooth over and twist the facts. He hadn't become a lawyer for nothing, after all. And maybe that's also why he went into diplomacy: it was nothing but a crooked business that suited his crooked nature. Diplomacy was horse-trading, polite blackmail, amicable intrigue. If there was any point to it besides looking after tourists, athletes, and businessmen abroad, it was to prevent things from happening. And rightly so. Preventing wars—that was the point of diplomacy. Or preventing an attack on the rain forest by construction machines. This justified using any means at his command.

He didn't have the talent to formulate protests against the destruction of the rain forest. He was no politician. As a lawyer his particular strength lay in negotiating behind the scenes. As a lawyer you had to be diplomatic. Preventing a trial sometimes made more sense than putting up a flimsy defense—even if it wasn't as spectacular. And you always felt a little sheepish getting together with the prosecutor for the horse-trading "entre hombres."

Once, a student under investigation for libel appeared in his office. He had written a lampoon in which he insulted three West German state premiers, the Chancellor, and the President. From his brother Fritz, who was already a poet and was studying literature at the time, Harry had learned about the "narrative persona": that's when an author lets a character in a novel speak or think for him. The character who does the insulting is, logically, the one to be held responsible, not the author of the book himself—at least as long as the whole thing deserves the name of art or satire. Harry had arranged to meet the public prosecutor for lunch. His name was Hütel, he came from Stuttgart, and he maintained that he was a liberal.

Over the salads they had for lunch, attorney Duckwitz asked Prosecutor Hütel if he knew what a narrative persona was. He didn't. Harry explained it to him, and the prosecutor dropped the case.

Duckwitz found himself thinking about that now. You reached an agreement with an opponent beforehand, prevented a dispute, and the interests on both sides evaporated like magic.

They approached Quito. Harry was looking forward to seeing Rita and Helen. What a piece of luck that Helen was here. He'd been lucky, period. His second woman wasn't as fat as Señor Dünnbier's, he didn't have an atrocious hacienda, and these stupid Andes weren't his home. He'd be able to leave them once and for all at the end of the year. Besides, Duckwitz was a better name than Dünnbier.

Although he'd already made up his mind about the road-building project, he wanted to get Helen's seal of approval. Could he do something for a vile character with vile motives in order to prevent something vile from happening?

"Don't make such a fuss!" said Helen. And then she burst out laughing: it was just too funny to see Harry brooding like some character in a play by Schiller.

But Harry wouldn't give up. He wasn't brooding, really. The fellow wasn't any better than a Nazi asking someone to prevent the construction of a concentration camp outside his mansion because it would ruin his view from the window as he played chamber music.

"Stop it!" said Helen. "Your comparison is all off!"

Harry said she had once used comparisons like that all the time; he got it from her.

"I used to," said Helen.

Taking care of the matter turned out to be simple enough. Duckwitz wrote to the Foreign Office expressing his reservations about the observance of export regulations in the case of the deal that was being planned. As expected, the central office responded that they weren't sure, either; they could not preclude the possibility of a violation. If that was the case, the deal would have to be nullified. Harry had the letter translated into Spanish in such a way that it suggested the Foreign Office would not hesitate to prohibit the sale. Harry played the letter into the hands of a high official, along with a forged exchange of letters between two other German construction firms indicating that the construction machine company in question faced bankruptcy. A deal worth millions collapsed. That's how simple it was.

Duckwitz felt like he had set off a bomb. It wasn't exactly edifying. For the German construction company it would probably mean instituting short hours and firing people. And all this so that on the other side of the world Eduardo Dünnbier could have some peace and quiet. So that a diplomat by the name of Duckwitz could have the satisfaction of having done a good deed after ten years of mindless busywork. And with regard to the artillery cylinders whose delivery Dünnbier actually did prevent, they would probably be snapped up by Chile or Iraq.

Harry felt uneasy. Instead of crusading loudly and openly against the injustices of this world, he had chosen a sneaky backdoor approach. He wasn't much of a shining hero. His was just a tiny light.

The year 1986 came to an end and with it Harry's time in Ecuador. He was due for another foreign posting, just as he had been after Cameroon. Harry was in his early forties. More than ever, he was now too old to be letting himself be sent here and there just as it pleased the people at the Foreign Office. He went into action. He wanted to go back to Bonn. Rita would just have to get by with the Conservatory of Music in Cologne. There'd be an official request, and a bit of transatlantic telephone lobbying.

"Why did you become a diplomat if you're constantly wanting to return to Bonn?" asked the voice of a Swabian in Personnel who would perhaps rather have been gadding about the world. "Don't ask me," replied Duckwitz. He'd see, said the man from Personnel. Duckwitz ironically threatened to commit suicide if it didn't work out, which was a bit shabby where Hennersdorff was concerned, since he really had killed himself in Africa. "Not that!" said the voice from Bonn; we've already had three suicides this year—more than our allotment.

Harry was a little concerned that moving to Bonn would require clarification of his pleasantly ambiguous relationship with Helen. He wanted everything to stay the way it was, but he didn't want to press Rita or Helen for a decision. This kind of threesome worked only if there was no pressure. Harry had learned at least that much during the past two years.

Rita raised the subject before he could. "You'll stay with us in Bonn!" she said to Helen, rather irresistibly, Harry thought. He was glad the offer had come from Rita

and that they were apparently thinking along the same lines.
Nevertheless, it did show that she clearly preferred a life
with him and Helen together to a life with him alone.
Although he felt that way too, it was still a little painful.

"If the gentleman of the house approves," said Helen.

•   •   •

No different from other world travelers, diplomats like to
take home souvenirs. In contrast to the common tourist,
however, the diplomat has no problem finding room in his
luggage. His move is planned for him. No matter how volu-
minous his household has become, it's shipped in full and at
no cost to him by experienced movers. Such preferential
treatment tempts many a diplomat into large-scale buying.
Artworks of all kinds, gold and silver jewelry, carpets,
antiques, sculpture large and small, high art and folk art—
whatever his heart desires—disappears into luggage protected
by diplomatic immunity. Of course, there were rumors that,
under the protection of this immunity, diplomats carried on
outright trade in antiques and archeological artifacts; but it
couldn't be proven. As long as they didn't have heroin in
their suitcases, it was no one's business but their own.
Heroin or shrunken heads, that is—their export was also
prohibited. In Cameroon, there was always a considerable
amount of native sculpture stowed away in the transport
containers of diplomatic colleagues. And no one took note of
just a little ivory. One of them had taken along precious
wood by the cubic meter for the floor of his very own home
in Bonn. From Singapore and Japan, diplomats brought back
consumer electronics, the latest generation of computers, and
huge audio towers that were as cheap there as they would be
only six months later in Europe. And then, of course, there
were Japanese motorcycles.

Harry hated this legal smuggling. And he couldn't understand why people who were by no means poor would stand in line in duty-free shops at airports or on board ship just to buy scotch for a laughable couple of marks less than the regular price. He wanted no pottery, no copper kettles, and no wooden cups from the Andes, no llama-wool blankets, and no real or imitation madonnas in that awful Latin American Jesuit baroque. Rita's little-used motorcycle and her much-used piano were the only bulky items awaiting the luxury of a ship's crossing.

It's also customary for a diplomat to undertake a farewell trip through neighboring countries, since he usually doesn't have a chance to get acquainted with them during his posting. Harry didn't feel like doing that, either. He wanted to leave right away. He'd had enough. Rita was undecided. Helen, on the other hand, was toying with the idea of doing a tour of Latin America. Harry vehemently advised against it. Helen couldn't seriously want to see the harebrained offspring of modern architecture in Brasilia or the ruins of no-less questionable Inca culture. Making a pilgrimage to centers of Inca culture in Peru to contemplate the enigmatic ruins of Machu Picchu or the old Inca walls in Cuzco doesn't make you any smarter. You can stare at them as long as you want, but you'll never be able to figure out whether or not the Inca state was hell on earth. And in order to determine that the cathedrals of the Spanish conquerors all look like police barracks, you need only a couple of postcards or coffee-table books. All this damned traveling around was a vice of people who couldn't stay seated on their hindquarters. "Down with tourism!" Harry cried out. "Long live the travelogue, photography, and the film documentary!" Films of iguanas lumbering around on the Galápagos Islands were a hundred times more educational than a trip to the Galápagos, where nesting Darwin finches, already threatened with extinction, were disturbed by gaggling American chicks—who interfered with the view as well.

Helen said she would still like to have seen all that— even disappointment should be authentic. But she didn't go on the trip. A publisher in Munich or Hamburg suddenly made her a good offer for an interesting translation, a fat catch, and it couldn't be put off. So the three of them would travel together after all.

Duckwitz's successor arrived in Quito ahead of schedule. He was in his early thirties and had two children and a pregnant wife. Harry wondered if that could possibly work. The family was going to take over Duckwitz's house. The move began. Harry hardly had to give it a thought. Indians from the moving company quietly packed their belongings. And of all people to make arrangements for the move, it had to be that timid cucumber at the embassy, the one who acted like an East German and looked like her name should be Gertrude or Hiltrude, the one who had smiled at Harry exactly once during his three years in Ecuador—his enemy. "Is that your crate of books, or does it belong to your acquaintance?" she asked maliciously. "My friend doesn't have any luggage," Harry said as witheringly as possible. "She even travels without a purse, imagine that!" She actually wanted to exclude the tons of books in Helen's crate from Duckwitz's diplomatic baggage. To be more precise, she wanted to let him know that she'd caught him red-handed. Illegal use of gratis moving privileges.

For their last days in Ecuador, Harry, Rita, and Helen moved into an old hotel in Quito. At breakfast they talked about what they should call the country they would be flying back to in a couple of days. Germany? No. Federal Republic? Ridiculous. Okay, where were they going? Home? Back home? That sounded so cozy. Back to Bonn! At least they could say that. That was neutral.

"You people have problems!" said Rita.

"It's our country of origin," said Harry. "It's where I come from"—he could identify with that. No home sweet home, no nationalism. He thought of it more as a lap than as a country, he said.

"Of course," said Helen, "*l'étranger*, the great outsider, the man who appears out of nowhere. 'He's a real nowhere man,' here comes Harry Has-no-land."

Harry changed the subject. "What would it be like to have lived in the twenties and thirties? We would have had nicer suitcases, and I'd be wearing a straw hat. We'd have gone rattling by train across the Andes to Buenos Aires, we'd have danced the tango in bars down at the harbor, and we'd have been waiting for the next steamer to Europe. Maybe we'd have given even less thought then to being a threesome than we do now."

"What do you mean? What bothers you about it now?" asked Helen.

Harry said he sometimes didn't quite know where he stood, couldn't talk about everything openly, in short, he thought an erotic combination like theirs might have been taken more for granted in the twenties.

Helen turned to Rita: "Did you hear that? He calls it an 'erotic combination'!"

Rita giggled the way she had years before in Africa. As if Harry weren't even there, she said to Helen: "He should be glad he doesn't know where he stands!"

She was right. It was better to have the present complications than to mourn bygone steamer voyages. It would have been rather superficial to stand at the railing in a straw hat, Rita on his right arm, Helen on his left, Harry the ladies' man about to cross the Atlantic. They heard jazz coming from the hotel lounge. These new versions weren't very satisfying. Maybe the pieces that were so popular today were superficial back then, too, and had gained in depth over the decades. Maybe the charm of that supposedly wild

era had been mere mind-blowing silliness; maybe the frivol-
ity had just been a mask for serious inhibitions. We don't
even know that, so how can we possibly bring to light
anything about life among the Incas!

Besides, said Helen, the Nazi period would still have
been ahead, and the second world war. No thanks! She'd
rather get on an airplane now, while 1987 was still young,
and go bumping back to the Old World.

12 *How Harry von Duckwitz returns to Bonn with Rita and Helen, and how and where they set up housekeeping. About a party they give and how they set the table for the occasion. In addition to some information about Harry's work at the Foreign Office and his particular way of taking part in diplomatic social life. How Helen rents a house in the Eifel region near Cologne, Harry develops fraternal feelings toward his brother Fritz, and the women wonder who has the prettiest legs. In addition to some comments on dirty politics, photography, and music, and a colleague who's the image of a British colonel.*

Out of the question! They couldn't possibly be expected to live in that row house in Bad Godesberg the Foreign Office had arranged for them to rent. At least as far as Harry and Helen were concerned. Rita's Asian side emerged again. The house wasn't so bad, she said: it had been renovated, it had a little yard, and it even had a washing machine in the basement. She already knew where she wanted to put the piano.

Harry shook his head. "Not again," he told Rita. He'd had enough of life in a row house the last time they were in Bonn. And this particular row house was especially ugly. Just look at that front door, the glass, the door handle, the two fake stone steps, the little spruce tree next to the entrance—a cemetery, a chicken coop. The ruin of anyone who lived there!

Helen started looking around and soon found an apartment near the center of Bonn. It was in a big, run-down older building. There were Turks living in the same building, Italians, Greeks, and pensioners on the same street. It wasn't even a trendy student quarter. No diplomat or politician had ever lived here. This was a place where you could breathe.

There was a big room for each of them and a spacious living area. Rita mourned the loss of a laundry room, so to console her Harry gave her a grand piano. Never in his life had he bought anything so expensive—18,000 marks. Could you pay for it with just one check? "But of course, sir," said the piano salesman.

Rita was happy with her grand piano, and for the sake of fairness Harry bought Helen the most recent French encyclopedia, all 28 volumes.

There was plenty of money. The idea that diplomats earn a lot, especially with all their perks abroad, was a legend that was constantly denied but nevertheless contained a good deal of truth. When they were transferred, there was even an allowance for buying new drapes. The government thought of everything. Harry didn't know what to do with all the money. Besides that, Rita got her stipend from her father every month. Helen absolutely would not let herself be supported by Harry; she earned her share by doing translations.

He had enough money, enough women, and work that left him a lot of free time. He had enough of all the things that had always been in short supply. Yet he wasn't proclaiming his happiness on the hour every hour. Paradoxically enough, thought Harry, the deficiencies of existence are revealed most clearly to people who experience no deficiency. People who must run after love or money usually fall exhausted into bed at night, with no energy to spare for pleasurable doubts about the meaning of it all.

In January 1987, when they came back from Ecuador and moved into the apartment in Bonn, the Chancellor had been reelected to another term of office, just as everyone expected. Rita's lack of interest in West German politics was infectious; for Harry and Helen as well, politics was about as important as a fart. The Foreign Minister was reappointed, so nothing was going to change. There were certain advantages to this, although Harry would like to have seen a new Foreign Minister throw out those characters who populated the Foreign Office's upper echelons. He would like to have seen senior officials beset with fear about who was going to survive the purges.

Harry usually walked to the office, first making his way through the busy but provincial pedestrian mall in the center of town, then through the Hofgarten, and then along the banks of the Rhine to the picturesque stairway that led up to the little dead-end street where the entrance to the Foreign Office was located.

A few months before, a bunch of crazy terrorists had assassinated one of their undersecretaries. You saw a lot of police patrols in the area now. The time when you could sympathize with terrorists had passed. Ten years ago, Harry had wanted to defend them. That was during the politically charged autumn of 1977. The question then had been the familiar one of what you would do if a terrorist came along looking for a place to hide. Naturally, you'd have hidden him in the broom closet for the night. Now you'd call the police.

Sometimes the Rhine was too melancholy for Harry; it was a mood he knew from his days as a Frankfurt lawyer. Then, he would walk down Adenauerallee, loud and ugly as it was, past the Mexican embassy, whose noble but crumbling façade was like a greeting from the better part of Latin America. The years in Ecuador had come to an end only a short time ago, but they were already being transfigured in his memory.

The people in Personnel were rather apologetic, because the only position they had for Duckwitz was in Public Relations/Domestic. With his legal training, Herr von

Duckwitz was naturally overqualified for this job, but no one had expected him to be transferred back to Bonn. They thought he'd be appointed to the ambassador's post in Dakar, in Senegal—after all, he'd written such excellent reports from Cameroon. "But unfortunately, your wife's musical training made that impossible," said the fellow in Personnel.

That just can't be, thought Duckwitz. They'd really read those stupid reports here in Bonn! Rita, by the way, did get a job at the Conservatory of Music in Cologne. She taught and studied piano, and worked as an accompanist.

The Public Relations/Domestic job was generally held to be boring, and Harry groaned dutifully. But actually he was delighted. It was exactly the right place for him. His job involved bringing up to date the Foreign Office's pamphlets on the Third World and German cultural policy abroad. Some of them had pretty kitschy titles, like "Bridges Across Borders," and their texts were held together with every sticky cliché you could think of. But they didn't contain any nasty propaganda. In fact, they were full of well-meant and even self-critical expressions of good will. The black-red-and-mustard-striped pamphlets were stacked by the hundreds in the basement of the Foreign Office and at the printer's warehouse in Coblenz, just waiting to be ordered. Bringing them up to date often meant nothing more than replacing the photograph on the first page with a more recent one of the Foreign Minister. He'd been in office for 13 years now.

The pamphlet Harry was currently working on bore the winning title "Our Foreign Policy," and a wonderfully pedantic subtitle added, "Its Aims. Who Conducts It. Whom It Serves." This pamphlet was to be subjected to a didactic overhaul by a Third Secretary who ran around with a chronic cough. In the man's previous incarnation, he'd worked for a few years as a teacher. Duckwitz was in charge of the pamphlet's content, but he did not bear responsibility

for it. There was no way a person could take responsibility
for the things it said about the new image of the Foreign
Office and its extreme usefulness as an institution. It was
full of lies, but at least they were white ones, not the kind
you use as a lawyer in court. The political divisions in the
Foreign Office actually did bear something like responsibility. But in the pamphlet office where Harry worked, you
could, in good conscience, feel that you had none. Especially
since no one was interested in the publications anyway.

The head of his office had, however, recently become
interested in the pamphlets; he wanted the material to be
snappy, more up to date. One time he had them show him
a revised pamphlet for which the ex-teacher had thought up
a new chapter entitled "Our Field of Labor: The World."
Harry had added a subtitle in boldface: "**Too much money
spent on weapons!**" He was quite pleased when the head of
the division said: "You're right to tell it like it is, Duckwitz!"
They were all against weapons.

On the whole, Duckwitz felt he had a good reputation
with his superiors and his colleagues, but for safety's sake he
didn't rely all too much on his intuition. When he was a
lawyer he'd thought he was a well-liked member of the firm,
and then he'd overheard the secretary and the pretty intern
pick him to pieces. So as soon as he found out that people
at the office were gossiping about his apartment, he went on
the attack. Wouldn't you know it'd be someone from Public
Relations/Domestic who'd camp out in the Turkish quarter
like a would-be poet. Duckwitz invited a large group of his
superiors and colleagues to dinner. Some of them came
dressed in suits, but most of them came in blue jeans
because they thought that would be better suited to Harry
von Duckwitz's casual style. Harry himself was dressed to
the nines.

When diplomats invite people to dinner, they're particularly careful to use their most select china. The Foreign

Office even provides financial assistance so diplomats can equip themselves appropriately to fulfill their social obligations. But Harry's table looked like a stand at a flea market: a jumble of glasses and mismatched china, family silver next to hotel flatware and cheap tin spoons from a cafeteria. Still, the food was good and the apartment was clean. His guests were confused, didn't quite know what to make of it all. Then Duckwitz gave a speech. For his part, he said, he rejected the self-imposed isolation of the diplomat in a diplomatic ghetto. Harry said he preferred integration. Integration, not isolation. The ivory-tower diplomat was a thing of the past. Nowadays, diplomats should live where immigrants live, to provide an official counter to the growing hostility toward outsiders in Germany. And finally, said Harry, he found older buildings with their large rooms and high, stuccoed ceilings more dignified than those cramped little chicken coops in Bad Godesberg, where there wasn't even a place to put a grand piano. Just that moment, Rita began to play a lilting prelude by Chopin.

Harry's guests were drunk, delighted, utterly won over. The fellow from the protocol office—Duckwitz knew him only fleetingly from the cafeteria and thought he would be particularly shocked—was obviously pleased and thanked Harry for a truly unconventional evening: "The Foreign Office could use more people like you, Duckwitz!"

Another surprise was that there was evidently not a guest among them who took his two-woman household amiss. Rita and Helen had obliged Harry by sharing the housewifely duties that evening in utterly beautiful harmony.

However, life with the two women wasn't quite as easy or as enviable as it appeared to be. At least not all the time. Occasionally it was downright enviable. But the whole thing was beyond his control. Sometimes, the erotic tension doubled at the same time that sexual activity was reduced by half. Then just when Harry thought he had worked out this new law of nature, they'd find themselves in the middle of a great romp, snaking and wriggling around, disproving all the formulas he'd developed to explain the secrets of their shared existence. Often, though, nothing happened. Nothing at all. For days. Two slender, good-looking women, and nothing happened. Things were comfortable, they were pleasant, but nothing happened. As if there were no such thing as being horny.

Once, Harry recalled that old game, the way he'd run his stocking foot up Helen's leather-clad leg under the table at the pub. Where were those pants? Helen shrugged her shoulders. Gone. Threw them out years ago. Out of fashion, all worn out. You shouldn't be so careless with souvenirs of past desire! Harry drove to Cologne and searched in vain, then drove to Düsseldorf, where he finally found what he was looking for in a little boutique with a slick salesclerk.

Helen and Rita said he was crazy when he came home with black leather pants for both of them. Size 8 for Helen, size 6 for Rita. "I had an urge to write another check," he said, then offended Helen with his erotic raptures about his "twin motorcycle queens." Helen told Harry he was kitschy and chauvinistic. Harry said she was an enemy of desire, and when he reminded her about playing footsy under the table, she said he was trying to bring back the past.

Harry took part in Bonn's diplomatic social life as rarely as he could, Rita even more seldom, Helen never. Out of the blue, Harry asked Rita and Helen to go with him to a reception given by the French ambassador—wearing their new leather pants. Rita thought this was going too far, and Helen said she wouldn't let herself be used for his premeditated provocations. Why don't you just order two call girls?

On the evening of the reception, though, Rita and Helen gulped down a couple of shot glasses of courage, slipped into their twin leather pants, and accompanied a surprised Harry to the French ambassador's residence. It was a great day for Harry. A day that would change everything. Harry von Duckwitz appears with his hard-rock queen and his hard-rock girlfriend at a diplomatic reception where ladies wear fancy dresses!

Rita and Helen left all the other women in the shade. Sensuous and beguiling, wild and audacious—at least that's the way Harry thought they looked. He was quite proud. It was absolutely majestic the way they ignored the unwritten dress code. The other women immediately began giving them dirty looks and whispering. And how they whispered—but in admiration! They thought Rita and Helen looked enchanting. If she had a figure like those two, Duckwitz heard the wife of the head of his division tell the wife of the deputy head of protocol, she'd be the first to wear pants like that. Smashing. "Düsseldorf," said Duckwitz as he went past them, "twelve hundred marks apiece."

The attempted provocation was a failure. And at the office he was allowed to write pacifist thoughts into his pamphlets without any objections. Evidently, it was impossible to disrupt diplomatic life.

Helen laughed as he complained to her about the high level of tolerance in the Foreign Office and told her that postmodernism with its motto, anything goes, had taken hold in Bonn. One of these days, Harry said, he was going to box the American ambassador's ears at some fancy diplomatic function. He was going to wait till the ambassador started praising the U.S.'s revolting foreign policy, then give it to the apple-cheeked boy, right and left. The only thing was, that cub scout might take it sportingly. On the other hand, if he really did lodge a complaint, Harry could probably depend on the Foreign Office to back him up. Everyone in Bonn hated the fellow for his arrogance. The only people who found anything positive in this character and his wife were the ones from the "house beautiful" magazines. Maybe, thought Duckwitz, he should play the part of an imp and blow in the wife's ear in public, if possible in the presence of the President. In that case, they'd probably encourage him to have himself declared *non compos mentis* and he'd be sent into early retirement for reasons of health.

"Don't you dare," said Helen. The prospect of having Harry around the house all day wasn't very enticing.

•   •   •

Occasionally, Rita would bring home from the conservatory a Japanese fellow with a squarish face. He was a tenor, and he didn't speak or understand a word of German. But he sang a more flawless German than all German singers put together. You could understand every word, and it didn't even sound artificial: "Was vermied' ich denn die Wege / wo die andern Wandrer gehn. . . ." Duckwitz found the Schubert song quite moving. Classical music had its gems, too. And of all people it was a squarish Japanese who unlocked these beautiful lines. "Don't you feel jealous when you see the two of them together?" asked Helen.

Helen found a house in the Eifel region that they absolutely had to rent. She'd always complained about the polluted air in Bonn. She wanted to be close to nature again, wanted to see fields and meadows. Besides, she and Rita needed a place where they could get away. The rent wasn't too steep, the house was nice, the area was ugly. A refuge. Out there, Harry could make up for his lost honeymoon with Rita, said Helen. Harry thought renting a house in the country was going too far, that it was simply too fashionable. But Helen was undoubtedly right. The air was better, and there were still herons. You could get milk that turned sour immediately, and there was an amateurish compost heap in the yard. In the end, Harry was quite content. Rita's motorcycle had a place of its own in an empty barn near the house, and there was a pizza parlor in the village.

Harry asked his brother if he wouldn't like to come out more often. Fritz lived in Cologne, and the Eifel was just a stone's throw from there. Harry had never had much to do with his poetic brother Fritz, but sometimes he had the feeling he should do something for him. Did he earn enough money from his books? Shouldn't he give him some financial support? Helen said: "The man is a year younger than you. He's not a child anymore."

Fritz made his living in radio, and he didn't live too badly. He had a girlfriend. There had been talk of her when Harry was in Bonn the last time, in the early eighties. Helen had met her once in Cologne. "She's not bad looking," she said. Harry didn't trust Fritz to write great literature or have a great woman, but he was curious. She was divorced and had two or three children, they said, and she was a doctor in a hospital.

The first time Fritz came to the house in the Eifel, he came without his girlfriend. "If you like," said Harry, "you can fix up a room for yourself on the third floor. For writing poetry and that sort of thing." Fritz laughed: "What strange ideas you have!" He said he needed a place to set up his computer.

"You're all crazy," said Harry. Helen had also bought a computer, that is, two computers. And they gawked at her in both Bonn and the Eifel. "You look like a case worker checking her files," said Harry, who was feeling slightly offended.

"That's pretty good," said Fritz. "A case worker. Yes. The writer as case worker. There's something to that."

The next time he came, Fritz brought along his girl-friend. Her name was Inez. Her ex-husband could think of nothing better to do with his weekends than take care of two of their children. Fritz thought this was an ideal solution. Inez brought along only the smallest of the children, because it was still nursing. Without hesitation, she bared her pretty little breast and offered it to the baby. Harry didn't know whether he found it provocative or simply the most natural thing in the world. He lit a cigarette. "Go and smoke outside! There's a baby in here!" said Helen. "It's all right," said Inez. "He doesn't smoke very much." The baby was nine months old, but Inez had been divorced for two years. "Well, am I finally an uncle?" asked Harry.

No, said Fritz. Inez's ex-husband was the father of this baby, too. She still had a very good relationship with him. It must have happened one of those times when he came to pick up the kids for the weekend. Fritz laughed.

Harry thought the baby was pretty cute. "Take him for a minute," said Inez. Harry didn't dare. "Nothing can happen," said Inez.

She was in her mid-thirties, two years older than Rita. She was built about like Rita and Helen, and her hair was dark, too. When she smiled, her lips slid up over her long front teeth.

Fritz and Inez didn't spend the night there. When they had gone, the conversation naturally turned to Inez. What did Harry think of her?

"Pretty good," said Harry.

"I didn't like her as much this time," said Helen.

"I like her," said Rita. "The baby is sweet."

Harry was glad the problem of children had been solved for him. He had colleagues whose wives had pestered them for years about having children, and then when the kids arrived, the husbands became even bigger martyrs. Good old Rita without a uterus. Was she sad when she saw a happy mother?

"Can you imagine going to bed with her?" Helen asked.

"Right this instant," said Harry. "She has the longest teeth!"

"Periodontitis," said Helen.

"It doesn't matter," said Harry, "the main thing is they're nice and long."

Then Helen and Rita started comparing legs. Inez's legs weren't bad. "In any case, they're longer than mine," said Rita.

"That's not true," said Helen.

"But she has nice heels."

"My heels aren't bad, either!"

"I didn't say they weren't!"

"She sort of shuffles when she walks."

"You women are the worst machos of all!" said Harry.

"I don't understand how she can wear such a dowdy skirt," said Helen.

"Her skirt was divine!" said Harry, and he recalled Elizabeth Peach from Cameroon and the Renaissance painting she'd shown him: three beauties and a swooning Paris, who was supposed to select the prettiest.

•   •   •

May arrived. A year before, there'd been an explosion at the Chernobyl nuclear reactor in the Ukraine. It had contaminated part of the globe and had supposedly altered the consciousness of mankind. The three of them had been in Ecuador at the time. In safety. Since their return to the lightly contaminated soil of central Europe, Helen's fears had begun to get on Harry's nerves. He was prepared to shoot the entire nuclear lobby, to stab them, strangle them with his bare hands, especially that piece of nuclear waste they called a Research Minister. Absolutely! Anybody who recommended the stuff, let alone made and sold it, should die a thousand deaths. At some point the party's over. But Harry didn't feel like being exposed to constant discussion of the danger of nuclear energy on top of his constant exposure to actual radiation. He hadn't protested yet, because Helen was right about being careful and right to be concerned. But it was beginning to get to him. If things went on this way, he'd have to plug his ears every time she brought up the subject. The same way the environment can absorb only so much pollution, his consciousness could absorb only so much information about all these new environmental catastrophes. After all, consciousness is a stream, and you can pollute it the same way you can pollute a river. Harry noticed that just to hear Helen mention the "becquerels" contained in every wild mushroom and every trout—simmered or fried—was enough to pollute his mind and drive him wild.

Once, Helen asked Inez how she handled that with the children, especially the baby. The stuff was even in mother's milk. "Oh," said Inez, "there's nothing you can do. You just get on with it." Though this wasn't an answer, it did have a kind of folksy wisdom to it. And since Inez was a doctor, what she said was rather comforting, even to Helen. If Inez and her baby didn't dissolve in the radioactive rain, then maybe things actually would go on. Harry was taken with the incomparable way Inez said the word "becquerel." Not a trace of hysteria. It bubbled up like freshly opened mineral water.

Sometimes Harry invited some of his colleagues to the Eifel for the weekend. There actually were a few people who, in their own congenial way, had had enough of the Foreign Office. It was too bad Hennersdorff wasn't alive anymore. One time, Harry brought the chinless Count Waldburg to the house. Fritz and Harry found him entertaining. Rita was delighted to find that he played the piano quite well. Helen and Inez agreed that Waldburg was a nice enough fellow, but unfortunately his squawking got on their nerves.

Another time, Harry's colleague Willfort came for a visit. Harry knew him from the time they were at the diplomatic training center together. Willfort had been in Jakarta, and now he worked in the office responsible for cultural policy abroad. All anyone was interested in was the shit, said Willfort. Good ideas didn't stand a chance. He drank like a fish, told good-humored stories about his miserable work in Bonn, and raved about the years he'd spent in Indonesia. He kept telling Rita: "I'm going to pay court to you, I really am." Willfort knew all about French philosophy. Helen could talk with him about postmodernism, a subject nobody else in the house had the slightest interest in. Harry had been refusing for years to pay any attention to all these trendy ideas. You'd just figured out what it was all about when the trend had passed, he said. He'd also let all the bunk about structuralism go right past him in the early seventies—and what do you know: now no one even knew what structuralism had been about. The same thing would happen to postmodernism. Naturally, Harry secretly read every essay on postmodernism that appeared in the papers. After all, you couldn't be ignorant on the subject! Ignorance had to be feigned.

Helen thought Willfort looked like a British colonial officer and told him so to his face. Harry was startled, because he found the remark tactless. After all, who wants to look like a colonial officer. But Willfort was delighted. She could picture him in a pith helmet, said Helen. Harry had never heard Helen talk to a man this way before. He tried to figure out how he'd feel if Helen were to have an affair with Willfort. The idea made him uneasy. In any case, he wouldn't let on. Not at all. There's nothing more ridiculous than a man who doesn't accord his women the same rights he claims for himself.

Helen saw to it that Willfort was invited more often. Every time he came, he clicked his heels and greeted them as Colonel Willfort. One time Helen said: "You should shave off your mustache, it doesn't suit the image of a colonel. It turns you into a sergeant!" The next time Willfort came, it was without his mustache.

The house in the Eifel improved their lives considerably. Helen always had the best ideas. But she didn't always have the best taste, thought Harry. Instead of those wonderful antelope leather pants from Düsseldorf, she wore billowing skirts and baggy pants. "If you love me," said Harry, "at least take out those awful shoulder pads." Helen often stayed alone in the Eifel during the week, working on her translations. Or did she meet Willfort there? The devil only knew. She was translating a cultural history of the coiffure from French into German. There'd been a cultural history of every niggling thing lately. By now, someone had probably written a cultural history of the fart. Apparently, cultural historians couldn't come up with anything better. There was a cultural history of the light bulb, of the locomotive, of fragrances, and of odors. "It's all a bunch of smart-ass nonsense," said Harry, who knew every title from the hours he spent reading the newspaper. Strangely enough, Helen didn't contradict him. All she said was that she'd rather earn her money with nonsense like that than to look on and do nothing—like a diplomat—while the world was destroyed by the arms trade. Harry asked her if someone had written a cultural history of the pith helmet yet. No, not that she knew of, she said, but she understood that someone was working on a cultural history of trousers. Maybe it would have a chapter on black leather pants; that might be of interest to Harry.

Sometimes Rita spent the night in Cologne. Supposedly with a friend from the conservatory. When Harry found himself alone in the apartment in Bonn, he'd turn up the jazz from the good old days when jazz didn't dilly-dally around but wailed with dignity. Once in a while he'd take out his trumpet and play a little, at least till the Turk down-stairs started banging on the ceiling. Or he'd listen to Aretha Franklin and Tina Turner belt out their songs from the late sixties: "You're no good, heartbreaker, you're a liar and a cheat." And although this was the kind of thing a teenager does, it made him feel completely grown up. At least more grown up than he did at the office or the embassy, where he did self-important but childish things.

They almost always spent the weekends together at the house in the Eifel. Not much went on. Inez's baby started to walk. Otherwise time stood more or less still.

At the beginning of September, though, the people in Protocol began to reel. That most bourgeois of all commu-nists, the head of East Germany, was coming on a state visit. Ridiculous old goat. It was more amusing to listen to the oaths being sworn by that totally flipped-out premier of Schleswig-Holstein. He swore he hadn't spied on his politi-cal opponent, but he got caught deeper and deeper in his lies, committed perjury. You weren't offered a show like that every day. Finally they found the fellow dead as a doornail in a hotel bathtub in Geneva. Duckwitz loved it. The wind-bags at the Foreign Office and everywhere else in Bonn, in every newspaper in the whole stupid republic, could talk about nothing but the decline of political culture. The affair had caused immense harm. It could hardly be rectified. And there were actually dozens of colleagues sitting on the edge of their seats, shaking their heads about the quagmire that had been revealed and about the press, which had not balked even at taking pictures of the premier's body in the bathtub. "I beg your pardon!" said Duckwitz. "We need a good show like this more often!" It's great when the quagmire finally comes to light and reinforces the lessons of history we keep forgetting. It doesn't make any difference whether its political bribery, tax evasion, or prying into someone's private affairs—when the dirty tricks come to light, it's just one more piece of precious evidence that politics is the dirtiest business of all.

•   •   •

Once, they took pictures at the Foreign Office, on the stairs leading down to the Rhine. Trees, a balustrade. It was a downright stage, with the Rhine flowing decoratively in the background. Rita, Harry, and Helen. "What's all this nonsense for?" asked Helen. Harry thought that, every few years, you had a right to take some photos to remember yourselves by. He'd asked Helen to wear something that didn't have shoulder pads—that is, unless she wanted to get mad later at how ridiculous she'd looked in 1987. Rita said it would be easier to ask someone to take the picture than to go through the whole business with a tripod and a timer. Harry answered: "I know you inscrutable Orientals don't have any inhibitions." As a European, doing something like that was embarrassing. Photography is a form of self-gratification, and you don't ask anyone else to take part. Besides, he looked even more uncomfortable in pictures someone else had taken. Harry walked back and forth, placed Helen here and Rita there, and himself in every conceivable position in between. Helen soon lost her patience, stuck out her tongue, and then the film was all used up.

Some of the pictures were pretty good; even Helen had to admit that. For weeks, they left them lying around at the house in the Eifel, showed them to all their guests. Fritz laughed, and Colonel Willfort said it was pure Chekhov. The only thing that could have intensified the sense of melancholy would have been himself in the role of the officer from the big wide world. "And one more thing, dear

Duckwitz—you should by all means have worn a light-colored suit."

13 *How Harry von Duckwitz makes an effort to see something positive in fidelity and gets all tangled up in hypocrisy. In addition to what happens when he and Inez go out for a bratwurst, and a few thoughts on AIDS and tight skirts.*

"Who'll go for a walk with me?" Harry asked after lunch, for appearances' sake. As usual, Helen had disappeared into her room to work on a translation. Fritz yawned the way he always did and said he wanted to take a nap. He missed Rita's piano playing, he added. Rita was on a concert tour in Holland. "Today she's playing in Rotterdam," said Harry. Helen had flown from Rotterdam when she came to Quito. She was still with them. It gave Harry a start; it had been four years now. Rita was accompanying a Korean tenor on the piano. Schubert songs. "That's great," said Inez, who was also yawning. But she did think it would be sensible to get a little exercise, so she said she'd go with Harry for her own good. Harry asked himself again whether this lack of emotion was real, or whether she was pretending in order to avoid suspicion. But probably his asking whether anyone wanted to go for a walk sounded like indifference to Inez, too, even if he'd been itching for hours to be alone with her. "Go on, you two," said Fritz, as if he knew everything. He couldn't possibly know. As soon as they were beyond the curve in the road and no one could see them from the house, Harry tried to pull Inez to him. She seemed distant and tense. It was still too soon.

Inez said, as she so often did, that it was hard to bear. She kept asking herself whether the whole thing was worth it. Harry begged her not to ask questions like that. A love affair is always worth it, no matter how high the price.

The price was secretiveness, and that's what was causing problems for Inez. Harry would say: "Fritz is my brother!" Openness is fine, but you can't openly have an affair with your own brother's girlfriend. That would be going too far. That would be distasteful. If the affair couldn't be avoided, at least it had to be kept secret.

Inez sighed as the same old subject came up again. She saw things differently, but she didn't have a solution either.

The problem wasn't just his brother, Fritz. Harry didn't want anything to disturb his tranquil existence with Rita and Helen, either. If there was one thing that spoke against an affair, it was this. Rita would hardly feel disturbed at all, thought Harry, but Helen would consider it absolutely intolerable. She would drive him crazy every morning at breakfast with her reproaches. It would torment her, but she'd say it didn't bother her at all, that it was none of her business. Sorry, it was just no way to treat her; it was disgusting the way Harry couldn't get his fill. Harry wanted to spare himself and Helen this animosity, and Rita shouldn't be put in the position of the betrayed wife. People who've been betrayed lie when they get angry. They either exaggerate, or they play down how much it hurts. By keeping it a secret, Harry thought he was preventing the flood of mutual lies that would wash over all of them if the sweet secret became public. The moment of its disclosure would have something of the confession about it; but there was nothing to confess. A love affair is not a crime, and therefore it follows that it doesn't have to be confessed.

As they always did when they were alone together, Harry and Inez talked of nothing but the problems of their relationship. The more hopeless and complicated it seemed, the more impassioned Harry's defense. Finally, he seemed to have placated Inez, and she relaxed.

It grew dark and they turned back. Here was the barn where they did it the first time. Standing up. Harry had pulled up Inez's skirt. It was tight and didn't slide easily over her hips. "That's not a skirt, that's a foreskin," said Harry, though not very knowledgably since he was circumcised. "Do you think that's what it's like if you have a phimosis?" Inez, the physician, interrupted her unexpectedly wild necking and laughed out loud. Before that, Harry had been crazy about her; from that moment on, he was in love.

"How long has it been?" he asked her now.

"Almost a year," she said. They'd grown more refined. They didn't do it standing up anymore. Unfortunately. But they still talked the same way. Doing it. It wasn't exactly an unusual choice of words, but it had become their own. Where should we do it? When can we do it again? And then the crowning touch: Do it with me!

It wasn't easy, doing it. There wasn't enough time, there wasn't a place. Inez was not only close to Harry's brother in some unfathomable way, she had three children by a former husband. Two of the children went to school, but there was also this little squirt of a latecomer. It was difficult to do it at Harry's. It was silly to rent a hotel room in your own town, and it would be in poor taste to take Inez along as an appendage on a business trip. But it was just as tasteless to do the opposite: go to some medical conference with Inez and play escort. Harry had felt like an obedient dog the one time he did. They'd tried everything, rejected everything.

And here they were again, talking about how beautiful and how difficult their story was, and again Inez used the word "relationship." Again, Harry suffered as he heard it. Harry had asked Inez to avoid this slickest of all words, but on that score Inez was incorrigible. She's right, thought Harry, you don't solve the problem by avoiding one stupid word. Besides, there were more and more people who made fun of the lingo used in group therapy. In fact, mocking the lingo was almost as much of a cliché as the lingo itself.

"Our relationship is very stressful for me," said Inez, and Harry swallowed even this second trendy word patiently and lovingly.

The fact that Inez came from Bavaria, where Harry had grown up, made her seem even more familiar to him. Her last name was Miller; he liked that. He liked writing it on envelopes. Inez Miller—an "i" looks so much better than a "ü".

Although they were walking slowly, they were rapidly approaching the house. All of Inez's rigidity had disappeared. It had taken two hours, the way it always did. They could have used another two hours.

Before they came within sight of the house, at the same place where Harry had tried without any luck to embrace Inez when they left, they fell into each other's arms. Harry was surprised, just as he always was, at how wildly Inez would suddenly kiss and pant, once her reservations had been overcome. "Just look, just feel how alive it makes us," said Harry. "Why did we spend two hours talking about all the complications—we should have spent those two hours doing it!"

Inez didn't say anything, and Harry asked himself whether her silence meant yes or no. He was irritated he'd said anything at all instead of simply pulling up that foreskin of a skirt that she was wearing again today and doing it on the spot, right there on the path no one else would walk along. I'm not brazen enough, he thought, and then they were home. But at least the embers had been stirred up a bit.

Fritz was reading the newspaper, and Helen had put water on for tea. "You were gone a long time," said Fritz, playing the distrustful husband. Harry forced himself to smile. It was revolting the way Fritz was always acting as if there something going on between Harry and Inez, especially since there really was. It was a pain, because it made you feel doubly deceitful. But it was also a relief since you could hide the real deeds behind playful confessions. The falsehood took on an ironic cast, and that way it didn't carry so much weight, thought Harry.

Any scruples they could possibly have were nipped in the bud by the thought of how rarely he and Inez had a chance to splurge for a night. They could manage it only every four to six weeks. Inez's children had to be taken care of and they had to be healthy, that was the crux of the problem. Several of their little trysts had been called off because one of them had suddenly come down sick. And then Fritz and Inez couldn't have any plans, because as a friend of longer standing, Fritz's rights went back further than Harry's. The best time was when Fritz was in a creative phase and needed peace and quiet. That's when Inez felt most free. Inez's ex-husband wasn't a threat, although it sometimes happened that Inez had all her healthy children tucked safely away with school friends and the apartment was finally free for a big romp, and he absolutely had to speak to her. He had to talk to her about a joint tax return from the years they were married; some deadline had passed. And then, of course, there were the emergency calls from the hospital.

There were fewer obstacles on Harry's side. He only needed to tell Helen and Rita that he had to go away on business. As far as work was concerned, the slightest call from Inez took precedence over anything he was doing. "My job is ideal for lovers," Harry had once told Inez. Just think, if he'd been a doctor or a lawyer, they'd never be able to get together—either his practice or his law office would have gone bankrupt.

After days of discussing when they could get together, after all the commotion, they'd have one of those rare opportunities when they could consummate what in a divorce proceeding might be called a "breach of marriage." It had been years since Harry worked as a lawyer. He had only vague and negative memories of his divorce cases. He'd never want a divorce from Rita. No separation from Helen, no divorce from Rita, and certainly no end to his relationship with Inez. It would be barbaric to leave one woman because of another. No leaving, no being left, no renunciation, no abnegation. It would be miserable without Rita, without Helen, without Inez. It would be pretty hard to take Rita or Helen alone; it was better with the two of them together, but it didn't exactly mean there was twice the passion. The resulting hunger could be stilled with Inez—or not, since there was so little opportunity.

Inez and Harry had made an agreement in order to keep from putting too much of a strain on their frenzy: she wouldn't tell him anything about her relations with Fritz, and Harry didn't need to reveal anything about his life with Rita and Helen. Inez had made the suggestion, and Harry agreed to it immediately because he agreed with everything Inez suggested. Still, nothing could have interested him more than the relationship between Inez and his brother, Fritz. It was absolutely baffling. It would have interested Helen, too. And he would have enjoyed talking about this odd arrangement with Rita and Helen.

Harry had not thought for one second about leaving Rita and Helen for Inez. At least not seriously. Sometimes, when the reprehensible idea forced itself on his thoughts, he'd give in to it for a while: a break so clean it wouldn't leave a trace of unhappiness behind with Rita or Helen or Fritz. Everyone would be happy with the solution, and off he'd go with Inez to a new life. London, Madrid, Palermo— it didn't matter where. They'd do it at least three hours a day. Panting, gasping, writhing, romping. Burying their noses in each other's hair, which Inez liked—and not wasting a thought on Helen, who couldn't stand it. Bringing Inez's kids Beatles records, both winning hearts and laying the basis for a decent taste in music in the little brats' souls. It was reassuring that the records were still available after twenty years. And then every year the whole clan would have a reunion at which they would enthusiastically agree that it had been the right thing to do: Rita would get herself a terrific singer, Helen a philosophy professor who didn't like to bury his nose in her hair, and Fritz a muse who was so good-looking that Harry would begin to get restless again. That dream would last about ten minutes.

The other solution Harry dreamed of was that Fritz got himself a new muse, Inez moved into the house in the Eifel—which was big enough for the children—and Rita taught them to play the piano. But Helen and Inez together would never work. Not even in Harry's imagination. Even Harry wouldn't have known how, under the same roof, to balance his uncontrolled craving for Inez with his well-tempered affection for Rita and Helen. There was no other solution than for things to stay the way they were.

•   •   •

In the kitchen, the water was starting to boil. Helen looked at Harry and said without any warning: "The future is in fidelity."

"That's interesting," said Harry, rather startled. He asked whether Helen had found this wisdom in the work of some fashionable French philosopher whose latest book on cultural history she was translating. No, Helen said with pleasure, she'd read it in a women's magazine. She'd taken the liberty of reading the women's magazine Inez had brought along. Helen said "women's magazine" as scornfully as she could. Or was Harry imagining things?

Helen asked if Harry could make the tea. After all, she was the one who put on the water. This might have been a

snide remark, too, but he couldn't really protest. Harry
didn't like to leave the room at times like this. He wouldn't
have put it past Helen to unleash, in his absence, some kind
of pointed remarks in Inez's direction. Though Helen
couldn't really know anything about this business.

As Harry came back into the living room, he heard
Helen say: "For most people, there's just too much stress in
being unfaithful."

It wasn't the first time Harry had the feeling Helen
could read people's thoughts. Thoughts were in the air, why
shouldn't you be able to read them? But now he was really
annoyed. It sounded as if Helen had listened in on the
conversation they'd had on their walk.

"What do you mean, stress?" asked Harry. He didn't
want to leave unanswered the assertion she'd snatched from
that women's magazine. After all, it just happened to be
Inez's opinion, too. You do get something out of it, he said.

Oh? And how would you know? asked Helen. She
didn't believe a word Harry said. In her opinion he was only
verbally unfaithful, he confused his fantasies with reality; he
had nothing to contribute.

Harry looked over at Inez as deadpan as he could. She
avoided his glance. You could see that she felt dishonest. At
least Harry thought you could see that. The passion that had
just been rekindled had gone to the devil for sure. It wasn't
good for all of them to meet here in the Eifel. But it was
unavoidable. Harry couldn't forbid his brother to come to
the house or ask him to come without Inez. Especially since
he wanted nothing so much as to see her. He'd rather see
her under these conditions than not at all. After all, they
weren't living in the nineteenth century. You no longer shot
yourself if you were in love with another woman, nor did
you leave the country. Whatever you do, don't give her up!
You just have to organize things, coordinate, make appointments, cancel them, rearrange them. That's how to make

room for a lover on the side. It's exhausting and often enough so nerve-wracking and humiliating that he and Inez sometimes felt more relieved by a postponed date than by one they could keep. They both admitted that they found the delay refreshing. They would laugh, and agree that while postponement wasn't as good as being together, it was a nice substitute. You just couldn't give up. I don't have anything against abortion, Harry had said to Inez, but I am very much against aborted love affairs. Inez liked that. Her eyes flashed when he said things like that.

One of the unpleasant consequences of their secret infidelity, thought Harry, was that they were accused of being faithful. They couldn't talk about the take. They were like thieves who can rummage through their stolen treasures from time to time but can never show them to anyone. A perfect robbery, and you have to suffer the accusation of being merely a would-be thief.

There were all kinds of disadvantages to being unfaithful, but it was worth it anyway. It's worth it, it's worth it, it's worth it, Harry kept telling himself. It makes the soul grow. After all, life is all about gathering experience.

Since he began his affair with Inez, he again liked being with Helen. He could take her billowy skirts and baggy pants better if he could pull up Inez's foreskin of a skirt from time to time.

Inez was defiantly leafing through the magazine Helen had referred to so scornfully before. Then she began reading out loud: "One of the reasons for the trend toward the new fidelity is to be found in the fear of AIDS."

"New fidelity!" Harry repeated derisively. If there was anything he couldn't stand, it was this kind of talk about trends. What drivel. Relationships were evidently supposed to be clean and healthy, as clean as the environment. Infidelity as erotic pollution, that's where this new trend was leading.

Helen wanted to know how long Harry had been using the word "relationships." The word "trend" is even worse, said Harry loudly; he couldn't stand the word "trend" anymore, or the word "new," and least of all the word "fidelity." He couldn't stand the word "AIDS" anymore, either. They'd fought for years for sexual freedom, he said angrily, and now someone comes up with this damned new fidelity!

Helen laughed. "Fought! Did you all hear that? Harry *fought* for sexual freedom!"

Harry remembered the German title of a film: *Ich kämpfe um dich,* I'll fight for you! He didn't know if he'd seen it, didn't know who directed it or what it was about. Didn't remember a thing. But what a title: *I'll Fight for You!* Just as kitschy as it was true. I'll fight for Inez, he thought, I'll fight for this love of Inez.

"AIDS really is a problem," said Fritz. Harry thought the remark a little flat-footed for a poet, and he said so. Besides, AIDS is the worst reason to be faithful, said Harry. Even the anti-AIDS ads on television recognized that. They weren't pushing monogamy, after all, just the use of Trojans. "I grew up with condoms," said Harry. Since the early sixties, he hadn't left the house without a condom. A baby would have been just as fatal to him as AIDS. He'd carried the same condom in his wallet for five years before he finally had a chance to use the trusty piece, at the age of twenty. It didn't bother him to run around with condoms in his jacket pocket. You just had to be careful not to play around with the little plastic package when you went out to get a bratwurst. In your horny preoccupation, you might confuse it with the mustard, and not every woman would appreciate the unintentional symbolism of the still-life you'd create by squeezing it onto your plate next to your sausage.

It had happened to Harry the last time he left the Foreign Office and drove to Cologne to have dinner with Inez. She had to be back in the operating room in half an hour, so they only had time to grab a bratwurst at a stand. Harry had driven back home, cursing the need for secrecy that kept him from amusing Helen with the story of his misadventure. She would appreciate a good joke like that. But you couldn't try to get a dirty laugh out of Helen over something that had provoked a dirty laugh from Inez just a few hours earlier. That would be a betrayal. Harry enjoyed telling Helen the story now, in this anonymous way, though she didn't seem to find it very funny. Inez, on the other hand, cast him a glance in which Harry read respect for his nerve in telling it.

"It isn't the danger of AIDS that speaks for fidelity," said Harry. "It's the non-fatal but ominous danger of doubling." Harry paused for effect. To his disappointment, no one asked what he meant by the "danger of doubling." The danger of doubling, he explained anyway, consists of the possibility that the unfaithful person could get into similar situations with various partners. That has to be avoided, and avoiding it is one of the painful side effects of infidelity. "Assume that I'm having an affair with Inez," said Harry.

"I'm sure you'd like to," said Helen, asking if Harry hadn't noticed that Inez wasn't interested in men like him.

"Just assume it's the case nevertheless," said Harry. Inez gave him a crooked smile.

"If I were," said Harry, "I'd probably like to go see Visconti's *Ossessione* with her. And she'd like to go with me. However, I'd also like to go with you, Helen. The only thing is, it would be in poor taste to go with one and then the other. This would represent a more unforgiveable violation of intimacy than any amount of screwing. Or suppose I'm sitting at an Italian restaurant with Helen, eating appetizers. And I find that the artichoke hearts squeak when I bite into them. And I ask Helen if they do the same thing in her mouth. Two days later I'm sitting there with Inez, eating artichoke hearts. They still squeak.

It's not very important, but I want to say something about it to Inez and ask her what I asked Helen, namely, if they do the same thing in her mouth. But I can't do that. It would be a breach of style. Or suppose I'm lying in bed with Inez. We've done it together. While we're resting up for another go at it, I feel like telling her what I read in the news-paper—that sales of men's pyjamas have declined by 80 percent over the past few years. The probable reason is not that more and more men are sleeping in the buff, but that more and more of them are sleeping in their jogging suits. I'd also like to have a good laugh over it with Helen while we're resting up for another go. But I can't do that. This sort of doubling would be mean to both of you. In conclu-sion," said Harry, resting his case, "not only the faithful abstain, the faithless must also abstain, if they have any character."

"Be serious for once!" said Helen.

"Oh, come on," Harry replied. "Can anyone take the subject of fidelity seriously anymore? I'm sorry, but when I hear the word fidelity, what occurs to me is half-witted and German—oaths, Wagnerian pap, and Nibelung nonsense. Fidelity comes in handy for church and state because it keeps the people in line. Fidelity is dull, and sticky, and all botched up. It's only conceivable as a perversion of some-thing else. Maybe the oath of fidelity is the most extreme form of masochism. It may be great for those who like it. Subjecting yourself to an archaic code of behavior may have its appeal, the same way chains and self-flagellation appeal to some people." Harry knelt down: "Come, beautiful Helen, command me to be faithful so that I can put myself obedi-ently in chains and not have to pant over the unattainable Inez anymore. Yes, there could be something to that," said Harry.

"You idiot!" said Inez.

"Cut it out!" said Helen angrily. Harry was not only a

rotten diplomat, he'd been a rotten lawyer, and that's probably why he'd had the idea of changing over to the Foreign Office. Was he crazy? Attacking fidelity because of its Christian background was the most primitive thing she'd ever heard. After all, you don't go around killing people just because the church considers killing a sin. Of course it isn't about AIDS, or about Christian morality; no one in his right mind is interested in that anymore. The joke is that everyone's sleeping with everyone else and no one has anything against being unfaithful anymore. Infidelity is constantly being practiced and propagated. It's the most normal and bourgeois thing there is. If Harry's heart were still in the right place, he'd have to plead the case for fidelity!

Maybe Helen's right, thought Harry. She'd been right back then about free love. What was right then might be wrong today. Helen always had a good nose for the changes society needed to make.

Harry suddenly remembered a television talk show he'd watched recently in his untiring consumption of the media. He hadn't told Helen or Inez anything about it. First, because he was embarrassed, at the age of 40, to have watched a show for teenagers—live, hip, everyone on a first-name basis, no one over 23. Second, because he again sensed the danger of doubling: he wouldn't have known to which one of them he should have confessed watching this terrible show, Helen or Inez. And third, because one of the subjects they discussed on the show was fidelity, and the biggest jerk of them all was this slick fellow who breezily propagated what Harry had just espoused: he said he was happily married, but he made love to whomever he pleased; he thought this was his right, and his wife felt the same way. His marriage wasn't threatened by it, said this New Age Don Juan. Harry could have boxed his ears. The unfeeling know-it-all. The man's soul was the dispassionate result of genetic engineering. Harry swore that he would never again plead the cause of open marriage. It's better to maintain you're faithful, especially when you aren't. Big fat lies are a thousand times better than all this sick talk about openness that comes out of some psychological test tube.

One girl on the show actually took the view that she would preserve her virginity for marriage. No premarital sex. Her view was a relic of the Middle Ages passed on in the fifties through religious instruction at school. And here it was being spouted in 1988 by a twenty-year-old. The incredible thing was, the girl wasn't full of Catholic inhibitions or covered with pimples—she was sassy, and her huge eyes sparkled promisingly. To his horror, Harry had been able to imagine being faithful to a gentle, beautiful, old-fashioned creature like this the rest of his life. After the show, he'd crawled repentantly into Helen's bed and curled up against her so closely that she had woken up and asked: "What's gotten into you?"

"Okay," Harry said now, "I'll play the role of public defender of fidelity. It's high time we improve the social standing of fidelity. The defenders of fidelity are members of an ostracized, or at least ridiculed minority. They deserve our protection. The proponents of infidelity, on the other hand, enjoy broad respect. Nowadays, any idiot can allow himself to be unfaithful. Every spaced-out psychologist, every gussied up or run-down sex counsellor says the unfaithful are right, and this fact alone should make us stop and wonder if fidelity isn't at least the more tasteful point of view."

"Bravo!" said Helen.

Fritz said: "Why don't you ever have any cookies to go with the tea?"

Harry cast an apologetic glance at Inez before continuing: "The faithless have no class, they're foolish characters from some light comedy or operetta, they're the customers at sex shops. Society gives its approval to the uninhibited activities of these characters and regards their screwing around as a form of self-realization. They make the proponents of fidelity look like inhibited nincompoops. There are no moral reservations about infidelity anymore. But there are reservations based on questions of good taste. The practice of infidelity is not to be rejected because of the danger of illegitimate children or AIDS, nor because it involves too much stress and too many complications. The essential place of stress in our lives has been recognized for some time now, and complications are what make us grow. Infidelity is to be rejected because it enjoys the silent complicity of an unsound society. All the discussions about self-realization are just empty phrases. What is truly original is faithfulness, because it is so rare. Fidelity is an admirable goal. Infidelity is a matter of course."

Harry rose and lay his hand on Helen's knee: "Your Honor, when I touch a person I've known well for years, it doesn't cause the same turmoil as touching someone I don't know as well." Harry clasped Inez's slender knee and found his hand too fleshy. "Erotic tension," he said courageously, "does not necessarily stem from a person but from the degree of that person's unfamiliarity. Such an injustice must not be furthered by praising infidelity. If infidelity cannot be avoided, it should not be openly promoted, but skillfully concealed."

"A little skimpy," said Helen. "Is that all?"

"No," said Harry, "that's not all, but it's time for a recess."

Recess, he remembered, was essential in the midst of court proceedings. You really needed a little peace. The peacefulness of a faithful marriage, however, was an awful idea. If all you do is long for other women but can never run after them, you never find out how prickly the ones you dream about really are. Inez was prickly, too. Thank God. It made it much easier to live with Helen.

Tomorrow he'd call Inez and suggest they take a little break to recuperate. That was the only solution. To rest up a little. They shouldn't see each other for a couple of months. Contact forbidden. But what if Inez acquiesced too readily? It would be just like her.

After Inez and Fritz had gone, Harry picked up the women's magazine Inez had left behind. He wanted to find out more about this trend toward a new fidelity. Helen sat down next to him on the sofa, took the magazine out of his hand, and said: "Don't think for a minute that you can take a rest now."

14 *The effect of the historic events of 1989/90 on the everyday routine of the Foreign Office and on the strenuous labors of its diplomats. How Duckwitz does not look forward at all to his next assignment abroad, and what the Foreign Minister says while airborne. On false advertising from the left and the right, and on the nature of politics. As well as some thoughts on the origins of love and how many ways a one-syllable word can be pronounced.*

"Well?!"

All of a sudden there was this new greeting, drawn out and arch as a question mark. You'd be crossing the parking lot, standing in an elevator, walking through the lobby, and some colleague would call out: "Well?!" In the cafeteria, too. Before you could even sit down, somebody was saying: "Well?!"

"What is all this nonsense?" asked Duckwitz. He wanted to know if the new "Well?!" was peculiar to the Foreign Office or a new fad all over Bonn. He went to the Postal Ministry cafeteria next door. They were saying it there, too, though that could have been the influence of the dozens of people from the Foreign Office who ate there because the Postal Ministry cafeteria was supposedly better than their own.

It took a while for Duckwitz to figure out what they meant. In May of 1989, the Hungarians had cut through the barbed wire at the Austrian border without so much as a by-your-leave. It was the beginning of European communism's bankruptcy proceedings. Things happened so fast that just six months later, when the Berlin Wall fell, the process was as good as complete. The most nimble leftists immediately began to act as if they had known it all along, which they may have, but they hadn't exactly said it or written it very clearly. Others hesitated, not wanting to come around too quickly. It wasn't easy for them to give up the schizo-phrenia they'd grown fond of over a period of decades. It had, after all, allowed them to pick on both political systems without the slightest hesitation. Liberal newspapers featured heated debates about whether communism could be saved, whether it should be saved, or whether its demise should be acknowledged without a tear. Conservative columnists, on the other hand, commented with obvious pleasure on the decline of an ideology they had always considered hair-raisingly unrealistic.

It was during the months when the East was opening up that the word "Well?!" made the rounds at the Foreign Office in Bonn, and most likely at the embassies abroad. It probably also circulated in every official office, editor's office, school, and factory—"Well?!" It was an exclamation, a comment, and a rhetorical question all rolled into one.

Rightists in particular enjoyed throwing it at leftists. That is, the more conservative staff members at the Foreign Office said it to the less conservative ones—there could scarcely be any talk of right and left at the Foreign Office. "Well?!" It was the discreet cry of a winner not yet sure of his victory. There was a touch of gloating in it, a certain sense of triumph: Well, what do you have to say now? Well?! It looks like you bet on the wrong horse! Well?! You look pretty foolish! Well?! Now I guess the cat's got a good hold of your tongue!

When two of the more conservative diplomats ran into each other, the emphasis was different. The exclamation was shorter, less arch: "Well!" A brief confirmation. An exclama-tion marks a victory. "Well!" We certainly showed them! And then there was the unemphatic, almost shy "Well" of the losers. With two question marks: "Well??" What are we going to do now? During that time, in the summer of 1989,

Duckwitz had come to know his colleague Knesebeck a little
better. "Well??" Knesebeck had said to him one day as they
were waiting to use the photocopier. Duckwitz had always
taken Knesebeck for an ultraconservative because he wore
such ultraconservative collars and had such ultraconservative
knots in his ties. Wrong. The collapse of communism led to
another revelation: Knesebeck was a dyed-in-the-wool Social
Democrat. Left wing. The ruling order had never enjoyed
his approbation. He'd always favored a just distribution of
wealth and was against the exploitation of the Third World.
His views had never caused a stir—after all, who isn't in
favor of a just distribution of wealth and against the exploitation of the Third World?

From the beginning, Duckwitz's reputation at the
Foreign Office was that of a leftist, a red baron. They
thought his unconventional talk was leftist. They had given
him a label that he, as a non-reader of Marx and Engels,
did not really deserve. At least, he felt, not from an
ideological point of view. Still, he wore the label gladly. The
false labeling appealed to him.

The events of that summer and fall, constantly extolled
as historic, gave Duckwitz another opportunity to mock
German ways and freshen up his image. Now that being a
leftist was growing increasingly unpopular, being one gave
him special pleasure. Even as a kid, he'd felt a certain
satisfaction in losing at dice and cards. Whether it was at
the copying machine or in the cafeteria, whether he ran into
someone by chance or at a reception: when he met people
who showed even a spark of nationalist feeling in face of the
political developments in Germany, he gave them a dig
wherever he could.

It seemed as if the unification of Germany was
unavoidable. You couldn't even exclude the possibility that it
was the lesser of two evils. But it was far from being a cause
for joy. At a morning meeting, someone solemnly reported

on one of the Foreign Minister's great feats, something they'd all heard on television the night before. His negotiating skills had secured the free exit of droves of East Germans. Some of the people at the meeting began to feel very grand. For just a moment, diplomacy appeared to have a higher meaning. Then there was muffled laughter from somewhere near Duckwitz. He had whispered to his neighbors that political intercourse between the two German states was at the least a violation of the rules of the Kama-sutra. Good lovers, he said, no matter how strong the urge, take time for foreplay. "This is just pitiful," said Duckwitz. "They're all suffering from *ejaculatio praecox.*"

Colleagues who thought you shouldn't make jokes about something as sacred as the German nation tried to rise above Harry's leftist indiscretions by ignoring them. And every time another leftist politician was swept away and leftist illusions crumbled a little more—about once a week— they took their revenge by calling out the word of the season with particularly snide satisfaction: "Well?!" As if he had ever had any illusions. As if he had ever put his money on communism.

Knesebeck didn't hide the fact that he thought Duckwitz's polemics weren't to be taken seriously. But he was evidently of the opinion that true and not quite so true leftists had to stick together. He may also have been affected by the fact that Duckwitz was being subjected to more scorn from the right than he deserved. However, not even the critical situation of the political left brought Knesebeck and Duckwitz any closer, especially since Duckwitz didn't find the situation critical at all. The collapse of communism was, as he put it, a pleasurable affair, as is almost any collapse. As a voyeur, he was getting his money's worth. Knesebeck thought this was both frivolous and cynical. He was afraid that German nationalism would come welling up again and that capitalism would dig in even more brutally than before. "It will attack without mercy!" said Knesebeck.

"Please!" said Duckwitz. "Restrain yourself!" He'd heard that Knesebeck was from a wealthy family. Typical. Still, you could hardly hold that against him. So Duckwitz said: "You're the last living example of that dying breed, the drawing-room leftist!"

"If ever there was a drawing-room leftist, it's you!" said Knesebeck. Raising his voice, Duckwitz replied: "Me? A drawing-room leftist? Say that again and I'll join the last remaining Marxist party on the spot!"

In the meantime, the conservatives' understandable sense of triumph had grown a little more subdued. Soon it was submerged beneath the zealousness that dominated the work of the Foreign Office. Like civil servants everywhere, the staff always complained about the amount of work it had, or pretended to have. Suddenly, with the preparations for the union of the Federal Republic of Germany and the German Democratic Republic, there really was something to do. They were continually having to work something up for the tireless Foreign Minister. And they had to make it clear to all 160 countries with which West Germany maintained diplomatic relations that the new Germany would be the most peace-loving, most harmless country in the world. Colleagues from the political affairs division spoke wearily of their 13- to 14-hour workdays. Preparing for German unification was a back-breaking job! And then there was the Europe 1992 Project. Work, work, work! The people in the office of East European Affairs were talking about 16-, even 17-hour days! The news reached Bonn from every corner— from Brussels, Geneva, and New York: Hard labor is the order of the day. "Once more, with feeling!" added a counselor to the European mission in Strasbourg.

It was as if all the members of the diplomatic service— whether they were members of the senior, higher, clerical, or

inferior service—were teaming up to lay to rest the myth of
the diplomat's leisurely life, to impress upon each other the
recognition that their job was just as hard as that of
businessmen. But the funny thing was, business executives
had long since stopped boasting. It was no longer the in
thing to do. In the mid-eighties, you could still make an
impression on people by talking about your 100-hour work
week. In the meantime, the toughest of the top executives
realized that it made them sound a little dim, as if they
could never get their work done. So now they were boasting
about their leisure time. Having time for women and for
sports was what defined the successful man now. The
Foreign Office was a couple of years behind. Again. They
had also been years behind in computerizing. From time to
time, the fact that they hobbled along behind the latest
trends and the newest developments in technology almost
made the Foreign Office appealing to Duckwitz.

"Of all the industrialized countries in the world, we
have the smallest but most efficient Foreign Office," he had
said recently. His comment had left him open to the scorn
of the others at the lunch table. When everyone else was
talking about unification and nothing but unification, about
the currency union, the date of admission of the German
Democratic Republic, the date for the first all-German elections, when the question of whether Bonn or Berlin should
be the capital, the only thing you heard about Protocol was
that it had purchased a new red carpet in July.

Duckwitz had been on call in the Press Office at the
time. With a certain pleasure, he had prepared a press
release concerning the purchase of a length of coconut
matting 36 meters long by 2.44 meters wide, 88 square
meters overall. What does a thing like that cost? A laughable 5000 marks. The old carpet had lasted 30 years, and
was walked on by Adenauer and de Gaulle, Kennedy and
Mother Teresa.

State receptions and parades were the height of the ridiculous, but the business with the coconut runner was even better. Especially the price. Every row-house wife in the country, every couple of years, wanted her sweetie of a husband to come up with new carpeting for their cozy domestic landscape. In the meantime, the price had gone up to more than 10,000 marks, as Duckwitz very well knew. Helen had also had the idea of doing some renovating at the house in the Eifel. Protocol's red carpet served the entire country, lasted at least 30 years, and cost less than a round-trip ticket to Latin America.

His colleague from Protocol didn't have much of a sense for the irony of the red carpet story. Instead, he told everyone who would listen that the West German Foreign Office had to do nearly twice as much work with its 6000 employees as the English Foreign Office with its 12,000. Even the staffs of almost 10,000 people at the Quai d'Orsay in Paris and at the State Department in Washington didn't have anywhere near as much work. In his own half-touching, half-insufferable way, the man from Protocol was proud of their tremendous German efficiency. The same way the average German praises his car for its incredible performance and great mileage.

The Press Office was also busily distributing the many verbose statements being issued by the Foreign Office. But in Public Relations/Domestic, where Duckwitz was, there wasn't much to do. In these turbulent times, no one was interested in the self-portrayal of the Foreign Office. In late 1989, German unification was as good as certain, and who knew whether Berlin wouldn't be the capital after that. There was no point in bringing up to date government publications in which the structure and function of the Foreign Office on Adenauerallee was explained to high school government teachers who were, strangely enough, interested in the subject. The undersecretary had planned to freeze operations until the whole German Question was finally settled. It was a very sensible plan—and one that Duckwitz was able to talk him out of. The transition period, he said, had to be given its due in later publications, and so it was especially important to observe and document it carefully now.

The undersecretary was persuaded, and Duckwitz was able to keep the job no one envied him. Nothing was happening in his office. He read newspapers and got paid for it. He was the only one at the Foreign Office who had the time, and so he was better informed than all the hustlers and bustlers whose industriousness he mocked.

Sometimes he tried to stir up his colleagues: the Foreign Minister was robbing them of the fruits of their labor. They read and researched and dictated and rewrote their detailed reports all day, said Duckwitz: "And what happens to them? The Minister is informed about them by his advisers as he's entering a room for important negotiations, and then they're reduced to vague promises or admonitions, whatever he happens to need." All they did was turn exact numbers and precise research into friendly ambiguities. And that was called top-level diplomacy. The Minister didn't even know anymore where he was going, whether it was Moscow, Washington, Paris, or Prague. The main thing was to rush from one important capital to the next, sit down in front of some fireplace for a photo opportunity with his high-level negotiating partners, and be on his way someplace else three hours later. Where are we going? asks the Foreign Minister as he drops into a seat on his government plane. To London. And what do I say there? You say loudly and unmistakably: Diplomacy has been given an opportunity, and we must seize it! The Foreign Minister nods and drops off for a nap. "That's international politics," said Duckwitz. "We might just as well be using doubles."

•   •   •

Duckwitz had been due for another foreign assignment for almost a year now. He'd been able to put it off again with the argument that his wife's training as a pianist did not permit such a posting. As little as he liked the now larger Germany, he didn't at all feel like spending the next three years in a place like Dar es Salaam or Lusaka, Bangui or Niamey, N'Djamena or Ouagadougou, engaging in the schizophrenic labor of development aid. That was where he'd probably be assigned as ambassador. The idea of playing His Excellency on the world's hind end was absolutely ludicrous. No one even knew where these places were—you had to tell them: Tanzania, Zambia, Central African Republic, Niger, Chad, Burkina Faso. Nor did he want to be sent to Tokyo and the authoritarian-minded Japanese. He'd be just another cog in the embassy machinery, in charge of the legal aspects of all those revolting computer deals. Singapore and Manila were out of the question as well. He didn't want to go any place at all, thanks. He didn't want to be separated from Inez, not even from his brother Fritz. He wanted everything to stay the way it was. Maybe New Zealand—but then he could try for that post when not a tree was left standing in Germany. Latin America? Not again! The U.S.? No thanks! Eastern Europe? Interesting, but to be perfectly honest, too complicated at the moment. Duckwitz had recently been talking to a man in the Office for East European Affairs who had just come back from a stint as counsellor at the embassy in Warsaw. The man was steeped in the spirit of reconstruction. "The countries in the former Eastern Bloc are nothing but one giant repair shop!" Duckwitz told him.

"I see! You'd rather declare than repair. The fine gentleman doesn't want to get his hands dirty!" the man had countered.

"That's right," said Duckwitz. "As long as there are still
so many people hot to do the cutting and patching, I don't
see why I should lift a finger."

It was not unusual, actually, for someone to defend
himself against arbitrary assignment abroad with plausible-
sounding arguments, preferably family problems. Limited
availability wasn't exactly good for a person's career, but
Duckwitz didn't think this was such a bad thing. There was
nothing more interesting to him than his private life.

While the 1600 people at the Foreign Office in Bonn
were constantly busy with the question of German unification during those wildly busy months of 1989, while even
Foreign Office chauffeurs were constantly in transit, Harry
did what had to be done as quickly as possible, read his
newspapers, and thought about love.

Why was he more crazy about Inez than she was about
him? Or was he wrong about that? And why was he so
crazy about her, period? Why did he have the feeling he'd
known her forever, even longer than Helen, whom he really
had known forever?

One early afternnooon in October, he suddenly had the
answer: Inez's slightly open mouth, her dark hair, the cut of
her eyelids, and something about her nose reminded him of
the cover on a box of condoms he'd admired at the age of
13 or 14, in a dispenser at the men's room in a pub, or
rather at an inn in the Bavarian Alps. You got three for one
mark in those days, but it wasn't the rubbers he was thinking of. The face of the woman on the box was what had
impressed him. It was a fuzzy, coarsely made photograph.
This must be ecstasy, he had thought. Abandonment.
Happiness. Love. The tilted head, the slightly parted lips,
the sexy wave in the hair, the closed, artfully made-up
eyes—complete concentration on pleasure. This was Inez.
Harry hadn't purchased the box at the time. Maybe he was
too afraid he'd be caught with it. Maybe he was too embar-

rassed because he didn't know what to do with the rubbers inside. They had nothing to do with love. That much was clear to him, even then. But the woman on the box—that was love.

15 *How Duckwitz gives an election-night party at his apartment in Bonn, along with a little election analysis and a short summary of Harry's futile deeds—both foul and heroic—while in the diplomatic service. How something nearly happens to Fritz, Inez gets angry, and Rita and Helen both yawn. How Harry is unexpectedly promoted, and finally a recollection of how, once upon a time, they collected the empties at the Foreign Office.*

"Shut your trap!" said Duckwitz as the Chancellor began to speak. The Chancellor continued, completely unmoved. He'd been asked by a reporter whether he would reshuffle his cabinet following his election victory. The Chancellor told the reporter he could appreciate the question, and he realized the reporter had to ask him the question, but he had to ask the reporter to understand that he couldn't give him an answer to his question at this point in time. Yes, of course, said the reporter, he appreciated this, but he hoped the Chancellor would show some understanding for the question. The Chancellor replied that, as he had already said, he fully appreciated that the reporter had to ask the question—then he turned to another microphone. Although it was a mild day for December, he then thanked everyone at the grass roots level for helping bring about this great election victory on such a bitterly cold day. "Shut your trap!" Duckwitz yelled at him again, and everyone laughed. Rita giggled, put her arms around Harry, and said: "No one says that better than you!"

It was still early in the evening, election day, December 2, 1990. The first actual numbers were beginning to flicker across the television screen. As expected, the people had voted for this bizarre colossus for a third time. It was the first all-German election, but the government had not been able to convince people that it was something special. The German Democratic Republic had been dismantled two months before, and reunification had been carried out. But this was already yesterday's news.

This time, Harry had assembled not only the hard core of the Duckwitz clan—Rita and Helen, Fritz and Inez—he'd also invited a couple of his colleagues: Knesebeck and Sachtleben and their wives, and the chinless Count Waldburg, who had been appointed to oversee cultural affairs at the embassy in Helsinki or Stockholm, in any case, somewhere in Scandinavia. He happened to be in Bonn on home leave. There was also a mild cynic from the Office of Protocol who reminded Harry of the Uncle Benedikt of his childhood days. Aunt Huberta's mysterious admirer. Harry openly called him Uncle Benedikt II. There were also a few black diplomats from Ghana and Cameroon; they made Harry think of Hennersdorff—the longer he was dead, the closer Harry felt to him.

They'd turned on the television and were consoling themselves with the usual jokes about the homely stupidity of the now united German folk and about how ideally suited the Chancellor was to this homeliness and this stupidity. The black Africans laughed and showed their wonderful white teeth. They said they couldn't understand what all the excitement was about. Harry said: "It's easy for you, with your black skin and beautiful white teeth!"

Harry began to expound on his "tumor" theory. He found it better than the usual intellectual theories, which maintained that a dreadful Chancellor was the well-earned punishment of a dreadful people. The Chancellor is a growth, he said. You can see this by the fact that there are secondary growths. Most of the people in his immediate circle are like him. The executive secretary of his party, for instance, has just as disgusting a physiognomy as the

Chancellor himself. Helen said she was tired of Harry's theory. Inez said that in the case of a growth, the important question was whether it was benign or malignant. She said she thought the Chancellor must be malignant if there were so many secondary growths. Uncle Benedikt II asked Inez what she did for a living. When she told him she was an anesthesiologist, he said she should chloroform the entire Chancellery.

"That's right," said the chinless, but today rather rakish-looking Count Waldburg. Harry piped up: "Chloroform, not reform, that's what we need!" When no one showed the proper appreciation for his wit, Harry thought of Elizabeth Peach back in Cameroon. She'd always been partial to slogans like this. She must be a dozen years older now! Tomorrow he'd give her a call from the office.

Inez said she thought the election results weren't funny but depressing. In 1987, Harry thought the results were depressing, but this election left him cold. Helen had been left cold by the elections in '87; the last time she got excited was in 1983. She said Harry hadn't been upset in 1987, either. "You should know," said Harry. Political excitability was evidently some sort of force that lets up with time, at least as far as a particular party is concerned. Surprisingly enough, it was Inez who got angry this time. Inez of all people, the apolitical doctor who had probably been a well-behaved and industrious student who never dreamed of criticizing the way society functioned. Inez of all people was the one who said reunification in general and these elections in particular made her want to puke.

Harry said he was beginning to think it was childish to expect intelligent and appealing faces. It was a contradiction in terms. Intelligent people don't go into politics, nor do the people you find appealing. Scoundrels are evidently better at politics—it's sad, but it's also somehow a relief.

Inez said the problem was that you didn't know whether the scoundrels were harmless or dangerous.

Waldburg didn't see any danger at present. He even thought it possible that the Chancellor's thick skin was a political advantage. For instance, he said, this newly strengthened conservative government might resist sending German soldiers to areas of international crisis out of sheer pigheadedness—in other words, it could do the right thing out of stupidity and complacency. A coalition government made up of Social Democrats and Liberals, on the other hand, might happen upon the idea of supporting American troops in the Gulf with a few German volunteers—as a sign of Germany's goodwill.

"That's outrageous!" shouted the left-leaning Knesebeck. "It's exactly the other way around!" Helen warned that there'd be no stopping Harry if he got started on his theory of the negative universe, where the dumbest people always do the right thing and the smartest people always do everything wrong.

At least, said Harry, the way politicians and reporters talk to each other has changed. Just four years ago, a politician asked by a reporter immediately after an election about his concrete plans would have thundered that the question was absolute nonsense. Nowadays politicians and reporters keep assuring one another that they appreciate the other's position. They still play the game of empty questions and pointless answers, but in the meantime they let you see that they find it ridiculous.

"Is that progress, or is it even more perverse?" asked Knesebeck.

"Progress is perverse," said Duckwitz.

"It's glasnost: openly kicking the people in the ass!" added Helen.

Derisive laughter could be heard from the television. The Chancellor had just thanked dear God Himself for the good condition he was in. He really had. Dear God Himself! It was only his good condition that made it possible for him to fulfill the duties of his demanding office.

"That's all politics is anymore, a matter of condition," said Harry. "He's right about that."

"Ninety-nine percent condition, one percent inspiration," said Fritz, "to not-quite-quote Oscar Wilde."

"That's good, that's good," said Uncle Benedikt II.

Then Harry had to tell the story of the banquet the Foreign Office had recently given for the Chancellor, to lighten up his rather tense relationship with the diplomatic corps. Of course, he didn't really have the time because of all the circus about unification, but in the long run he couldn't resist a seventeen-course meal. The Chancellor sat next to a dried-up undersecretary who had once been ambassador in Washington or Paris, an incredibly skinny count. No, not Waldburg, said Harry. The Chancellor sat there silently chomping away. After a while he asked his neighbor, "Do you know what I envy you for, Count?" And while the count was courteously shaking his head, the Chancellor said: "The fact that you can eat so much without getting fat." When the Chancellor made the same supposedly witty remark for the third time, evidently in the belief that it was folksy, Duckwitz rose, tapped his glass, and recited an old saying: "The scoundrel alone knows hunger, / The rabble eat till they burst. / An aristocrat watches his figure, / That is, as long as he has one first." That's good, the Chancellor had said loudly, he'd have to remember that. Somebody should write it down for him. He just couldn't use it in East Germany, he added.

That had been some time during the summer of that supposedly historic year, 1990. Duckwitz had never had a chance to observe the Chancellor that long from so close up. His knowledge of people, on which Harry could usually depend, melted away in the face of this monstrosity. "For example, was his reaction to my little performance clever, or dumb?" Harry asked.

"We'll never know," said Uncle Benedikt II. This major diplomatic secret inspired Harry to talk about the minor riddle of his years as a diplomat. Why didn't indiscretions have the slightest effect on a diplomatic career? While he was in training almost 15 years before, Duckwitz had launched a fierce attack on Germany's close allies the Americans, but had merely earned extra points for it. During his first foreign assignment in Cameroon, he had not only frequently misbehaved—at the table, among other places—he had also neglected his duties. He hadn't promoted the interests of German business. In fact, he had sabotaged them. He had called the military attaché a pistol-polisher in front of the whole embassy, and he had helped German tourists out of tight spots only reluctantly—and not without making it clear to them that they had no business being on that continent.

Harry evidently had some of that force that always wants to do ill yet manages to do good, said Fritz.

"Our little Mephistopheles!" said Helen. Rita made horns by holding her hands to her forehead, then gave an amazingly obscene wiggle with her rear end.

"I had no idea you were a devil," Inez said, in what Harry considered a wonderfully suggestive way.

"He's an angel of peace!" said Sachtleben. He then recalled how, at a big morning meeting in the fall of 1981, Duckwitz had challenged the Foreign Office to send a delegation to the peace demonstration that was to be held in October at the Hofgarten in Bonn. Quite apart from his own urge to demonstrate against the modernization of NATO weapons, Duckwitz said, he was willing to bet that a delegation of a few diplomats would effectively counter the Foreign Office's dubious reputation as a collection of petty idlers. Even this grotesque suggestion had not been taken amiss; it had simply been ignored.

"My God," said Duckwitz, who was a little embarrassed at the memory of his unsuccessful revolutionary outburst. "I had just come back from Cameroon. That was nine years ago."

Later, in Ecuador, he had harassed all kinds of diplomats with his dirty jokes about their S.O.B of a Chancellor. And just as he had in Cameroon, he let German companies run aground there, too. Sometimes he'd felt like a secret agent, but he didn't say that now. On the quiet and without attracting any attention, he had turned down the requests directed to the embassy by German companies, and though his tricks hadn't prevented the construction of a road through the rain forest, he'd at least been able to delay it. On his own authority, he'd even turned down requests by German writers who wanted the embassy's support in visiting Quito and Guayaquil to read from their works on their tours of the Goethe Institutes in Latin America. "That wasn't heroism," said Helen, interrupting Harry's reminiscences, "that was just plain nasty."

To Harry's relief, his brother Fritz was of the same opinion he was—German writers didn't belong in the Goethe Institutes, and certainly not in Latin America. You don't travel halfway around the world to read your work to a couple of former Nazis and their mixed-up offspring. Just a few months before, Fritz had turned down an invitation to Kuwait. There was no Goethe Institute there, but a German cultural center had made him a regal offer: 6000 marks and 14 days in a first-class hotel, and all for a two-hour reading. When Fritz told them about it in May or June, everyone urged him to accept, even Harry, whose ulterior motive was that it would be easier to see Inez while Fritz was gone. But Fritz had remained firm. He wouldn't read his work to a bunch of tedious engineers for all the money in the world.

When the Iraqis attacked Kuwait in August and the Westerners who were there weren't allowed to leave, Harry was overcome with guilt at the very idea that his poor brother Fritz had just barely escaped becoming a hostage.

The story of Fritz's near tragedy led to an outpouring of emotion among the guests at Harry's election party. As if Fritz had just that moment escaped mortal danger. "What do you mean?" said Fritz. "By now I'd be back. Besides, I'd like to have become better acquainted with some of those German gangsters in Baghdad."

And then something happened that irritated Harry tremendously: Inez took up Fritz's comment and spun it out. The Germans down there were utter criminals, unscrupulous arms dealers and weapons technicians. She absolutely could not understand why people got so upset over them. If war did break out, they would deserve to be blown to bits by the stuff they made and sold.

"Bravo, madam!" said Count Waldburg, applauding. Harry was speechless. Inez had never before acted like an ordinary wife, picking up a comment Fritz had made. And she'd put an even more radical spin on it!

Finally Harry said: "You're right," and tried to kiss her hand. But Inez withdrew it, saying: "You're one of the gang, too."

Uncle Benedikt II said loudly: "Turn off the boob tube, we don't want to watch our oaf of a Chancellor anymore, this is much more interesting!"

Then they poked fun at German unification and the President and, of course, the Foreign Minister. And Harry once again had to tell the story, which Uncle Benedikt II hadn't yet heard, about how he, Duckwitz, had slighted the soccer team while he was in Quito and had been reprimanded by the Foreign Minister, surprisingly enough one of the few times such a thing had happened during his diplomatic career.

When he was in Quito, Harry had made sure that no one from the embassy was there to welcome the victorious German soccer team at the airport. However, the ambassador had insisted on a reception for the team at the embassy, nothing fancy you understand, just a drink. And not at the residence. The team was offended. In Santiago and in Lima, soccer fans of German descent had formed an honor guard and the ambassadors had given glittering parties for them in their residences. Duckwitz had finally exploded. "Which one's the captain?" Everyone thought he meant it as a joke, for the captain was as well known as an emperor. There wasn't anyone who didn't know him and, naturally, Duckwitz too knew his face from the newspapers and from television. Duckwitz then yelled at the captain that he'd be damned if he'd go to the airport to pick up such a low-class bunch. Soccer, he said, is the sport of idiots, for idiots. The head of the German Soccer Federation had later lodged a complaint directly with the Foreign Minister. About six months later, Harry received a light reprimand from Bonn. He regretted the incident, Duckwitz answered, for criticism of soccer was actually beneath him. Next time he'd call golfers a low-class bunch.

"That's great!" said Uncle Benedikt II when Duckwitz finished telling his story. The only trouble was that fine reports like that didn't get read at the Foreign Office, as Duckwitz himself knew best. Even official dispatches were ignored unless it was a question of a war or a kidnapping. However, more dangerous than insulting a soccer captain was inciting an entire team to seek asylum—encouraging them to desert East Germany, which, thank goodness, was no longer possible. But just a few years ago this had actually happened on Cyprus. The West German ambassador in Nicosia had offered asylum at his embassy to the East Germans! He just couldn't imagine that they wouldn't want to come to the free West. But they didn't. Instead, there

was a hail of protests from East Berlin, and the Foreign
Minister, who otherwise didn't have time for anyone or
anything, summoned the man back from Nicosia and reprimanded him personally. But since the Foreign Minister was
a liberal man and the ambassador a strict conservative, the
Foreign Minister probably had not, in Uncle Benedikt II's
opinion, given the slightest indication, not even a nod, that
he actually approved of the deed on a human level. "What
do we learn from such cases?" asked Sachtleben. "We learn
that at the Foreign Office only political dolts get into
trouble. Badmouthers like Duckwitz are forgiven their
misdeeds."

"The daring red baron brings a little color to our gray
office," said Knesebeck maliciously.

It was shortly after midnight. Inez looked tired. Her
cheeks were sunken the way they always were when she'd
been on night duty several times in a row. Harry found it
especially attractive. Inez and Fritz left. The others gradually
took their leave as well. The election returns had long since
been analyzed and commented on. As expected, the Foreign
Office would remain in the hands of that perennial winner.
Duckwitz had been in the diplomatic service for fifteen years
now, and he'd never witnessed a change at the top.

Helen yawned crudely, at least as far as Harry was
concerned; he thought about Inez's charming yawn. He went
over to Rita, put his arms around her a little awkwardly, and
said: "I'm sorry I dragged you here to this stupid country.
How can you stand it?" He hoped Helen would go to bed
so that he could go to Rita's room without Helen noticing.

They sat around unable to make themselves get up and
go to bed. Harry said he didn't know whether it was a bad
thing or a good thing that the election results seemed so
unimportant to him. "Maybe it's normal not to be interested
in all this nonsense anymore."

"That would be a good subject of discussion for New

252 Joseph von Westphalen

Year's Eve," said Helen, going off to bed. Rita yawned unerotically and disappeared into the bathroom. Harry put on a Duke Ellington record and took the wine glasses out to the kitchen. Was Ellington overrated? All of a sudden, the good old pieces from the thirties seemed flat and inconsequential. He tried King Oliver, 1929, Chicago. This was good, not so upbeat.

Harry liked slowly cleaning up after a party, listening to music, and pursuing his thoughts without interruption. It couldn't go on this way, this diplomat's life. For a couple of years he'd enjoyed the pointlessness because it was in keeping with the pointlessness of life altogether. But the fifteen years he'd spent puttering around this way were simply too much. He had to call it quits. But what then? He'd never go back to being a lawyer, he knew that. Suddenly he had the feeling that his life was in shambles, and he poured himself a tall glass of whisky. In any case, he wouldn't quit. They'd have to want to get rid of him. The fact that his presence in the diplomatic corps hadn't become intolerable didn't speak well for him, he concluded ruefully. But it was difficult to get rid of a civil servant, period. That was the problem. In business, you could just throw someone out. There was a fight over severance pay, and then they were gone. But only top foreign service officials could be suspended when they were no longer politically tolerable. Discreetly, they were given early retirement. Only from the rank of minister counsellor upward were you important enough to become a liability. In the diplomatic service, this was the equivalent of an ambassadorial post in a mid-sized country, two steps above Duckwitz. He'd have to stay with the diplomatic service another eight to twelve years to make that kind of exit. That was no solution.

Harry washed the glasses and plates by hand. The dishwasher was so loud that it drowned out the music. The old jazz did him good. The King Oliver album ended with

"Call of the Freaks" and "The Trumpet's Prayer," and Harry
was thinking that a three-minute piece by a black jazz
musician was worth more than all the speeches of the
Chancellor and the Foreign Minister put together. And he
was thinking that he was a damned sissy. If he'd been fed
up with being a lawyer, he should have had the courage to
become a musician, and if he hadn't been good enough to
make it as a trumpeter, he could at least have set up a
recording company. He could have reissued the old recordings, written album cover copy about the great King Oliver
—and all of it would have been more meaningful than this
pitiful job as a diplomat. Inez was right to look down on it.
Harry von Duckwitz. It was a name for a diplomat. But it
could also have been a name for a trumpeter.

While he was putting on Clarence Williams' "Long,
Deep and Wide"—1928!—Harry was thinking that about
two years before, in 1987, it really should have come to a
blow-up at the Foreign Office. That was the time to have
been thrown out. There had been a heated public debate
about a doctor's statement that all soldiers were "potential
murderers." It had been in all the papers. A neurotic army
officer pressed charges, and the doctor was actually found
guilty of slander. Harry thought the judge should have been
flattened on the spot, like a pesky wasp. The decision had
been reversed on appeal. Harry was upset about the appellate
judge's opinion, which carefully avoided any discussion of the
truth of the statement. He should have come right out and
confirmed it! Everyone who talked to the media was upset
by the decision; even the President, in a speech to a group
of potentially murderous officers, had shaken his head over
the deplorably liberal decision. "Nothing but a palaverous old
windbag!" Harry announced at the cafeteria. Naturally, everyone was on Harry's side, because the President's preachy
manner got on everyone's nerves.

Still, they were glad to have him around. "He's

catalytic," Duckwitz said. "He tries to neutralize the pollution the Chancellor causes." Everyone laughed. Duckwitz was in top form. "That's exactly what he is," Knesebeck called out with delight, "a catalytic president. Pure platinum, the lofty gentleman."

"Even a catalyst can be toxic," said Duckwitz, but the others had lost interest.

Then all of a sudden there had been an opening for one of his planned provocations. A journalist from the so-called "alternative press" had asked Duckwitz, who sometimes worked at the Foreign Service press office, what the Foreign Office thought of the court's decision. "I can't speak for the Foreign Office," said Duckwitz, "but personally I think the decision is a good thing, even if it is laughable. It merely confirms that we can tell the truth without being penalized for it." And then he added that the statement, "All soldiers are potential cadavers," would be even better, because it made you stop and think.

When Duckwitz was quoted in the paper, it raised some hackles. The Defense Ministry in particular was appalled. Duckwitz wrote a summation of his defense on the back of his payroll statement—the one piece of paper a good German civil servant anxiously tries to keep secret. He was summoned to the office of his immediate superior. But at that moment communism was collapsing in Eastern Europe, and the Defense Ministry had other things to worry about, as did the head of Harry's division. The grass had long since grown over the whole affair when this 2nd of December came and went.

Harry emptied the ashtrays, straightened the rug, and opened the windows to let in some fresh air. It was half past two. No point in going to bed. He danced around the living room to the "Kansas City Man Blues"—or was it the "Mean Blues"? As good as those numbers were, they were oddly interchangeable. Then Harry lay down on the sofa, put his feet up, glanced at the newspaper, and dropped off to sleep.

•   •   •

When everything finally came to a head, he wasn't expecting it. So often things had simply petered out. Suddenly, it all went very fast. A week after the elections, Duckwitz was summoned to the office of the head of his division, who waved a fashion magazine in his face. On the cover was a picture of a woman with huge earrings and a neck as long as a giraffe's. "Have you seen this yet?" he asked. No, Duckwitz hadn't seen it.

The man opened the magazine and handed it to Duckwitz. The title was in big, bold letters: "What we think of united Germany." Fifty people had been quoted. Duckwitz didn't have to search very long—the passage had been heavily underscored. There was a photo of him the size of a postage stamp, one of those from his straw hat series. Where did they get it? From Rita? Next to the photo he was quoted as saying: *Why, I wouldn't even wipe my ass with a black-red-and-mustard rag! Harry von Duckwitz, Foreign Office.*

"Incredible," said Duckwitz.

His boss was breathing loudly. "A catastrophe. The magazine has been on the stands for ten days. No point in a temporary restraining order."

"It would also kick up too much dust," said Duckwitz.

"So what do we do now?" the man asked.

"Ride it out," said Duckwitz. "You have to ride out a scandal like this one, in good old Bonn fashion."

"You have to issue a denial," the division head said sharply.

"But that's what I think, that's the way I talk. What's

there to deny?" said Duckwitz. "I just didn't authorize them
to print it, that's all."

"Then you'd better come up with something," the
official said loudly.

It was pretty clear: if Duckwitz didn't issue a denial, if
he tried to tough it out, they'd have to do something. A
nice clean denial, something about a farcical mix-up, and he
could probably get off again scot-free. But if he issued a
denial, he'd make himself look ridiculous. What was really
ridiculous was getting so upset about a statement like that in
a silly fashion magazine, getting upset about an eager young
journalist who had no idea what's on the record and what's
off. What should he do? His career was over, one way or
the other. They'd relegate him to working in the archives or
something.

Helen was on a trip to Paris. A translators conference.
Out of touch. Wouldn't you know. He called Inez at the
hospital. "It's about my future," Harry said when she
sounded irritated at being disturbed at work. "You'll have to
figure it out yourself," she said. "You've been wanting out of
that place for a long time."

Harry left the office. He couldn't think clearly there.
He fought the urge to call Fritz as well. He went to his
apartment and killed some time. Two o'clock, three—too
late to issue a denial for tomorrow's newspaper. No one
knows where Duckwitz is. Best not to do anything. An old
lawyer's adage.

Harry didn't want to be disturbed, so he took the
phone off the hook. He wouldn't be able to get around
buying an answering machine in the future. The question
was, what's the future going to look like?

After a while, letting the receiver just lie there seemed
silly, so he called Knesebeck. Knesebeck had told him the
story of the empties years ago, while they were still in training. Fifteen years ago, to be exact. My God, where does the

time go? Hadn't done a thing since then. Just nonsense.
Harry pictured Knesebeck in his tiny office. Before
Knesebeck came back to Bonn, he'd been ambassador in
Maputo, Mozambique. All kinds of servants. That couldn't
have been much fun for a leftist like Knesebeck. He was
about to be sent to Quito. "Poor thing," said Duckwitz
when he heard about it. "The embassy there is in an
atrocious building."

Knesebeck laughed. "We're probably going to move
into the East German embassy," he said. "You probably
don't know it. No Western diplomat ever strayed into that
building."

"But I do know it," said Duckwitz. "It's nice. You
should be pleased. Congratulations."

When Knesebeck answered the telephone, Harry asked
him to tell him the story of the empties again.

"It must have been the late sixties," said Knesebeck
readily. "The former Foreign Minister took some sort of
ideological inventory here at headquarters. The ultra-conser-
vatives, that is, the arch-reactionaries, or to be more exact,
the former Nazis among the diplomats were particularly
noticeable, given the governing coalition of Social Democrats
and Liberals. They'd grown especially cheeky, making nasty
comments about the government's policy toward the Eastern
Bloc. You can't make any concessions to communists, they
said, not one."

"It would be interesting to size up the anti-communism
of those days from our vantage point now," said Duckwitz.
"What would have happened if we'd completely ignored the
Eastern Bloc? The Cold War would have been even colder,
but maybe communism would have collapsed ten years
earlier. Which means that a pigheaded, idiotic policy would
once again have been the more efficient one."

Knesebeck said he didn't have time, unfortunately, to
get into a discussion of Duckwitz's favorite subject. He'd

love to discuss the fateful laws of the negative universe with him some other time, but he was waiting for a phone call from Romania. Something was up. The only thing more pressing than Romania was the crisis in the Gulf. But he did have time to tell the story of the empties. The point had been to rid the Foreign Office discreetly of a dozen or more senior diplomats who had become an embarrassment to the diplomatic corps. So they got rid of them like so many empty bottles. One, two, three, their service was counted up, and they were sent into retirement with pensions that reflected the years of service already rendered. There had only been one thing wrong with the way they collected and got rid of the empties: they were told why no one wanted them around any longer. This may have been fair, but it wasn't very smart. According to civil service regulations, senior civil servants can be taken out of circulation, but not for specific reasons. They are simply taken out of circulation, and no one tells them why. Evidently the lawmakers had wanted to spare them the necessity of hearing what every failure in the business world is told straight out: You're finished; you've become a burden. Civil service law loves silence. The old empties' lawyers protested their early retirement and won their case. They couldn't be gotten rid of, all you could do was take away their work. That meant they received their last full salary as ambassador or envoy, and later they got their full pension. "And they lived happily ever after," said Knesebeck.

"Thanks," said Duckwitz. "It's a nice story," and he hung up.

•   •   •

"Too bad I couldn't get hold of you the other day about the denial. Maybe we could have ironed the whole thing out,"

said the undersecretary a week later. It was the first time
Duckwitz had been in the man's office.

Duckwitz stared at the undersecretary without blinking
an eyelash.

"I get the impression you aren't taking this whole thing
too seriously," the man said.

"Could be," said Duckwitz.

The undersecretary handed Duckwitz a piece of paper.
"Dr. Harry Baron von Duckwitz, Counsellor to the Legation
First Class, is herewith promoted to Minister Counsellor
First Class, effective immediately. Bonn, October 17, 1990.
The Minister of Foreign Affairs of the Federal Republic of
Germany."

"Something's up," said Duckwitz.

The undersecretary reached across his desk to hand
Duckwitz a second piece of paper. "Dr. Harry Baron von
Duckwitz, Minister Counsellor First Class, is herewith
granted early retirement, effective immediately. Bonn,
October 18, 1990. The Minister of Foreign Affairs of the
Federal Republic of Germany."

"An elegant solution," said Duckwitz. "But where's the
statement of grounds?"

The undersecretary laughed. "You're no empty," he
said. "We won't make that mistake again." He told
Duckwitz that the early retirement business interested him,
so he'd worked it out himself: Duckwitz would receive 70
percent of his pension, currently about 3600 marks a month.

"If you had resigned," said the undersecretary, "you
wouldn't have received a penny. What more could you want?
You don't really intend to quit working?"

"The promotion trick is a good one," said Duckwitz.

"We got a few pointers from the Interior Ministry.
They've had to play this trick fairly often. You're the first
one here at the Foreign Office."

"But at least I was a ranking political appointee for 24 hours," said Duckwitz.

"Relatively speaking," said the undersecretary. "We saved ourselves the expense of promoting you to an undersecretary. That would have been even more lucrative for you, of course."

"Wouldn't you like to follow my example?" asked Duckwitz.

"Sometimes I would," said the undersecretary, looking out the window at the Rhine. "I was happiest when I was ambassador to Copenhagen. Where were you the happiest?"

Duckwitz suddenly got a warm feeling. Several years back he would have laughed out loud at a question like that. Happy? What was that? He still didn't know, but suddenly he realized that the question didn't sound as silly as it used to. "Maybe I'm happiest right now," he said, "and I just don't know it yet."

"Reading through your dossier," said the undersecretary, "I almost get the impression that you were headed for this from the start."

"Maybe," said Duckwitz, lost in thought. "Maybe that's the case."

Somehow, neither of them could bring the discussion to an end. And so Duckwitz asked whether the undersecretary knew Duckwitz's namesake, who had been at the embassy in Copenhagen during the war and who then became an undersecretary.

"Georg Ferdinand Duckwitz, yes, he was a good man. Unlike you, his birth wasn't aristocratic—but his bearing was!" The undersecretary laughed with pleasure at his own wit. "He helped save Danish Jews during the war, helped them escape."

"I know," said Duckwitz. "I didn't save anybody's life. I wish I could have." For a moment he almost felt like crying. "Thank you. I'll be going now. It's not a very grand exit."

"No," said the undersecretary, "you can't have everything. But you're still young!"

"Young? I'm 45!"

"There you have it."

16 *How Harry von Duckwitz enters the Foreign Office one more time to pick up his belongings, then hears a remarkable program about Germany on his car radio but can't find a place to pee. In addition, Harry's inability to decide whether he should drive to Cologne to see Inez, or to the Eifel where Helen and Rita are staying. Finally, how he fills his tank and listens to some music, then succeeds in not letting his mood be ruined by the situation of the world as 1990 comes to an end.*

Duckwitz and Sachtleben had agreed to meet at half past two. "Yes, on Saturday. In the lobby of the Foreign Office. The 29th. That's right, of December. 1990, you clown."

It was already two forty-five. 1445 hours. Where was Sachtleben? That's what you get for not saying 1430. But nobody does that except train conductors and soldiers. Hitler had told the Reichstag on 9-1-39 that the German army would return fire as of 1745 hours. That was war talk. The only consolation was that civilized people still hadn't let themselves be talked into wearing digital watches. At the beginning of the eighties, they'd been all the rage, but the nonsense hadn't caught on. At least for their wrists, people still wanted something with a face and hands, even if every radio, stove, and automobile was now fitted out in digital. The only people who were still wild about digital watches were the blacks in Africa and the Indians of the Andes, and that was only because time didn't matter to them.

Duckwitz had been going in and out of the Foreign Office since 1976, for fourteen years. Foreign Office headquarters, Adenauerallee. He'd spent three years in Bonn after his assignment in Cameroon, four years after he'd come back from Ecuador. He'd gone through the lobby a couple of thousand times, but he'd never had to wait for anyone there. Now he was a visitor.

Ten minutes to three. 1450 hours. Where was Sachtleben? He'd been urging Duckwitz to come and pick up his things. Following his removal from active service two weeks before, Duckwitz had been forced to vacate his office pell-mell. As if one day more or less made any difference. But all of a sudden they were picky. They had their instructions, after all—and civil servants follow instructions. That day Duckwitz hadn't driven his car to the office, since it was in for repairs. He'd asked if he could leave his personal belongings in Sachtleben's office for the time being. Sure, he'd said, your very own temporary storage facility! At least nuclear technology was good for a bunch of new metaphors.

Five minutes to three. Something must be wrong. The Saturday before New Year's. There wasn't a soul in the lobby. Somewhere in this building today there were people on stand-by duty. Harry had always thought the building was the worst bit of architecture he'd ever seen. Now that there were so many modern buildings that were even uglier, the familiar old concrete block seemed more like a hospital where you could actually get well—or a school where you could actually learn something.

Finally Sachtleben showed up. He didn't apologize for being late, and he was obviously annoyed at having to come to the office the Saturday before New Year's to get rid of things an ex-colleague had left in his keeping. He'd asked Duckwitz to pick them up any number of times, and today of all days Duckwitz was finally willing to come.

As they walked down the empty hall toward his office, Sachtleben became a little more conciliatory: Duckwitz knew how cramped things were in those little offices. The same old song and dance, the same old complaints. He needed every shelf. In January he had to work on a draft for the EC—comparative pricing of agricultural products. The price

of an egg in the EC and in the countries applying for
admission. The Turkish egg, the Hungarian egg. Sachtleben
shook his head—sometimes it made you wonder. In any
case, he'd ordered forty ring binders for January 2 and he
needed room for them. That's why he'd been so insistent.

Duckwitz nodded. Sachtleben unlocked the door to his
tiny office. As Duckwitz entered the room, he knew why
he'd been putting this off so long. There was nothing worse
than having to part with things. You should never part with
things—not with women, not with your possessions. Parting
with old opinions wasn't easy either, but at least you didn't
need boxes to put them in.

"What should I put all this stuff in?" asked Duckwitz.
Sachtleben was annoyed. Duckwitz should have thought of
that before he came. There wasn't a crate or carton anywhere. Duckwitz knelt down in front of the only bookcase
in the room. The three bottom shelves were full of his
belongings. He pulled out a sheet of paper. It was a letter to
Marida Böckle in Quito. Never mailed. It had been pretty
shabby of him to take off the way he did. After all, they'd
been having an affair, even if it hadn't been the greatest.
Sometimes, when there was nothing going on with Rita or
Helen or Inez—and that wasn't exactly seldom—he'd indulge
himself with lewd memories of Marida. To want just one
thing, with a woman who wants the same. This was the
spirit in which he'd written to her in November of 1987. It
was a mixture of things—one-fourth guilty conscience
because he'd left without a word, three-fourths fence-
mending in case he ever saw her again. Making an open
reservation. What a soft-soaper he was. Duckwitz couldn't
decide whether to crumple it up or file it away as a
document.

"Would you please. . ." said Sachtleben, rattling his key
chain.

"Just a minute," said Duckwitz.

My God, here's a postcard to Inez, from Geneva. Didn't send that either—seemed too affectionate. Then there was a postcard to Helen, also from Geneva. He'd spent two weeks at the German delegation to the U.N. office there. You could tell that he'd written the postcard to Inez first. How hypocritical.

"Please!" said Sachtleben. "I've got other things to do today!"

"Just a second," said Duckwitz, glancing up at him. "You're making me nervous standing there like that!"

Sachtleben wasn't about to leave. Where should he go, anyway? He couldn't wait outside like a school kid who'd been thrown out of class.

"Don't make such a big deal of it," said Sachtleben. "You're not exactly conducting an autopsy!"

"Oh yes I am," said Duckwitz. "That's exactly what I'm doing." He asked Sachtleben to give him the key to the office and to go on out to the parking lot. "I'll be right there," he said. "I just can't go rummaging around in my past with someone looking over my shoulder. It's driving me nuts!"

"Absolutely not," said Sachtleben. What was that supposed to mean? Did Sachtleben think he was a spy? Did he have instructions not to leave Herr Dr. Harry von Duckwitz unobserved on Foreign Office premises? He wouldn't put it past them. Or was Sachtleben worried that Duckwitz would go rooting around in his desk? "You were a spy for the East German Stasi," said Duckwitz, "and you're afraid you're finally going to be uncovered, is that it?"

Sachtleben laughed out loud. "You're some comedian!"

"You never know," said Duckwitz. "In any case, I'm a spy. I'm spying on my own past."

"Just take all your trash with you and be done with it," said Sachtleben. "You can sort out all that stuff at home, damn it." He had to take his daughter to a birthday party in

Bad Honnef and his son to one in Königswinter, and then he had to drive his wife to her mother's in Düsseldorf. Duckwitz apparently had no idea how difficult his situation really was. Suddenly Sachtleben laughed again: "You don't have any children. You have no idea how hectic it gets. And all the problems with school! Children who constantly get bad grades and have to repeat a year. Changes in schools, private schools, sinfully expensive. And a wife who's constantly threatening to get a divorce! That's a little different from having to clear off a shelf."

Duckwitz leafed self-consciously through a half-empty photo album. The pictures had been taken in Ecuador in '85 and '86. One man and two women, taken with an automatic timer so that all three of them were in all the pictures. They were pretending that everything was harmonious. Actually, it hadn't been unharmonious. Rita, Helen, and Harry on the terrace outside their house in Quito. It was a downright impressionistic composition—wicker furniture, tea cups on the table, and above it all the Andes. Then there was a trip to the country. Three figures. From the back. A man and two women looking at the mountains. Posed but not untruthful. Harry with Helen's straw hat—Helen always wore a straw hat. She was afraid of getting skin cancer at that altitude. But the hat didn't suit her at all, and she knew it. She took it off for photographs. Harry found that a hat was too much of a bother, and he wasn't afraid of cancer. Besides, Helen's hat suited him well, so he put it on whenever pictures were being taken. They complemented each other quite nicely.

Sachtleben groaned: "What you need are plastic bags; otherwise there's no point to all this."

Where was Duckwitz supposed to scare up plastic bags here at the office on a Saturday afternoon? Sachtleben swore under his breath and said he'd check in the basement.

Alone at last! Duckwitz rummaged around some more.

He found a spinning top that he'd planned to take to Inez's daughter, and a Norwegian matchbox—the kind they once made out of wood shavings. He'd never been able to make up his mind whether to give it to Helen or Inez. There was also a Chopin recording and those awful monthly salary statements. And then there was a yellowed slip of paper with a note on it: "The main concern is to establish a business-like atmosphere in which proper procedure is guaranteed." What kind of nonsense was that? Duckwitz studied the puzzling words for a minute, then remembered that his boss had made the nonsensical statement last year at a meeting about some crisis or other. Duckwitz had written it down for his collection of utterances void of meaning. He'd started collecting them years ago, and there had to be a shoe box somewhere in the apartment in Bonn or in the Eifel with the label "Null and Void." He had dozens of statements like this—his own private minutes of meetings he'd attended.

He was always keeping things that should be thrown away. It was a real specialty of his. Joseph Beuys had at least been able to pass off his trash to museums as works of art, lucky fellow. Every man an artist. Somehow it was true. Everyone can become a millionaire, say the millionaires. This stuff is worth a hundred thousand marks for sure. Please do not touch. Title: "Foreign Rubbish." There was a snapshot of Rita and Helen on the motorcycle. Null and void. They didn't ride the motorcycle anymore, and they'd never been real motorcyclists. It was a lie, but a good picture. Two she-knights, just as they're supposed to be—bold and beautiful.

He was in his middle forties and incapable of throwing junk into the trash. Somehow it was true—it was art, and you don't throw away art. And then the worst of it: a really terrible TV magazine he once bought because the woman on the cover looked like Inez. Some rising or falling TV star. She smiled at the spectator the way Inez did—her lips decently parted, her expression both impassive and sultry. Her legs were crossed, and her short skirt slid up the way Inez's foreskin of a skirt did. Since Harry didn't have any photos of Inez, not to mention one of her in that skirt, he'd kept the magazine.

And finally there were a couple of photocopies and a letter from the visiting government adviser he'd tried in vain to provoke in Quito. "As you can see from the material I've enclosed, Herr von Duckwitz, you are part of a long tradition," the adviser had written to him in Quito in March of 1986. The letter was written on Chancellery stationery. The photocopies were of a book entitled *The History of Diplomacy,* which had just appeared. There were big red exclamation points in the margins, and some passages had been marked. For example: "A certain degree of tension between the central office and the embassies is part of the everyday life of every country's diplomatic service. There has never been a shortage of complaints from either side. Count Münster, Imperial Ambassador to London and Paris, referred to the Foreign Office on Wilhelmstraße in Berlin as the 'Central Cattle Yard' and to the staff as 'cattle.'" This passage was followed by a witty description of the well-known story of Napoleon spending half an hour cussing out Talleyrand, who'd been thrown out of office: "Livid with anger at the equanimity of his victim, the Corsican lunged at Talleyrand as if to slap him in the face, screaming, 'You're just a heap of shit in silk stockings!'" In the margin next to this passage, the adviser had written: "Idea for Duckwitz!" On another page the man had alluded to Harry's two-woman household; he hadn't missed a thing. The book was discussing Count Kaunitz, who'd been one of Empress Maria Theresa's envoys before he became Chancellor. He kept mistresses in Paris, Brussels, and Vienna, and he never so much as went for a drive without the company of a mistress, a singer, or a dancer. When he had appointments to keep, they waited outside in his coach. "Once, when Maria Theresa was reproaching him for his conduct," the author wrote, "Kaunitz replied, unperturbed: 'Your Majesty, I am here to discuss Your affairs, not mine.'" This passage was followed by a reference to the numerous affairs of Metternich, three times married and constantly in love: "He did, however, grant his wives the same freedoms he claimed for himself: only a few of their eleven children were his."

Duckwitz folded up the sheets of paper and put them in the inside pocket of his jacket. He'd have to read them out loud on New Year's Eve. The day after tomorrow. Inez had been on duty Christmas Day; New Year's Eve she was going to come out to the Eifel with Fritz and her children. Harry was looking forward to it.

What a pleasure it would be to read these passages out loud to his harem! And the discussion afterward! What does this passage tell us? That monogamy is a crime, of course. A lie propagated by the chronically possessive and faint-hearted. Go forth and do it, that was the message. Do it the way Metternich and Kaunitz and Prince von Pückler did. Nobody can be satisfied with just one person. A man needs three women, and a woman needs three admirers, otherwise this filthy world is unbearable. Did you hear that, Rita, Helen, Inez? Come on! Love me more, let yourselves be loved more, drive more men crazy! There's just one rule— that you do it with style. Abandonment is an art, and it mustn't have anything of the soap opera about it. The only thing that can free your head is free love, and only a person who loves and is loved can laugh at the hare-brained idea of the love of God. That kind of love was thought up by pious characters who wanted to pass it off on people without any pluck. Pure pabulum. People who beg for God's love are only halfbaked. The only effort worth making on this earth is that of running after women and seeing a few of them run after you. Quotas for politicians! What nonsense. As if

270 Joseph von Westphalen

there weren't already a number of old battle-axes in politics. It's not women who have the better policies, it's people in love who do. That's why politics is so abysmal.

"Well, I'll be damned!" Sachtleben was standing in the doorway. "You haven't made any progress at all!"

He was carrying a bundle of the kind of plastic bags their embassies had been handing out for the past few years. They must have been an invention of some little bureaucrat from the public relations division. Tourists, business people, and traveling M.P.s are always needing plastic bags, whether it's in Canberra, Kuala Lumpur, Cairo, or Ankara. And since a plastic bag is a chance for some free advertising, they bore the company name: Federal Republic of Germany. Below that, the name was repeated in Arabic, English, French, Spanish, and Portuguese—it was just a wonder it wasn't there in Cyrillic letters, especially since the greatest demand was registered in Moscow. There was a black-red-and-mustard stripe around the middle, and on the back a particularly ugly version of the national emblem, the eagle, sticking out its deceitful tongue.

The first thing Harry put in one of the bags was the TV actress with her Inez-mouth and her Inez-skirt. It took seven bags to empty the shelves.

"Finally," said Sachtleben in a pained voice. He picked up one of the half-filled bags in order to get Duckwitz moving. Duckwitz took three full bags in each hand and lugged them down the hall. Sachtleben impatiently held open the elevator door.

"The baron moves out," said Duckwitz.

"You look like a derelict," said Sachtleben.

In the elevator, Sachtleben laughed once again and said: "Somehow you're right. This place is the pits." In the parking lot, he helped Duckwitz heave the black-red-and-mustard striped bags into the huge trunk of the old Ford Duckwitz was driving now. "Don't look so bitter," he said.

"I can't stand the sight of those colors anymore," said Duckwitz.

Suddenly, Sachtleben punched him in the shoulder. They'd done that while they were in training, young and cheerful, and it had taken the place of grand words. Harry used to think it was terrible; now he was moved by the sign of affection.

"It's too bad," said Sachtleben, "too bad you're leaving."

"Why weren't we ever on familiar terms?" asked Harry.

"Well, you're so aloof," said Sachtleben. "You were always the unapproachable Herr von Duckwitz."

"That's a bunch of rubbish," said Harry. "Me, unapproachable!"

"Yes, you are," said Sachtleben. "But nice. A little arrogant, but nice. In any case, you'll be missed." He shook Duckwitz's hand and said: "And I mean that." Then he turned around and walked toward his car in the dusk.

Duckwitz closed the trunk of his car. He was glad that Sachtleben hadn't asked what he was going to do now. Professionally, that is. He had no idea. At first, nothing.

"That's absolutely decadent!" Count Waldburg had said recently with a sparkle in his eye as he heard about Duckwitz's ouster. His other colleagues were full of encouragement. "Perfect!" commented Knesebeck. "My respects!" said Willfort. Amusement, best wishes, and congratulations from all sides—the dashing baron had made a dashing exit.

Once he was in his car, Duckwitz realized that the situation wasn't amusing at all. He realized it because he couldn't find the right music for the mood he was in. Two dozen tapes in his glove compartment, and not one of them was right. His old jazz recordings left him cold, and neither Johnny Dodds' clarinet nor the cornet of the young Louis Armstrong worked their old magic. This was a bad sign. The blues guitars of Big Bill Broonzy and Muddy Waters, which usually made him so resistant, didn't have any appeal.

Nor did Memphis Minnie with her "Me and My Chauffeur Blues," which could usually rekindle his spirits. Not even the cat-like voice of two-hundred-pound Lil Green had any effect. Yet her 1941 Chicago recording of "Why Don't You Do Right?"—which always melted Rita, Helen, and Inez—ought to have made any reasonable person melt.

You should never be in a car without a woman. A man alone in a car is bad. A traveling salesman. Though it's better than two men in a car—that's the police. And a car with three or four men is positively criminal. They can only be on their way to some brutal board meeting. A passenger seat is supposed to be occupied by a woman, a woman who also sways in time to the music. That eighteenth-century Count Kaunitz understood why he never went for a coach ride without a woman. It also spoke for him that he didn't give a fig about titles and included the sons of shoemakers and Danube boatmen in his cabinet.

But if Duckwitz didn't have a woman in his car, he was at least on his way to one. The only question was, which one? Either he could go to Inez in Cologne or to Rita and Helen, who had been in the Eifel since Christmas.

In front of him, where the side street crossed Adenauerallee, he could see Sachtleben's car. His left blinker was on, pointing in the direction of Bad Godesberg. Duck-witz pulled up to the right of him. Both of them rolled down their windows.

"Thanks," said Duckwitz.

Sachtleben gave him a friendly smile.

"Will you still make it on time for the birthday parties?"

Sachtleben nodded.

"See you again some time," said Duckwitz.

"Sure thing," said Sachtleben.

See you again some time.... Those stale old phrases

felt good today. They were what held things together. Then there was a break in the traffic and Duckwitz turned right.

It was an unconvincing exit. No bang, no trumpets, no splendor, no style, and politically off the mark. What had Inez said on election day? If German hostages had bit the dust during a war with Iraq, they would more or less have deserved it. Of course, she'd been talking about those chemical-industry killers. That's what he should have told the journalist, not the nonsense with the black-red-and-mustard rag. That would have been something worth tripping himself up for. The situation was especially ticklish because a former Social Democratic Chancellor was the one who got the hostages out. Even the most rabid conservatives didn't dare publicly attack the gentleman's humanitarian mission. To have responded from a cynically pacifist angle would have been a perplexing violation of a taboo, something right up Harry's alley.

•　　•　　•

Gloomy Rhenish winter weekend weather was not only depressing, it got to your bladder. Harry hadn't wanted to delay Sachtleben even more by making a trip to the john.

Jimi Hendrix is no help, he just gets on your nerves. Same with Bob Dylan. Even "Ramona," which could almost always save you, was a letdown today. Janis Joplin was too shrill. Pretty bad to hear some especially unpleasant political type say "Bobby McGee" was his favorite song. "Freedom's just another word for nothing left to lose"—wisdom growled by a frustrated college girl in the late sixties. Now it was being applauded by conservative M.P.s.

It was deadly to be driving on the autobahn in this kind of mood. Deadly might be a little exaggerated, he certainly didn't plan on having an accident—no reason for that. He wasn't living in a country where some government official hands a person his walking papers, lets him leave the room, then snaps his fingers for a thug to appear and do the dirty work. Duckwitz knows too much, says the official, and his sinister assistant understands what he has to do—tamper with the brakes. He wasn't living in a country like that. You don't know too much, you know too little. And so you don't have to die, you just have to watch out. An accident would be too easy a solution. You have to stick it out, persevere. Civil perseverance. Why not? Now that the distinctions between left and right weren't very clear anymore, perhaps you should just define yourself as civil. What are you? A civilian, dear lady, and nothing more. I will not stand at attention, I'll spit on anyone I please.

How pleasant the winters in the mountains of Bavaria had been when he was a kid. If you went skiing there now, you were contributing to the erosion of the Alps; if you set off fireworks on New Year's Eve, you were diverting money from a charitable donation. This morning they'd said on the news that the Campaign Against World Hunger had launched its "Food Not Fireworks" crusade. Germans set off more than 100 million marks worth of fireworks each year. Animal protection groups had joined the campaign because the fireworks were making cats and dogs neurotic. Okay, he could do without fireworks. Harry didn't like the racket anyway—that was what war must sound like. But somehow it was part of the whole thing. Of course, a silent New Year's Eve would also sound like war. Right now everything sounded like war, what with the crisis in the Middle East. A few hundred thousand potential cadavers facing each other with a mixture of fanaticism and composure, fear and brag-gadocio. No one had expected a return to such fossilized thinking at the end of the twentieth century. You couldn't even think about it, otherwise the misery grew and grew. To speak of the "deployment of troops" was going too far already. I'm a civilian. If you want to kill yourselves in droves, do it somewhere else. Are soldiers really there just to be turned into cadavers? There was absolutely no point in trying to understand the madness of the people who gave the orders. What solution do you propose, Herr von Duckwitz? I'm not here to suggest solutions! Duckwitz yelled at the windshield. I'm not going to fix what other people have loused up. I simply want to point out that it's the same old shitheads who are at work again.

Just look at him, Rita, Helen, just look at the president of the United States: he's nothing but a squawking turkey, crazy with fear and defiance because he doesn't know what to do; a pistol-polisher just like his opponent. You can't even say they're crazy anymore, because that's the kind of thing the *Bild* prints on its front page. Maybe the best solution would be to get rid of them both as quickly as possible. Tomorrow morning at eight, I want to have both their heads delivered with my morning paper. I can lay down an ultimatum, too. At the insistence of the crazies in the U.S., the crazies at the U.N. have given the crazies in Iraq until January 15 to withdraw from that odd little country called Kuwait. Or they'll shoot!

Actually, thought Harry, we should run a help wanted ad for murder. That would be something! But it would have to be done right away, there wasn't much time. Hello, I'd like to speak to the classified ad department, please. I'd like to place the following ad, full page—yes, I know, it will cost about 30,000 marks, plus value added tax. No problem. Are you listening? Write it down as I dictate. No, I can't send a fax! I'm sitting in my car, damn it, and I don't have an autofax. This is the Duckwitz Crisis Agency, do you understand? I want to place an ad, a full page ad, please write:

"A call to murder!" In boldface. And below that: "A reward of 10 million marks for the murder of the U.S. president," yes, you heard right, "by" — well, let's say "January

10. Muslims and assassins from the Arab world need not apply. The issue is prevention of war, not revenge. Loyal U.S. citizen preferred, patriotic Vietnam veteran most welcome. No one mentally deranged. The assassin" — yes, assassin; after all, we are talking about a political murder! — "must be from the U.S. or a closely allied country, otherwise the whole thing could backfire. An ex-East German would also be acceptable, but only one without Stasi connections! We hope that puppy of a U.S. vice president will be frightened off by this attack, but if he isn't, he's next." What do you think?

Oh, you don't think, you just take the ads. Wait, you do think something? You think the ad is a little one-sided? Just a minute, I'm not finished yet. Draw a line or make three asterisks or something, then write: "10 million for the picturesque head of the madman from Baghdad. The same general rules apply: the assassin must be an Arab—the outcry following the murder is to turn inward, not outward. American sharpshooters need not apply. And now the exacta pay-off: 10 x 10 = 100 million marks if both gamecocks are rubbed out. That's 50 million per assassin." No, not dollars, the mark is strong enough. "Submit your applications, ladies and gentlemen, sharpen your scimitars, Mussulmen, your ruler's neck is rather sturdy! Adjust your sights, you true American friends, or hire yourselves some rain forest Indians with reeds and poison arrows. It would be a welcome change from the usual gunfire." — Have you got it? What, you don't think your boss will accept the ad? Let me speak to the sissy! He isn't there? He's on a skiing trip? He's ruining our Alps!

I beg your pardon? You think the ad is cynical? That surprises me! I think it's a thousand times more cynical to send a hundred thousand people to their deaths. Where is the money coming from? It's the 100 million marks saved by not setting off fireworks on New Year's!

•   •   •

Duckwitz still didn't know whether he should go to see Inez in Cologne or drive to the Eifel. He was on the autobahn driving in the direction of Cologne. It was raining. Cars were racing past him. He was doing 90 kph. At this speed, it would take him 20 minutes to get to Cologne; that left him time to think about where he should go when he got there.

It was almost five and already dark. Take a piss and get some gas, then the world will be a little more bearable. He found it puzzling that he didn't feel like listening to a single one of his favorite numbers. Maybe he was in a state of shock from being ousted? At least his eroticism didn't seem to have suffered from it. That was all he needed. Things like that happen. There sure hadn't been much passion lately, though, either with Rita or with Helen. The only chance for a screw was if one of them was out of the house, and that didn't happen very often.

"Are we getting old, or what?" Helen had said, but she didn't do anything about improving her love life, either. She was still wearing those rusty fall colors and baggy pants, too short and too wide. "I feel sorry for you, you're so dependent on externals," she said. That was Helen's stern judgment. Harry found it very Protestant. He suddenly felt more attracted to Rita; at least she didn't broaden her shoulders with those disgusting, superfluous shoulder pads. She usually wore normal blue jeans, not the gray kind that looked sooty and dirty and had just become popular. Harry thought they'd been invented by some sadist who took pleasure in making people look uglier than they already were.

And the time was evidently past for a three-for-all. Not because of him—he'd argued in favor of it long enough. Or maybe that was just it. He couldn't figure it out. Even in

Quito the three of them had slithered around in bed only
once in a blue moon. And since they'd come back from
Ecuador it had happened only once, as a kind of initiation
rite in new territory. And then again the other day, just
before Christmas. A couple of days after he'd been let go.
"Look how down our retiring Harry is," Helen had said,
putting her arms around him. Beneath the irony you could
hear something like affection. And suddenly Rita had
stopped playing the chaste Bach piece she was working on
and started playing an incredibly melancholy version of
Harry's favorite, "West End Blues." The chords cried out for
a throaty trumpet accompaniment. "Actually," she said, "I
wanted to surprise you with this on Christmas, but I can use
the practice: 'Take your trumpet, baby!'" But it never came
to that, because all of a sudden they were in Rita's bedroom,
and without any embarrassment, without the least bit of
venom, without a word, what hadn't happened for ages
happened again: playfully and without shame, gently but
fiery enough that they worked up a good sweat. Harry
sniffed Rita's and Helen's armpits and said it was wonderful
how different they smelled. Helen remarked: "Maybe now
our premature pensioner will find some meaning in life."
Rita shook with laughter, and Harry couldn't understand
why he was always running after Inez. But as they cheerfully
set about fixing dinner and Helen sniffed at the lettuce
Harry had just rinsed—suddenly detecting pesticides and
putting up a fuss because it clearly hadn't been bought at the
health food store—Harry remembered why he needed Inez.
Things were fine the way they were. His feelings for Inez
were a blessing. There were no bitter disagreements about
how chemicals were destroying the planet.

"You've always been something of a hysteric," Harry
told Helen without a trace of combativeness. And Helen
returned just as gently: "You've always been something of an

idiot." The matter ended there and they were in a good mood again, but love had gone out the window.

Harry turned on the car radio. A church choir that sang as if to put the fear of God in your heart was bellowing out a hymn. On another station, passersby were being asked about the glorious events of 1990 and how it felt to be a united German. One of them said that the hour of joy had come. Just imagine! He had the nerve to make a pronouncement on radio that could have come from the Chancellor! He couldn't think of anything else to say. Stuff the people's ears with dumb pronouncements, and the same dumb things come right back out again, like a fax machine.

What if someone were to ask me that question now? thought Harry. May I ask how it feels to be a united German? You may, he would answer. I used to be embarrassed to be a German, but now things have changed. Now I don't feel anything; I'm numb. I don't feel like a German *or* like a united German! How about a European? I beg your pardon! That would be a cheap way out. You may not believe this, but at 45 I feel like I'm too young for these questions. I'll have an answer when I'm 90. All I know is how spring feels, how autumn feels. Now that Christmas has passed, with all those pfeffernüsse, all I feel is full. That's what you should say right into the microphones of those idiotic reporters.

He had to pee and there wasn't a rest stop in sight. Why live in an industrialized country if there aren't even enough places to pee? As far as that was concerned, you were better off in the bush. Although that wasn't quite true, either. Africa, in any case, was pretty densely populated. You could stop on a road leading straight through the jungle, and some curious black would pop out from behind a tree and you had to put your willie back in your pants without having taken care of your business. Just so you wouldn't stand there looking like some uncouth imperialist.

Harry changed the station again. Another recap of
1990. A couple of intellectuals had gathered at the sound
studio—children of the Republic, as the moderator called
them. That meant they were about the same age as
Duckwitz. They were introduced as ex-leftists—I believe I
can put it that way, said the moderator, and everyone
remained remorsefully silent in the face of the accusation. A
woman's voice piped up: you can say what you want against
the Chancellor, but he did exactly the right thing by pushing
the unification of the two German states. And Harry
thought, my God, in retrospect some nonsense really does
seem right. But even if what their blimp of a Chancellor
had done wasn't entirely wrong, that was still no reason to
say it in public. That was going too far. Then the practiced
baritone of a political scientist. Yes, yes, said the professorial
child of the Republic, the time has come to tighten our belts
and roll up our sleeves. He really said that! And Duckwitz
drove right past a public peeing place, he was so stunned by
the political wisdom of his contemporaries. The woman said
you couldn't leave the reconstruction of the former East
Germany to politicians, it was time for everyone to pitch in.
They'd already failed once, in 1968, when people only
changed certain ways of thinking. This time it was a matter
of creating something, a new society. The whole thing
seemed an embarrassment to the moderator, who tried to
provoke a satirist who'd remained silent up to that point:
"And what do you think?" The satirist groaned and said he
felt out of place here in the studio; it was more like being at
a tea party with the President. Honestly, it left him speechless, all this drivel about responsibility. He certainly didn't
feel any responsibility, and he wouldn't accept any responsibility, either. You could hear the moderator's breathing.
Evidently his idea wasn't working. If he might, he said, he'd
like to note that the honored satirist had made wittier
remarks. He wasn't up to his usual form. The satirist

remained silent, and the other children of the Republic tackled the subject of the "multicultural society." It was the result of the number of immigrants flooding in from a collapsing Eastern Europe. This time Harry saw the rest stop in time and was spared the remainder of their comments.

It was a good thing it was dark. There was no john at this one, and standing next to a car to take a leak while it's still light isn't as much of a relief. You're constantly aware of the resentment of the feminists driving by. Things would probably go so far that for the sake of solidarity, men would have to pee squatting down, giving up the last of their male prerogatives.

An autobahn isn't always as bad as a case of chicken pox. And compared to a dark and lonely rest stop, it's more like a lifeline. There wasn't much traffic between the holidays, almost everyone was somewhere already. There were no accidents, no traffic jams. There was no ice on the road, no long report from the front lines about some traffic bottleneck.

The rain had let up. Duckwitz was going to get gas at the first opportunity, no matter where he was going to go today. At the sound of the tone it will be five o'clock, said the voice on the radio. The evening news is next. One group of statesmen thought war in the Gulf was unavoidable, another group that it could still be avoided. Chatter long enough, and the unimaginable is transformed into the imaginable. There wasn't a cleaning lady in the country that couldn't come up with a better policy than this. The news was to be followed by a background report. They had one of their Washington correspondents on the line, and he was going to tell the newsmen in the studio whether there was going to be a war or not. The two had the situation under control; they chatted as if they were talking about some international tennis match, as if the important thing was to make knowing comments on the athletic condition of the opponents. The man in Washington said that the Pentagon reckoned with no more than 2000 dead American soldiers and six times that many wounded in a first exchange of blows. According to unofficial polls, the American public was prepared to accept these losses; but if there were more dead and wounded, the tide could turn against the administration's policies. This was the president's main concern. Still, said the correspondent, a certain amount of censorship might have a positive influence on public opinion. And he quoted an American journalist who said that if there were absolutely no pictures of corpses on television, then the American public would be willing for a time to accept a war with heavy casualties.

Harry was relieved to think that he didn't have to participate actively in the failure of Western politics at their own failure of a Foreign Office. In the cafeteria recently, the chinless Count Waldburg had said that diplomacy was certainly not going to fail; rather, it would celebrate a triumph. He'd been taking care of some business at Germany's U.N. mission in Geneva, and there they regarded the whole situation rather coolly. The two sides were just playing their trump cards, bluffing, upping the ante, and that only works as long as the threat looks as real as possible, he said. Deploying war ships is part of the game. Of course there wouldn't be a war; this was exactly the way to prevent one. The others listened cheerfully to this happy message—which was nothing more than a laid-back version of the government's official stance.

All of them that is except Knesebeck, who merely shook his head. He couldn't understand why everyone was so calm. The peace movement seemed to be paralyzed. In the early eighties, hundreds of thousands of people had taken to the streets to protest against NATO's plans to modernize its missiles. But Chernobyl had changed many people's minds, and now, when the situation had really become critical, everyone seemed to be under a spell, just waiting for the ultimatum to expire.

The others shrugged their shoulders. No one could explain it.

Harry had brought up the word "eve"—the strange calm on the eve of war.

"Gothic horror stories!" said Waldburg. "You'll see, nothing's going to happen."

Here in the car, Harry suddenly thought of an explanation for the paralysis. Of course! It had to do with the dismal state of affairs on the left. Now that the communist utopia had dissolved in a puff of putrid smoke, leaving capitalism with its free market economy to declare itself the victor, leftists were rebels without a cause; so they were simply holding their tongues. Critics of the system who'd been taught a lesson by recent circumstances didn't want to venture back into the line of fire. Maybe American saber rattling was the right approach after all. Countering madness with madness. Maybe the irrational understand only the language of irrationality. Maybe that madman in Baghdad actually could drop an atom bomb or two. Maybe it really would be right to send a few German soldiers to the Gulf. Maybe that's the only way to save Israel. Maybe that's the only way to prevent a third world war. Maybe you had to be grateful to the Yankees for their damned readiness to make sacrifices. Maybe the American ambassador was absolutely right to hold out his hat while pointing to the 300 million dollars the peace-loving American taxpayer was willing to shell out every year on maintaining the peace—that is, on weapons, because peace without a price is only possible in fairy tales. So the peace movement and the leftists weren't making a peep. And if the blow-up came after all, they could always say they'd been against the arms race all along.

But if that really was the reason for the eerie calm on

the eve of war, thought Duckwitz, then there was a flaw in their thinking. Even if it didn't come to war, even if the madman of Baghdad withdrew and gave his solemn promise never to attack another country, even if he apologized to Israel, it was absolutely no proof that the American response was the right one. Because even that improbably peaceful solution would be, under the circumstances, a victory for the military, purchased with loud-mouthed threats to send hundreds of thousands to their death. That was bad enough. And if it did come to war, those responsible would present the butchery as the lesser of two evils. A victory by those Yankee criminals and their allies would immediately be turned into a justification of the arms industry and modern weaponry. Only a catastrophic defeat of the allies could, paradoxically, lead to a belated victory of reason and under-standing. Then maybe those responsible would admit that it had been wrong to respond to an idiot's raid like an army of idiots.

Gloomy thoughts. And a familiar stench. On the outskirts of Cologne the chemical factories smelled like a combination of condoms and smoked ham. Politics wasn't the only riddle; chemistry was another.

On with the turn signal and right into the gas station. When you're in a car with a nearly empty tank, a gas station looks like a safe haven. Sixty liters of super, leaded. Helen was constantly urging him to buy a smaller, cleaner, newer car. Harry's reply was that it's worse to throw away things that work than it is to use them to the very end.

Harry bought two apples and the newspapers. Gas stations have everything. Something's happening there day and night, unlike shopping districts, where everything's dead after the stores close. A gas station isn't a country town, it's a glowing metropolis. Even the craziest drivers are amazingly well-behaved there, at the source, where they have to get their stuff.

Harry pulled over to the side. It was time to make a decision: Inez or the Eifel. He bit into one of the apples. He could call Inez from here and find out if she was home and in the mood. For a change, the phone booth was empty. But he preferred to call from a phone booth around the corner from her place. When she asked him, "Where are you?" he could say: "Just two minutes away." Harry thought this was more worthy of a lover.

Or should he drive straight to the Eifel? But what would be the advantage of doing without Inez for the sake of a clear conscience? He'd have to suffer through Helen's flowery, rust-red outfit, and when he put on the Fletcher Henderson recording with Coleman Hawkins on sax, Rita and Helen, who seemed to find it boring, would both say: "Not that old jazz again!"

He had to make a decision, but it would certainly not be decisive. That would be something: to have to decide between two women. Either—or! Her or me! I'll give you twenty-four hours! So far, Harry hadn't had any experience of women who think that ultimatums are a sign of passion. That only happens in America. Hollywood hooey.

Harry gnawed on the apple core and looked through the newspapers. Why had he bought them? The British had named the Chancellor "Man of the Year." Typical, but no reason to get upset. It was a joke. Then there were those poor former East Germans. They wanted to drive fantastic cars but didn't have the money. Harry had the money but didn't want the cars.

As always, the human interest pages were a consolation. For the first time since 1953, the top wish on people's Christmas list was not good health but world peace. The wish for "harmony in the family and with your partner" had fallen to third place. Well, Harry guessed he could agree with that set of priorities, even if it did show that he was just an average citizen.

All in all, he'd been lucky. Lucky not to be an American, who thinks it's okay to go to war to defend his country
in the deserts of Arabia. Lucky not to be a president or a
speech writer to a president. The German President's Christmas address had been the embodiment of honest good sense.
He'd begun with a downright erotic call to Germans in both
east and west: "Let us meet each other openly to unite. Let
no one expect the other to come; go out and meet him
halfway." His speech was like something Romy Schneider
might have said in her role as the Empress Sissy, or like the
words of a church marriage counsellor. A speech that
dripped lukewarm common sense. Wasn't every truth that
didn't arouse laughter necessarily false? Wasn't this over-
whelming lack of wit part of the reason for the miserable
state of affairs in the world? Wasn't it high time, 2000 years
after the birth of that tragic figure from Bethlehem, to call
for the elimination of the pastoral tone that papers things
over even more thoroughly?

When Harry turned 45 in October, everyone made the
usual comments about what other people had done by the
time they were Harry's age. He should have been a cabinet
minister at least! Suddenly, Harry had been quite satisfied
just to be himself. And today, at a quarter past five on
December 29th, in a gas station, Harry the early pensioner
was suddenly quite satisfied again. Actually, everything was
just fine. Actually, things could begin now. Actually, anything was possible.

Harry finished his apple and put down the paper.
Drivers kept pulling in and filling up. He'd done the same
thing. Too bad we don't just run out of gas altogether.
Maybe that would still happen. Out of gas. That was a good
one. A thousand marks a liter. And then only for close
friends!

Just six months ago, maybe nine, they'd joked around
at the Eifel about how other dogmas would come unglued

now that the dogma of communism as a viable alternative had unraveled. There was the dogma of modern art, for instance. The collapse of prevailing artistic values. Fritz and Helen had said fine, but how do you provoke the crisis? Nobody takes to the streets because of modern art; nobody is interested in it. Nobody cares whether something has artistic value or whether it's marketed by dealers and traded like stocks and bonds.

Standing at a gas station on the autobahn to Cologne, Harry suddenly found himself thinking of what it would be like if the bottom fell out of the modern art market. He'd have to tell the others about it on New Year's Eve. He could just see it. It wouldn't even require a war in the Gulf. From one day to the next, gas becomes a scarce and precious commodity. You'd have a situation something like the one in 1945, when you traded carpets for eggs and ham. Before his eyes he could see an art dealer from Cologne drive his American limousine up to the gas station on his last drop of gas, letting the car roll to the pump. The huge trunk is half open, and you can see paintings sticking up out of it, large-format stuff, by anyone with some kind of name whose things cost millions—Baselitz, Penck, Lüppertz, and all the rest. All of it overrated. The dealer wants to get gas. Money has no value. Gas for pictures. The gas station owner still has a few liters, but he wants something of lasting value in return. He goes around the car to the trunk and looks at the paintings. "Just a year ago, that one was worth three million," says the dealer, holding up a painting. With a sneer, the man shakes his head: "I wouldn't give you half a liter for that!" And, of course, he comes up with that old argument: "I have a three-year-old daughter. She can do that, too." The art dealer runs his hands nervously through his hair. Does he understand that this is the truth? That he has supported the wrong system? That he's a member of a kind of politburo of art? That his hour has come? There among the paintings is a cheap art book he's had in his car for ages: *Masterpieces of European Painting, from the Renaissance to Expressionism.* "Let me have a look," says the gas station man. His daughter could really use something like that later on for school. "I'll give you three liters for that," he says. "That's just enough to get you to the next station."

Harry's vision of crisis propelled him into the best of moods. Down with modern art! Down with politics! Long live private life, empty gas tanks, long walks! Tonight it didn't make any difference whether he slept with Inez, Rita, or Helen, or—as was most likely—alone: tomorrow was Sunday and the day after tomorrow was New Year's, and they'd go for a walk then, no matter what the weather. The Eifel region is a dull place. He decided that when winter was over, he'd drive to the Alpine foothills to visit the places where he'd spent his childhood. First alone, then with Helen, then with Rita, then with Rita and Helen, and then with Inez. He'd walk along the old paths, and he'd show his women which stones he'd sat on as a kid and where Regina had ridden by on her bike, a brand-new NSU bicycle—or had it been a Wanderer, or perhaps a Miele?

He had time, and he had money. If there was no gas, they'd go by train, and if the railroad went bankrupt, they'd go by bicycle. If the country went bust and couldn't pay his pension, he'd get a job as a lawyer with some firm that specialized in bankruptcies. If they didn't have anything to eat, he'd trade his book on European masterpieces for ham and eggs. If the Chancellor was being sought by the authorities and took refuge in the house in the Eifel, they'd lock him in the basement and have a leisurely discussion of what to do with him. The same with the Foreign Minister. If there was no electricity because the Greens had been crazy enough to shut down all the nuclear power plants when they took office, it would be hard—Harry loved the telephone and electric lights, and he was especially fond of his record collection—but it wouldn't be so bad. He and Rita would finally have a chance to find out if they could play a passable version of "Little Red Rooster" on trumpet and piano. "St. James Infirmary," too. Then there wouldn't be any more of those ads with dolled-up women saxophone players, and the saxophone wouldn't be in fashion; he'd finally be able to buy one for himself. And Inez and Fritz would move out to the Eifel, and they'd start calling the Eifel house their Eifel bunker, and life wouldn't be half bad. What a merry life his aunts had led in the fifties, when nobody had anything at all.

Fritz had just written his fifth book, and Harry still hadn't read a single one. He made a resolution, a New Year's resolution, to read his brother's books. The fact that he was his brother just amazed him. Fritz was so blond— and so bald. Of course, there had been a different father at work there. Harry's hair grew just as abundantly and wildly as it ever had. "Your hair is the best thing about you!" Helen said sometimes as she ran her fingers through it. Unfortunately, it was none of his doing. Without the least bit of effort on his part, his contrariness simply sprang from his scalp. Not one gray hair, though, and that at 45! I'd like to see someone do better! Nowadays people ran around with snow-white hair at the age of 30. Had things always been that way? He'd have to look into that, too. Statisticians always overlooked the most important facts. It was a highly interesting phenomenon. Life was interesting, period. It was wonderful to be an early pensioner.

His skin and hair were in good shape—Inez admired his smooth skin, Helen his hair. What more could he want? He didn't have dandruff—in fact, he was the only diplomat in Bonn who didn't. That is, *was* the only diplomat. . . . At receptions, when they had to wear those ridiculous dark suits, the others all had a dusting of white flakes on their jackets, everyone, that is, but Harry. He wasn't fat, he wasn't dumb. He wasn't poor, he wasn't lonely. So there. He didn't have buck teeth. He did have a bad tooth way in the back, but that was something you had to put up with in your mid-forties. He didn't wear glasses and there were no signs of far-sightedness. With his good health, he could have become an airline pilot. Sometimes his back hurt, but surely that didn't mean he had cancer of the spine. Sometimes his testicles hurt a little, but that probably wasn't cancer either—more a sign of longing.

It's hard to judge your own appearance. And he couldn't ask Inez, Rita or Helen: Say, how do I look, anyway? Do you find me attractive? That would be awful. He'd never let things go that far—though it would have produced some nice sarcastic answers. One time about ten years ago, when they'd been screwing, Helen said to him: "You look like Wittgenstein." Harry didn't know Wittgenstein. He was a philosopher who wrote a lot of dumb stuff, like every other philosopher. Not as bad as Heidegger, but you couldn't really use any of it. Harry had actually gone to the university library to get books by and about Wittgenstein. He found some photos. If he looked like that, he could be satisfied, he thought. But then Harry picked up the allusions to Wittgenstein's homosexuality. He went to the men's room and looked at himself in the mirror. Did he look like a homosexual? But what did that mean, anyway—to look like a homosexual? Was there any such thing? There was such a thing as a queer's way of talking—that affected tone of voice. What caused that? Did he talk like a queer? Helen had always said that Harry should have turned into a queer because he grew up without a father. When he protested, she'd say: "See how you reject the idea! That's not normal. You're a latent homosexual, only you won't admit it!" Helen of all people! That anal little monster. Not being queer certainly made things easier. A ladies' man had an easier time of it. And then there was all that crap about AIDS.

That was bad enough. Everybody knew it was raging among the pansies. "Pansies." That was an expression you didn't hear anymore. Expressions like that just die out. He'd have to look into that, too.

Harry was in a good mood. He still had the taste of the gas station apple in his mouth. A boscop, treated with something. At 45 you begin to grow immune to pesticides. A fine mist was still coming down, but now he kind of liked the awful weather. His gas tank was full, his bladder was empty, he had money in his wallet, and in January he'd start getting 3600 marks a month for doing nothing. He wouldn't give any more thought to the humiliating way he left the foreign service; he'd start something new. He'd do everything better this time. He'd talk it over with Helen, Inez, and Rita. He'd consider the advice of beautiful women, and the advice of his brother Fritz, the poet. And then he'd do something sensible. He'd open a publishing house. He and Helen would put out terrific books. He'd set up a recording company, bring out forgotten jazz, manage Rita's concerts. He'd give anti-American concerts. You don't have to stop at just griping about peace. He'd get people all worked up—so they wouldn't always go around like dumb Christians, loving everybody in sight and blathering about the Sermon on the Mount, so they'd look down on the right people from time to time. Good music comes from contempt, not love. Anger at the obstacles to love was what produced the blues, early jazz, and the good old pop and protest songs. Do anything but sing on behalf of a cause. But sing the people in charge to death!

It was twenty past five. A gas station is an oasis. Harry didn't want to leave. He put in one of his twenty favorite tapes. The music had recovered its old power. "You say that it's over, baby," bellowed Janis Joplin. And then her velvety soft offer: "Won't you move over?"

Nothing was over except that ridiculous time he'd spent

as a diplomat. Now he could get started. What kind of a group had Inez just joined? Doctors Against Something or Other. Being against something was always good. Against nuclear war or nuclear annihilation. Though being against it was a given. Did this mean they were for conventional war, or what? The good doctors hadn't thought that one through yet. They needed an executive director. Duckwitz, for instance, with all his experience in public relations and the media. He'd go right to work fitting them out with a more aggressive image. An ad, for instance: "When it happens, we won't heal everyone!" Followed by a list of the dirtiest bastards in the country. And then the trials! Is a planned violation of the Hippocratic Oath a punishable offense? Or don't the courts recognize the Hippocratic Oath as binding? Is there such a thing in law as the premeditated, or threatened, denial of medical assistance? These were all intriguing questions. And what about an advertisement that calls for assassination? The call to murder as metaphor, as food for thought. He'd manage that somehow. Calling it merely "food for thought" was playing pretty rough, but if it served the cause of truth, then it was all right. Or could it be that the group wasn't really on the up and up?

He'd just glanced at an editorial in a leftist newspaper. The author had charged that, in light of the present crisis in the Gulf, this organization's position on Israel was inconsistent. Still the same old guilt feelings. As their media man or executive director, Harry would be able to steer the doctors on a more sensible course. Though the business with Israel really was pretty hairy. You couldn't avoid making mistakes. What dirty politics the Israelis had been playing. Their swaggering occupation-army mentality was partly responsible for the desperate situation they were in. Still, if you took a good look at Israel on a map, if you recalled the wrath of its Arab neighbors and forgot the images of Israelis shooting and beating Palestinians with clubs, then all you could do was sing the praises of the Americans and argue in favor of sending the German army to the Middle East with the support of the entire country—in spite of the yammering of the Social Democrats. That is, if righting a wrong was to be anything more than an empty phrase. This damned Israel problem is ruining the cause of anti-militarism! Just imagine someone gave a war and nobody came. That had been a nice peace slogan. But just imagine an Israeli woman flashes her eyes at you, puts a gun in your hand, and says that if you don't cover her and, if necessary, knock off a couple of those masked characters, it will be the end of her! Just aim and fire, like in a western! And now just imagine the same thing with a Palestinian woman: she flashes her eyes just as persuasively, looks just like the other one. . . . Better not picture it, that's all.

Harry tossed the newspapers onto the back seat. Off to Cologne! If Inez wasn't there or didn't have the time, he'd just turn around again. It was pretty silly to treat the whole thing as an existential question. It must have something to do with autobahns. These miserable autobahns change your way of thinking. There's something fateful about even simple exits and interchanges, as if there were no going back. . . . What nonsense! There may be wrong-way drivers, but they're certainly not tools of the Fates.

Bonn to Cologne, no distance at all. A good thirty kilometers. What is it that makes people yearn for the wide open spaces? They drive from Alaska to Tierra del Fuego, thousands of kilometers, and they aren't any smarter when they get there. Tierra del Fuego is ugly. You can have ugliness in the Eifel, much closer to home. Distance is foolish, a nightmare. Nearness and closeness are the real thing. Bonn to Cologne. Happiness should never be further than thirty kilometers away. At most fifty. You should be able to reach it on foot in emergencies. The future lies in the mini-state. United Europe is an anachronism. The Soviet Union was

destroyed by its size. Bonn-Cologne-Eifel—a small triangle,
but large enough.

Let's go! Right into Cologne for a quick beer. It had
been ages since he'd had a beer at a pub, had been alone at
a pub. It was always wine with dinner and always dinner
with women. And whisky, so he could put up with the
women and with life. "Whisky and Women"—this was one
blues number he wouldn't have to write. Harry the Home-
comer, Harry Has-No-Land arriving in Cologne. He had to
open the car window, show those sad sacks what music was
and still is: The Beatles, *Abbey Road,* "You never give me
your money." And then: "See no future, pay no rent, all my
money's gone, nowhere to go." Pure mockery: four filthy-
rich teenagers singing about poverty and desolation. "Oh,
that magic moment, nowhere to go"—they knew exactly
which way to go. It was a resounding lie and yet, strangely
enough, it was the truth and nothing but the truth. All of
the statements of witnesses and all of the decisions of all the
courts in the world were nothing compared with this nasal
little melody and its lazy rhythms. "She came in through the
bathroom window ... she said she'd always been a dancer,
she worked at fifteen clubs a day, and though she thought I
knew the answer, well I knew, but I could not say." Why is
such nonsense, when you sing it like this, so illuminating?
Let me put my arms around you, Fabulous Four, let me
hold you tight, you millions! To be perfectly honest, it was
pretty doubtful that all men would ever be brothers. It
wasn't even really necessary. "Every man a traveling salesman" fits Beethoven's melody just as well, and besides, it's
true. First Harry had sold clients to courts, then he'd sold
the Federal Republic of Germany to other countries, and in
the future he'd sell something else, hopefully not vacuum
cleaners. He'd rather sell something he believed in. "See no
future, pay no rent"—you could only sing about the misery
of life when you were on top. Now hear this, ladies and

gentlemen, snobs of Cologne: you can forget all the pop
music that's been done since the mid-seventies. Ninety-nine
percent of it is totally superfluous. A decade and a half
down the drain. Wrong turn. Dead end. I've been making a
mess of things for a decade and a half, too. Come on, let's
start over. Storm the radio stations, tie up the disc jockeys,
ban that mindless hippity hop music to the archives!

Harry sent John Lennon's "Stand by Me" booming out
onto the street. He drove slowly, looking for a pub that
matched his mood. A car honked behind him—go ahead
and pass! Drive defensively. No accidents please, death is no
solution. Death is the pits, no matter which way you look at
it. Death is out of the question. Death is a master from
America. Death is from Hollywood. Death comes from the
Gulf, from oil, from German factories. Death is something
for opera lovers, for people who can't accept the banality of
life, for people who can't live without a "finis." It's for the
Mr. Cleans, the criminals, and the neurotics of this world.
Islam is death—Christianity is death. Every religion is death.
Religion is pointless. Pointlessness is death. Death is no
joke. The American president is death, the Iraqi president is
death. Two madmen have the world holding its breath in
the name of religion. Well, so long, *servus!* as the Austrians
would say. That's why the head of the House of Duckwitz
recommends what everyone else has considered reprehensible:
escapism. Flight. Go fight your wars yourself. We quit. For
now, we're withdrawing into the private sphere.

He spotted a pub, but even from the outside it looked
unspeakable. Keep going. There's nothing better than driving
slowly into Cologne in one of these big buggies, like a
Turk's, looking for an inviting pub. Tomorrow is Sunday,
the day after tomorrow is New Year's Eve. He still had to
pick up the mandatory champagne, though no one really
liked champagne and it gave everyone a headache. Still, you

can't be against every tradition at once. Champagne isn't
better, it's just more posh.

Inez was going to bring her kids. He really shouldn't
raise the subject of overpopulation. Besides, the kids were
good for Inez and he thought it was exciting to have a lover
with children. Your usual mistress is, of course, childless in
the extreme. He'd never wanted children of his own. The
family men among his diplomatic colleagues had been
enough for him. He only had to think of Sachtleben! He
should leave the world a few songs instead of children. But
as far as legacies like that were concerned, things didn't look
too good. Nevertheless, one of these days he was going to
write a blues number for Inez. He was going to call it something like "A Mean Mother's Lover."

He also had to remember to get mineral water and a
bottle of whisky on Monday morning. Scotch, of course—
there'd be no bourbon in his house! Not just because he was
the last of the anti-Americans but because that particular
firewater didn't taste good. He also had to take the newspapers and bottles for recycling, the usual errands of an
affluent society. And Rita's motorcycle had to go in for an
inspection. No one ever rode it, of course, but it should be
ready to go nevertheless. You just have to assume that life
will go on.

Finally he spotted a pub that looked okay. He began
looking for a place to park. Of course Helen was right, a
smaller car would have been more practical. But he loved
this big old boat. It somehow suited Rita, Helen, and Inez.
He couldn't imagine them riding around in some shiny new
car, a Mercedes or a BMW. Awful! Inez sank into the worn
cushions of his *gastarbeiter* boat just like a Turk. One time,
Harry had driven out into the country with her. Inez had
asked for directions in the middle of nowhere. An old man
with a plastic rain hat had evidently thought they were both
refugees, and he told them: "Go back where you came from,

you pack of Turks!" They hadn't been angry, because the singsong of his dialect made his reactionary comments sound unreal, and because they both liked the idea of being undesirable aliens far from home. "My little Turk, my refugee!" Harry had said.

They'd driven a short distance and put down the reclining seats. A premiere. Harry had expected it to be more comfortable. It gave him a high to think that not every diplomat or anesthesiologist would be willing to screw in some old clunker of a car. Inez had pretended she was a Turk with a broken accent: "Do it good—good do it." And Harry had said: "Me good Turk, you good Turk, we Turk goods." He hadn't been able to get Inez to say this. And then he'd sung for Inez the last verse of that old children's song about hares that have been shot but aren't dead, because death is there so that you can outwit it: "And when they got their senses back / and realized / that they were alive, alive, / that they were still alive, / they hopped up and made tracks." That was the point—duck when the hunter comes, then run like hell.

• • •

After Harry had jammed his car into a parking space, he walked back toward the pub. The drizzle didn't bother him. He didn't have a coat, didn't have an umbrella, he had no cough, no tuberculosis. He'd been spared all that. No club foot, no beer belly, my God, how lucky he'd been!

Actually, he was in a most fortunate position. Actually, he could get off to a good start. The only question was, how? Actually, he still had his life ahead of him, and actually, the Chancellor didn't have to make any difference to him. Actually, he couldn't have cared less about the Chancellor. Professional satirists are actually better statesmen than those awful amateurs. And actually, people who turn up their noses at the word "actually" are the dumbest of all. Harry remembered that there was some kind of cult piece written by Adorno. What was it called? *The Jargon of Authenticity.* He'd never read it. He assumed it was some pointed critique of the actual cited by people who'd never actually read it. If they had, they certainly didn't understand it. Well, in any case—long live the actual. The actual is the opposite of arbitrariness. The actual is pure decisiveness, but it's not pig-headed. It's a judgment, but an open one.

Actually, it wasn't so bad to be married. Or was it? Actually, Rita is a very pleasant and attractive woman. Actually, she plays the piano very well. Actually, he should be damned glad she played a lot of Schubert, Mozart, and Chopin, that she didn't touch that mush by Brahms and Schumann, or Bach's sterile fugues, that she didn't plunk away at the modern stuff. It was also a good thing she didn't play the violin or sing. He couldn't imagine her singing those swollen arias all the time. Helen was actually a fantastic companion. Actually, she was usually right. And actually, Inez was a fantastic lover. Actually, it wasn't so bad that she was Fritz's girlfriend, and actually, Helen was also a fantastic lover. And Rita's quivering orgasm wasn't something to turn your nose up at either. And Fritz was actually the best brother in the world. Actually, his poems probably weren't so bad. Actually, Rita wasn't always going to church, to be exact, it was more like twice a year.

But actually, a person shouldn't make too many allowances, otherwise he'd wind up saying things like: Actually, it's not so bad if the Yankees blow Iraq off the map; then at least we'd have some peace and quiet. Or: Actually, an atom bomb is a pretty effective means of coercion. You see! See what? Actually, war should not be the continuation of diplomacy by other means. That's the way things used to be. Nowadays, the threat of war is actually the precondition for diplomacy. Isn't that the way things actually are? And isn't that enough to make you puke? It was doubly good that he was rid of his job as a diplomat. No actually about it.

Actually, Harry wasn't such a bad name, even if all kinds of people were called that now. It wasn't a diplomat's name; actually, it was a name for a trumpet player.

Harry ran up the stairs to the pub. He'd been right. No unpleasant surprises. Not too full, not too empty, and people you could bear to be around for a while. He was looking forward to his first sip of beer. He'd earned it. And a cigarette. Others smoked too much; Harry, of course, maintained that he smoked too little.

Harry shook the rain from his hair. Actually, it's a shame that men don't wear hats anymore. Why don't they, anyway? He sat down at an empty table. This was his world. No offices, no official residences, no hotel lobbies, no airports or any of the rest of it. The waitress smiled at him as he ordered his beer. There was a telephone on the wall between the bar and the door to the men's room. He was looking forward to asking the waitress for some change when she brought the beer. She'd have to go rummaging around in her big change purse.

Then he'd take his first sip of beer and go over to the telephone before someone else could get there to mumble for hours, ruining one of the pleasures in life. He'd call Inez. No, he'd try the house in the Eifel first, to see what the mood was like. Maybe they'd planned on his being there for dinner. An ouster banquet! He'd gulp down his beer and take off if that was the case. If they hadn't planned anything and he could assume that when he came home didn't make any difference to them, he'd call Inez. He'd listen to the phone ringing while looking into the eyes of the waitress at the bar . . . and look away the moment Inez picked up the phone.

Either he could go there today or he couldn't. If he

didn't, he'd go next week. They'd see each other on New Year's Eve in any case.

Oh, really?

Of course!

Things were just fine, one way or the other. Things would go on. Some way.

Acknowledgments

In completing the work on this translation, I have enjoyed the kind support of the Office of Cultural Affairs of the City of Munich. I am grateful for their generous invitation to work at the Villa Waldberta in Feldafing and for the opportunity it gave me to meet with Joseph von Westphalen to discuss the "Englishing" of Harry von Duckwitz's story.

To Breon Mitchell I owe a special debt of gratitude. He has been more than generous with his time, support, and advice at all stages of this project.

I would also like to take this opportunity to acknowledge a debt of very long standing. For helping to open up to me the rich world of the German language and for his interest and support as work on this translation progressed, I would like to thank my husband, Lutz Richter-Bernburg. Without our *Deutschstunden*, this English Harry would have been unthinkable.

My thanks as well to the special group of friends in Göttingen with whom I read and discussed so many German authors. In some ways, this translation grew out of the evenings we spent together.

Members of my family as well as many friends, acquaintances, and perfect strangers have discussed with me the intricacies of everything from steering knuckle bolts to the geography of Latin America. I thank them all.

Finally, I would like to express my appreciation to Robert Wechsler—a fair and gentlemanly publisher, and an invaluable reader.

Melanie Richter-Bernburg